The Colors of Violence

Sudhir Kakar

THE COLORS OF VIOLENCE

Cultural Identities, Religion, and Conflict

The University of Chicago Press
Chicago & London

The University of Chicago Press, Chicago 60637
The University of Chicago Press, Ltd., London
© 1996 by The University of Chicago
All rights reserved. Published 1996
Printed in the United States of America
09 08 07 06 05 04 03 02 01 00   2 3 4 5 6

ISBN: 0-226-42284-4 (cloth)
ISBN: 0-226-42285-2 (paper)

Library of Congress Cataloging-in-Publication Data

Kakar, Sudhir.
    The colors of violence : cultural identities, religion, and conflict / Sudhir Kakar.
       p.   cm.
    Includes bibliographical references and index.
    1. Communalism—India. 2. Violence—India. 3. Violence—Religious
aspects. 4. Conflict (psychology) 5. Hindus-India. 6. Muslims—India. I. Title.
DS422.C64K35   1996
303.6′0954—dc20   95-35971
                                                                          CIP

∞ The paper used in this publication meets the minimum requirements of the American
National Standard for Information Sciences–Permanence of Paper for Printed Library
Materials, ANSI Z39.48–1992.

For my daughter Shveta, also because she asked.

CONTENTS

PREFACE

This book is a psychoanalyst's exploration of what is commonly known as religious conflict. The hesitations—"psychoanalyst's" instead of "psychoanalytic," the qualifier "commonly known as"—are due to an awareness that such conflicts are complex phenomena, involving the interaction of political, economic, cultural, and psychological forces. To reduce their complexity exclusively to psychoanalytic notions is to engage in a psychological imperialism which has been deeply offensive to practitioners of other disciplines—history, political science, and sociology among others—who have traditionally engaged in the study of social conflict.

My own aspirations in this book are modest. They are to provide a way of looking at conflict—the psychoanalyst's way—so as to deepen the understanding provided by other disciplines. To their insights, I wish to add my own discipline's characteristic way of reflecting on issues involved in religious conflict. Taking the Hindu-Muslim violence of 1990 in the south Indian city of Hyderabad as my case study, I have tried to bring out the subjective, experiential aspects of conflict between religious groups, to capture the psychological experience of being a Hindu or a Muslim when one's community seems to be ranged against the other in a deadly confrontation. This means working with a notion of the group aspect of identity, which is constituted of a person's feelings and attitudes toward the self as a member of an ethnic/religious/cultural collectivity. This particular self-image is transmitted from one generation to the next through the group's mythology, history, ideals and values, and shared cultural symbols. Group identity is an extended part of individual self-experience, although the intensity of this experience varies across individuals and with time. It can range from feelings of nominal affiliation with the group to a deep identification or even to feelings of fusion, where any perceived harm to the group's interests or threats to its "honor" are reacted to as strongly as damage to one's own self. I have then tried to describe the ways in which social-psychological forces in a particular period of history bring out latent group identities and turn them to violent ends. With evidence drawn from interviews with men, women, and children, psychological tests and speech transcripts of Hindu and Muslim "fundamentalists," I have sought to analyze the fantasies, social representations, and modes of moral reasoning about the out-groups—"them"—that motivate and rationalize arson, looting, rape, and killing.

Chapter 1 describes the context of Hindu-Muslim violence: personal, social, and historical. After trying to understand the emotional reverberations of the Hyderabad riot of 1990, the central event of my study, I give a brief account of its setting—a social and historical portrait of the city of Hyderabad—before going on to trace the contested and contentious history of Hindu-Muslim relations.

Chapter 2 begins with my own memories of the violence between Hindus and Muslims at the eve of partition of the country in 1947. It examines the nature of such memories and the ways they are transmitted from one generation to another. It discusses the morphology of religious group violence, the sequence of steps leading to the formation of riotous mobs, the psychology of such mobs, and then briefly summarizes events leading to the 1990 riot.

Chapter 3 turns our attention to the "activists" of violence. These are the "strong men," the *pehlwans* and the *dadas* who take over the direction and organization of violence once the riot begins. The chapter views religious violence through their eyes and tries to identify some common themes in their psychological makeup and professional socialization.

Chapter 4 looks closely at one set of victims of the riot—the Pardis of Shakkergunj, a small Hindu community in an old part of the city who have been repeated victims of religious violence. Through interviews with members of one extended Pardi family, we see the different ways in which men and women experience this violence and understand how the Hindu image of Muslims is constructed. The chapter concludes with a discussion of children's representations of Hindu-Muslim violence.

Chapter 5 describes Hindu-Muslim relations and violence from the viewpoint of a poor Muslim family from the old part of the city of Karwan. The chapter analyzes the different "victim" responses of Indian Muslims and concludes with a discussion of the morality of violence, that is, with the ways Muslims and Hindus evaluate their various interactions with members of the other community, including such riot-time "interactions" as arson, rape, and murder.

Chapter 6 discusses the social-cultural impact of modernization and globalization in fostering fundamentalist and revivalist group identities. Its centerpiece consists of the analysis of a speech by a Hindu demagogue which shows the psychological steps through which such an identity is sought to be constructed.

Chapter 7 is, so to speak, the Muslim counterpart of the preceding chapter. It analyzes the speech transcripts of the *mullahs*, the most conservative spokesmen of the community, to describe the psychological construction of Muslim fundamentalist identity.

In conclusion, chapter 8 summarizes the various identity-threats arising from the social-cultural arena that bring the latent group aspect of our identity to the forefront. It traces the development of this aspect of identity, the conditions necessary for the release of its potential violence, and the role played by religion in its facilitation.

ACKNOWLEDGMENTS

I gratefully acknowledge the support of the John D. and Catherine T. MacArthur Foundation which made long periods of field work in Hyderabad and other cities possible. A National Fellowship of the Indian Council of Social Science Research enabled me to work on the preliminary aspects of the study. Most of all, I am grateful to my friend Vikram Lal for his support when it mattered the most.

I am thankful to Sujata Patil for her assistance in collecting the materials on the Pardis and for the many discussions on the project. I owe a special debt of gratitude to Sahba Hussain for her interviews with the Muslims of Karwan. Without her deep involvement and courage in locating and arranging interviews with the "killers," this study would have lost an essential intimacy with the violence of the conflict. I am also grateful for the assistance of my dear friend Ali Baquer and the help given by Mehdi Arslam and Javed Alam.

Institutionally, the Committee on Human Development and the Divinity School at the University of Chicago have been generous hosts for an academic quarter each year for many years, and that is where the plans for this work first took shape. I also owe a debt of gratitude to the Institute for Advanced Study in Berlin, where a fellowship allowed me to complete the writing of the book. Colleagues at the Institute, especially George Lowenstein and Aziz Al-Azmeh, were generous with their time and helpful with their comments and criticisms.

ONE

The Setting

The face of the two-year-old girl has come to occupy a permanent corner of my mind. Every now and again it rises to the surface of consciousness. Some of these occasions are predictable. There is little mystery when the disfigured face flashes across an inner screen while I am reading about, or seeing on television, episodes of violence between racial, religious, or language groups in different parts of the world. I can also understand, even as I resent, the little girl demanding attention whenever people talk of Hyderabad, whether they are praising its old-world charm and the deliciousness of its cuisine or lamenting its lost feudal glories. The connection of the face with other contexts is more obscure. Why does it suddenly bob up when a man in therapy is telling me of a painful encounter with his boss at work or a female patient weeps as she recalls memories of her humiliation at the hands of an elder sister? I know I will have to go through a long chain of associations to lift this veil of obscurity. I am rarely in the mood to make this effort since the girl is not a welcome tenant. She is a squatter.

I first saw the face in a newspaper photograph accompanying a report on the Hindu-Muslin riots in Hyderabad in December 1990. When I finally began this study in the following year, I encountered this particular photograph again and again in newspaper and magazine clippings. It had become the dominant image of that particular carnage. I do not know whether the girl is a Hindu or a Muslim, although a Telegu paper, championing the Hindu cause, identifies her as a Hindu. What you see in the photograph is the unkempt hair, matted with dust, of a child from the slums and then, shockingly, the deep gash of the scythe across the top of her face. The wound, not yet healed into a scar, starts at the right temple, cleaves the corner of the eyeball, and the bridge of a rather flat nose, to peter out in the sands of the left cheek. The stitches are not the careful job of a well-paid professional. They bespeak a harried resident doctor trying to cope with an overflow of the wounded and the dying in the emergency room of a run-down government hospital. The stitches are uneven crosses across the face, hasty scrawls of someone anxious to get over with a silly game of ticktacktoe. One arm of the girl is around a cushion, seeking comfort without finding it. The right side of the face and the injured eye rests against the edge of the cushion as she looks out through the left eye of the camera, the world, and, if I am not careful, at me.

There is an unfathomable numbness in her expression, the aftermath of a cataclysm that has shaken the little body and soul to a depth unimaginable for me. I try to look through the child's eyes at what must have appeared as a phalanx of giants, with black strips of cloth covering the lower halves of their faces, come crashing through the splintered front door. She sees one of the men raise an axe and club her father down, the sharp edge of the weapon catching him in the back of his neck as he turns and tries to flee. She sees him disappear as he falls, and the men close in with knives, scythes, and wooden clubs. She sees the mother standing transfixed and then hears her make a sound between a sharp cough and a scream as a spear slices through the base of her throat. The girl takes a step toward the mother when the scythe is swung. There is the burning pain beyond all her experience of pain. Blood streams into the eye and, then, oblivion.

I imagine, in that particular moment when her consciousness began the distinctive spiral which ends in the loss of all accustomed moorings, that the universe revealed its secret to the little girl. She caught a glimpse of the immeasurably vast stretch of indifference surrounding the pinpoint of light we call a human life and from whose odds and ends—birth, death, bodily functions, sexual feelings, relationships with parents, siblings, children—we desperately keep on trying to construct a meaning.

I shake my head to free myself of these fantasies and again turn to the photograph of the child with a stony face and one uncomprehending eye. I am aware that my flight of imagination is a failure rather than a success of empathy. The sheer magnitude of the violence done to her is too oppressive for me to employ that crucial tool of my trade, without which no psychoanalyst can grasp and make sense of what is going on within another person. Perhaps this is so because the child is so patently a victim. She is pathetic because she has been flattened by fate. Empathy requires its addressee to be tragic, someone who has helped to bring fate upon herself and was thus fate's active even if unwitting collaborator rather than its passive victim. Tragedy at least preserves a memory of one's agency and therefore holds out the hope of its eventual recovery. The unmitigated passivity of pathos, on the other hand, is a dead weight that tugs down at the spirit of everyone who comes in its contact. I cannot empathize with the child because I must defend myself against her pathos. It is far easier for me to pity her. Pity is distant. The girl's face, then, is not haunting but nagging, like a child beggar or a leper with his insidious whine, evoking an angry guilt that will not let you shout at the wretch, "Disappear! Die!"

At the outset, then, I am apprehensive whether I will be able to bring the essence of psychoanalytic sensibility to bear upon my conversations with the victims of the riots, as well as to my interviews with the agents of violence, the men who stab, bludgeon, and burn. It is not enough for me to take up the clinician's stance and, for instance, speculate upon the little girl's eventual fate: namely, if she survives the poverty and the neglect of a disfigured orphan (who is a female to boot) and grows up into an adult, she will become fearful of expressing any anger, will be easily startled by any physical surprise, and will have incomprehensible impulses to injure herself. I want to do more but am afraid that I will do much less as I leave my accustomed clinical moorings to enter the world of social violence with nothing more than what is called a psychoanalytic sensibility.

The core of the analyst's sensibility does not lie in clinical expertise or in a specific way of observing and interpreting people's words and actions. It does not even lie in a perhaps easier acceptance of the gulf between people's ideals and their behavior, in the analyst's greater difficulty in summoning up righteous indignation or in reluctance to carry out a lover's quarrel with the world. The core is empathy. Empathy is the bridge between the serene reserve of the clinician striving for objectivity and the vital, passionate, and vulnerable person who inhabits the clinician's body. Empathy makes me, as an analyst or scholar, step out of the anonymity of an impersonal enterprise and constantly recognize myself in it as a human being of flesh and blood. Without its vital presence, I fear that the creative tension between objectivity and impassioned involvement, between the stoic and the emotionally responsive perspectives, will be lost.

Shifting Perspectives

I began this study with a description of the reactions evoked in me by the little victim of the Hyderabad riot in the conviction that not only the observer but also one's state of consciousness belongs to the description of the phenomenon one seeks to describe and understand. The father, with his new Polaroid camera, photographs the child. As he holds up the print, the child is first pleased and then puzzled. "But, father," the child asks, "Where are *you* in the picture?" The father could have at least extended a leg to get his foot into a corner of the photograph.

Whereas quantum physicists realized the importance of the interaction of subject and object in the comprehension of reality—"We cannot describe the world as if we did not belong to it," was the credo of the pioneers[1]—this recognition has not generally taken place in the social sciences. Most social scientists have continued to exclude their own subjectivity from descriptions of psychological and social reality. They have not felt the need for putting imaginative flesh on academic bones. Subjectivity has been regarded as irrational. At best, it is irrational not in the sense of being against reason or constituting the not-understood but of being outside reason.

Perhaps the social scientists were unwittingly forced to choose a more convenient strategy when they kept the subject strictly separate from the object, since an attempt to grasp a more holistic world, the "really real," through the inclusion of their own subjectivity would have led to a degree of complexity which could have bordered on chaos. Psychoanalysts, however, were compelled to abandon this Cartesian stance because of the very nature of their discipline. Whereas in the early years of psychoanalysis, the feelings aroused in the analyst by the patient—countertransference—were thought to contaminate the analyst's objectivity, to be eliminated through a rigorous self-analysis, it was soon realized that the analyst's subjectivity was an essential source of information about the patient. In other words, the analyst understands the patient only in so far as he or she understands the disturbance the patient evokes in him- or herself. As the analyst follows the patient's productions and their effects, the analyst must be both an observer and the object of observation. Whether it is the individual patient or large collectivities, we will see with our experiences, hear through our memories, understand with our bodies. In my own account of religious violence, it is these different yet interdependent modes of engaging with the persons and events of this study, the keeping alive of the tension between the immersive and reflective parts of my self, the quest not to let the experiencing self get buried under the agenda of a self that would rather organize and interpret the experience, that I seek to capture in my writing of this book.

The City: "Unparalleled in the World"

The city of Hyderabad was conceived of as the new capital of the Deccan kingdom of Golconda after the old fortress city a few miles away became congested and unhygienic due to an acute shortage of water.[2] Mohammed Quli Qutub Shah, the founder of the city, named it Bhagnagar after his beloved Hindu mistress, Bhagmati. Officially renamed Hyderabad after her death—Hyder being the title given to her by the king—Bhagnagar continued to retain its popular name. Even a hundred years after its founding in 1589, travelers' accounts continued to refer to Hyderabad by the name of Mohammed Quli's beloved Hindu mistress.

Four hundred and two years old at the time of this writing, Hyderabad was envisaged by its founder to be a city "unparalleled anywhere in the world and a replica of heaven on earth." The benevolent ruler, with artistic sensibilities and literary tastes, who liked to flaunt his sensual excesses in verse, had the good sense to entrust the task of giving his vision a concrete shape to his prime minister, Mir Momin. The minister, who had grown up in the garden city of Isafahan in Persia, planned the new capital on the lines of the city he had loved as a child and brought in architects and builders from Persia to carry out the grand design. Mir Momin's plan favored a gridiron pattern with two main intersecting roads, each sixty feet wide, which divided the city into four quarters. The northwestern quarter adjacent to the intersection was reserved for the royal palaces and the eastern quarter for the residences of the prime minister and the nobles of the realm.

For the houses of the commoners, twelve main zones, spread over an area of ten square miles, were allocated. Each of these *mohallas* had schools, hospitals, mosques, inns, and gardens—with vegetable and fruit markets at the periphery—in an effort to make every *mohalla* self-sufficient. Later, during the short period Hyderabad came under the Mughal rule, the construction of a protective wall around the city was started. Completed by Asaf Jah in 1740, the wall had twelve gates which closed nightly at eight and opened at the crack of dawn.

The main roads were lined with fourteen thousand two-storied shops, and there were separate areas earmarked for state offices, public buildings, and foreign embassies. The pride of the public buildings were the Jami mosque and the Char Minar ("four minarets")—a square edifice with four broad and lofty arches and a minaret 220 feet high, at each corner—which has come to symbolize old Hyderabad and the faded glory of its Islamic heritage. Located at the center of the walled city, at the intersection of the two main highways, it was from Char Minar that the imperial power of the Qutub Shahis emanated outwards.

The French merchant and celebrated traveler Jean-Baptiste Tavernier came to Hyderabad in April 1641, during the reign of Abdulla Qutub Shah, who succeeded his father Mohammed Quli to the throne of Golconda in 1611 and ruled till 1672. Tavernier describes the city thus:

> A large river bathes the walls of the town on the south-west side, and flows into the Gulf of Bengal close to Masulipatam. You cross it at Bhagnagar by a grand stone bridge [Purana Pul], which is scarcely less beautiful than the Pont Neuf at Paris. The town is nearly the size of Orleans, well built and well opened out, and there are many fine large streets in it, but not being paved—any more than are those of all other towns of Persia and India—they are full of sand and dust; this is very inconvenient in summer. . . .
>
> When you have crossed the bridge you straightaway enter a wide street which leads to the King's palace. You see on the right hand the houses of some nobles of the court, and four or five *caravan sarais*, having two storeys, where there are large halls and chambers, which are cool. At the end of this street you find a large square, near which stands one of the walls of the palace, and in the middle there is a balcony where the King seats himself when he wishes to give audience to the people. The principal door of the palace is not in this square, but in another close by, and you enter at first into a large court surrounded by porticoes under which the King's guards are stationed. From this court you pass to another of the same construction, around which there are several beautiful apartments, with a terraced roof, upon these, as upon the quarter of the palace where they keep the elephants, there are beautiful gardens, and such large trees, that it is a matter of astonishment how these arches are able to carry such a weight. . . .
>
> On the other side of the town, from whence one goes to Masulipatam, there are two large tanks, each of them being a coss in circuit, upon which are some decorated boats intended for the pleasure of the King, and along the banks many fine houses which belong to the principal officers of the court.[3]

Hyderabad was cast in the mold of some medieval Persian cities. Imposing public buildings and palaces were to line its main streets. Secondary streets then led to self-contained neighborhoods or *mohallas*, with their narrow winding lanes often ending in blind alleys, small open squares, and densely packed low-rise houses with inner courtyards, many of them surprisingly spacious. The city was also Islamic both in population and in its mainstream culture which had roots in Arab, Turkish, and, especially, Persian ways of life. Since the Qutub Shahis were Shias, with strong links to their coreligionists in Iran, a great number of Persians streamed into Hyderabad over the years to seek their fortunes. The most important positions in the administration of the kingdom were held by Persians who had a tremendous impact on the art, architecture, literature, and culture of Hyderabad for nearly two hundred years after its foundation. With the establishment of the Asaf Jahi rule, Persian influence declined a little but nevertheless continued to shape the *hyderabadi* way of life, at least among the upper classes. Tavernier notes the fair countenance and good stature of its Muslim inhabitants as compared to the dark complexion of the surrounding peasantry, presumably Hindu, who had their assigned, mostly humble, places in the feudal order and whose native Telegu culture existed only at the fringes of the dominant Islamic ethos. In the cultural pecking order, the Persians were right at the top, followed by Turks and other central Asian immigrants. Native-born Indian Muslims felt inferior to both and were keen to establish the existence of Persian or Turkish blood in their lineage, a mind-set which has persisted till very recently. The anthropologist, S. C. Dube, quotes Hindus in the villages of Shamirpet outside Hyderabad in the 1960s saying: "A Hindu untouchable of yesterday becomes a Muslim today: and tomorrow he will start proclaiming that his forefathers lived in Arabia!"[4] Because of the Brahminical notions of pollution, the few Hindus who aspired to share the dominant cultural ethos could do so only on a limited basis.

The Perso-Islamic domination of Hyderabad's cultural and social life does not mean that Hindus were excluded from administrative positions and from a share of political power. Talented Brahmins and later the Kayasths could rise to high positions in the court. Another French traveler, François Martin, tells us of the heartburn among the Persian, Pathan, and Deccani nobles at the elevation of the Brahmin Madanna, who had become the most powerful minister of the king at the time of his visit.[5] Hindus were to hold high positions in the civil and revenue administration of the state well into the early period of the Asaf Jahi dynasty in the eighteenth century.

As the construction of the new capital gathered pace and the grand design of the city began to unfold, Mohammed Quli could not have imagined that the lowly Hindus would one day threaten its Islamic cultural suzerainty or that the city's decline was already presaged by an insignificant event taking place at the outer edges of his dominions. I refer, of course, to the entry of what would later be called the "modern West" through the East India Company, which began setting up a "factory" in the port city of Masulipatam in 1611.

For almost a hundred years, the city flourished in an approximation of

Mohammed Quli's vision. Even making allowances for travelers' hyperbole, Hyderabad seems to have deserved the accolades that came its way as not only a great but also a gracious city, with considerable hedonistic charm. Its Islamic ethos was not of the puritan kind but of the more pleasure-loving Persian variety. Martin gives appetizing details of his dinner on the evening of 28 June, 1681, with a Persian noble at Hyderabad's court—in fact, the brother-in-law of the king.[6] The number and quality of the dishes served on this memorable occasion far surpassed the fare of court feasts in Turkey. Every quarter of an hour, at the ringing of a bell, fresh glasses of wine were served. Female dancers entertained the guests and were offered as companions for the night as farewell gifts by a generous host.

Martin's evening, however pleasant for the participants, is not particularly remarkable. Irrespective of the period of history or region of the world, sensual indulgence has been a hallmark of the wealthy and the powerful, of what soap television today calls "the lifestyles of the rich and the famous." What is more interesting about Hyderabad is the percolation of hedonism into the lower strata of the city's population and its satisfactory partnership with the ends of commerce as well as the interests of the state. Tavernier, an epicure who loved good food and wine, tells us,

> There are so many public women in the town, the suburbs and in the fortress, which is like another town, that it is estimated there are generally more than 20,000 entered in the Darogha's [the Commissioner of Police] register, without which it is not allowed to any woman to ply this trade. In the cool of the evening you see them before the doors of their houses, which are for the most part small huts, and after the night comes they place at the doors a candle or a lighted lamp for a signal. It is then, also, that the shops where they sell *tari* [palm toddy] are opened. The king derives from the tax which he places on this *tari* a very considerable revenue, and it is principally on this account that they allow so many public women, because they are the cause of the consumption of much *tari*.[7]

Another Frenchman, Thevenot, notes the liberty enjoyed by the women of Hyderabad. Their marriage contracts had a clause that the wife would retain a complete freedom of movement and could even drink *tari* if that was her desire!

In 1685, Hyderabad was plundered by the Mughals. Two years later, it was annexed to the Mughal empire by Aurangzeb, but the period of its relative obscurity was brief. In 1725, Nizam ul Mulk, the Mughal's viceroy in the

Deccan, made himself virtually independent of his nominal overlord. Hyderabad again became the capital of a dynasty, this time that of the Asaf Jahis ("equal in dignity to Asaf, the minister of King Solomon"), the title given to Nizam ul Mulk by the hapless emperor of a rapidly unraveling Mughal empire.

The threat to the fortunes of the walled city (the walls themselves were demolished in the 1920s to relieve traffic congestion), however, did not arise from the quick changes that were taking place on India's political map during the eighteenth and nineteenth centuries. The impending danger was more from the process of modernization which picked up pace in the wake of the British conquest of India. Although the Nizam's suzerainty over his dominions was spared—he became a subordinate ally of the British in 1798—the political, economic, and administrative importance of the old city was now fatefully set on a course of slow erosion. With the coming of the railway in 1874 and the establishment of an incipient industrial base through the setting up of railway repair workshops and a textile mill, it was clear, at least in hindsight, that the northern part of the city outside the fortified walls held the key to Hyderabad's future.

The shift northward, across the Musi river, was accelerated by the floods of 1908 and the plague of 1911 which led the Nizam to move his residence and administrative offices out of the walled city to the north of the river. The ruler's example was soon followed by most of his nobility. The final blow to old Hyderabad was, of course, the integration of the state with the republic of India after the country's independence from British rule. This meant not only the dismantling of the Nizam's administrative machinery but also the disappearance of the feudal economic base on which most of the old city's population had subsisted. In addition, many of the Muslim elite fled out of Hyderabad, mostly to Pakistan. The old city was well on its way to becoming a ghetto. As Ratna Naidu in her sociological study of Hyderabad has observed, "Deprived of economic opportunities with the dismantling of the feudal structure, and deprived of its elite, who are usually the powerful spokesmen for the enhancement of civic amenities, the walled city as an area languishes in multiple deprivation.[8] The deprivation is not only material but also psychological and cultural.

Culturally, the history of Hyderabad is witness to a process of ever increasing heterogenization. Although the Hindus were always a part of what was essentially a Muslim city, their native Telegu culture was clearly a subordinate, "low" culture in the preeminently Islamic scheme of things. In the eighteenth and nineteenth centuries, many cultural groups migrated into

Hyderabad from other parts of the country and even, as in the case of the Arabs, from as far away as the Middle East. The Arabs, like the Marathas, came to Hyderabad to soldier in the Nizam's army. The trading communities of the Muslim Bohras from Gujarat and the Hindu Marwadis from Rajasthan became prominent in the city's commercial life. Then there were the Kayasthas and the Khatris from north India, traditionally the backbone of many an Indian state's administration, who played a similar role in the Nizam's affairs of state. These groups tended to cluster together in separate enclaves where they could follow their own ways of religious and community life. This is not to say that individuals did not leaven their traditional lifestyles with the dominant Perso-Islamic culture. Many (especially the Kayasthas, who are well known for their identification with the masters they have so ably served, whether the ruler be British or Muslim) would cultivate an appreciation of Urdu poetry or adopt the sartorial style of *sherwani*, the long buttoned-up coat with a high round collar and *gumi topi*, a cousin of the Turkish fez. They would prefer Hyderabad's distinctive cuisine and its gracious modes of public address and speech. Yet, on the whole, the lifestyles of the various groups in the rest of the population—their customs, mores, architectural styles, food habits—remained distinctive. In the seventeenth century, for instance, in the inns set up by the Qutub Shahis for poor travelers, Muslims received a dole of bread, rice, or vegetables already cooked whereas "the idolaters, who eat nothing which has been prepared by others, are given flour to make bread and a little butter and as soon as their bread is baked they cover it on both sides with melted butter."[9] As in the rest of the country, in the medieval period, Hindus and Muslims shared activities and experiences in the public realm "even though in private they were completely segregated, almost opposed to each other."[10] In short, it was a multicultural coexistence rather than any merger into a single, composite culture; Hindus and Muslims lived together separately. They were more than strangers, not often enemies, but less than friends.

After Hyderabad's integration with independent India, the heterogenization percolated even into the *mohallas* as Hindus began to replace the Muslims who had left for Pakistan. Thus from 1951 to 1961, the Muslim population of the old city declined from 69 percent to 55 percent while the Hindu population increased from 21 percent to 40 percent, a trend which began to be reversed only after the violence between the two communities became endemic. The recurrent bloodletting in the past fifteen years has had the demographic consequence that Muslims from the outlying areas began to flee to the old city as if to a fortress while the Hindu exodus was in the

reverse direction. Currently, the Muslim population of the old city is esti-
mated at around 70 percent.

Contemporary Hyderabad is certainly not a city for those with a par-
tiality for nostalgia. The Musi river has long ceased to be one. It is a stinking
sewer without the sewer's saving grace of flowing water which at least keeps
the garbage moving. The Musi now is but a marshy tract between the old and
the new cities, with slime-covered puddles and a sewage-borne creeping,
crawling, and buzzing life which, to me, makes Hyderabad the mosquito
capital of India. Like the river, there is no longer an "old city" of medieval
Islam. Leprous beggars asking for alms in the name of Allah are still to be
found but the nobles, taking the evening air dressed in flowing muslim ropes,
are long gone. There are no carriages clattering on the unpaved streets or
groups of veiled women, hinting at suppressed laughter and whispered assig-
nations, gliding through the brightly lit bazaars redolent with strong flowery
perfumes and the smell of fresh horse droppings, the shops stocked with
choice wares from Persia, Arabia, and the rest of Hindostan.

Today, the old city is barely one step ahead of being a vast ghetto of over
a million people, living in settlements, the *bastis*, and the *mohallas*, that are
homogeneous in their religious and caste compositions. Small houses
stacked side by side line winding alleys which are negotiable only by foot or
bicycle. Goats, dogs, and chickens, coexisting in the harmony of the chron-
ically hungry, rummage through the refuse littering the open spaces. Unemployed young men stride purposefully through the lanes, even if the purpose
is only to buy a cigarette from a corner shop or to impress any hidden female
watcher with their purposeful mien. Children play the staple games of the
poor—hopscotch for the girls while the boys run after an old bicycle tire,
kept rolling in a wobbly motion as much by their excitement as by the
strokes of the stick propelling it forward.

The economic picture of the walled city, described by Naidu, is dis-
mal.[11] The working population is around 30 percent of the total number of
inhabitants. The largest number, about a third, are skilled and semiskilled
artisans engaged in the traditional occupations of weaving, pottery, sandal
making, and food preparation. About a quarter of the working population
earns its livelihood from casual daily wage work, as pushcart vendors of vegetables and fruits, hawkers of trinkets, pullers of rickshaws, scavengers, and
other low-prestige occupations such as watchmen and messenger boys in
government offices. The fabled earnings of the Muslims who went to work in
the Arab countries of the Persian Gulf have brought only minor changes into
the lives and the living standards of their families. They have provided only a

temporary respite from pervasive economic hardship. The Gulf connection of the Muslims has had more social and cultural rather than economic consequences; for instance, it has resulted in a greater pan-Islamic pride which is visible in the sleek new mosques that have recently been built in the Muslim-dominated areas of the walled city.

The city is poor, but its poverty is more a general unkemptness and disorder than drabness. Economic deprivation has not smothered Hyderabad's vitality or dulled its desire for vivid definition. Even in destitute *mohallas* there are startling splashes of color. Here, only the front door has been painted; there, the wooden shutters of a small window. Green, the color of the faithful, is the most preferred. It ranges in hue from a bilious green to the freshly planted paddy green of those gleaming new mosques of the last two decades. Occasionally, there is a swathe of sunflower yellow across a house front, but another universal favorite of both the Hindus and the Muslims appears to be a cheap metallic blue, the color of the sky on glossy religious posters. Hyderabad's bazaars and the houses of its well-to-do citizens favor ornamental wrought iron grills for the shutters of their shops and gates. The work is intricate and distinctive, giving the impression of swirling curlicues and scimitars, of Persian calligraphy cast in iron.

Hindus and Muslims: Versions of the Past

My aim here is not to write a history of Hindu-Muslim relations in Hyderabad for the preceding three hundred years. It is both more modest and in some ways more ambitious. It is modest in that I would like to get for myself and convey to readers a general impression of the way Hindus and Muslims have felt about each other, whenever they have felt as Hindus or as Muslims or, in other, more psychological words, whenever overarching religious identities have become salient and dwarfed other group identities through which individuals also experience themselves. It is difficult because historians are of little help in an enterprise which is so contentious and where the interpretation of historical data is so inseparable from the historian's own political aims, ideological commitments, and the strong emotions these commitments often generate. Yet some sense of this past is utterly necessary for my enterprise, considering the myriad reflections in which I was to encounter it in the present. In an ancient country like India, where collective memories reach back thousands of years, cultural psychology can never be as ahistorical as it may be in a young country like the United States. Cultural psychology in India must necessarily include the study of the psychic representations of collective pasts, the way collective memories are transmitted through generations, and the ways the past is used as a receptacle for projections from the present.

The chief protagonists of the debate on the past of Hindu-Muslim relations which excites so much contemporary passion are the secularist (both Hindu and Muslim) on the one side and the Hindu nationalist on the other, with the Muslim fundamentalist and the Hindu revivalist on the sidelines, trying to inject their particular brand of venom in the proceedings. The debate has momentous consequences, its winner aiming at nothing less than the capture of India's political soul and the chance to shape its destiny in the coming decades.

The secularist faction—framer of India's constitution and politically ascendant since the time of Nehru—comprises most of the Western-educated liberal and leftist intelligentsia and is greatly influential in academia.[12] Hindu and Muslim, the secularist avers, are relatively recent categories in Indian history. Before the late nineteenth century, overarching religious entities and identities such as Hindu and Muslim did not exist. Among the Hindus, there were various sects frequently at odds with each other; nor did Indian Muslims constitute a monolithic Islamic collectivity. The secularist goes on to draw a picture of widespread Hindu-Muslim symbiosis of the precolonial and early colonial periods and the development of a syncretic popular religion, especially at the village level, which borrows elements both from Islamic practice and Hindu ritual while it reveres Muslim saints as much as Hindu holy men.

The secularist view makes a clear-cut distinction between the terms "religious" and "communal"; the latter is not used in its Anglo-American lexical sense, meaning someone who is altruistic and civic-minded, but in its specifically Indian meaning of one whose exclusive attachment to his or her community is combined with an active hostility against other communities which share its geographical and political space. Whereas religion is solely seen as a matter of personal faith and reverence for a particular set of icons, rituals, and dogmas, communalism is a more collective affair which involves a community's politics and economics as much as its faith. Communalism not only produces an identification with a religious community but also with its political, economic, social and cultural interests and aspirations. This identification is accompanied by the strong belief that these interests not only diverge from but are in actual conflict with the interests of other communities.

In this view, the precolonial and early colonial period conflicts between Hindus and Muslims were rare. Whenever they occurred, they were essentially religious in nature, that is, the conflicts were over religious symbols such as the route or form taken by a religious procession, issues of control over temples or mosques, and so on. Twentieth-century conflicts, on the other hand, have been initiated by communal ideologies and are basically over clashing economic interests. In the secularist view, even the religious persecution of Hindus by such eighteenth-century monarchs as the Mughal emperor Aurangzeb or, later, by Tipu Sultan in South India, were dictated by reasons of state rather than the communal ideology of any particular ruler. Aurangzeb's discrimination against Hindus and the destruction of their temples is interpreted as an attempt to reformulate the ideological basis of the late Mughal state, while Tipu's attacks on Hindu temples and the Hindu culture of the Kerala Nayars was a deliberate act of policy rather than of religious fanaticism.[13]

The secularist holds that communalism, and the consequent large-scale violence between Hindus and Muslims, began to spread in the late nineteenth century chiefly because of colonialism.[14] To counter a growing Indian nationalism, he argues, the British followed a "divide and rule" policy by deliberately strengthening Muslim communalism. The rapid diffusion of nineteenth-century Hindu revivalism and of pan-Islamism in the following century, again the products of Asia's colonial encounter with the imperial West, was another reason for the rise of communalism. Yet another factor was the decline of the syncretic warrior of the eighteenth century, who had been forged in the mixed bands of soldiers, Hindu and Muslim, who served various kings, again Hindu or Muslim, or foraged on their own in the anarchic political conditions which prevailed in India as the Mughal empire unraveled.

The basic fabric of India, though, remains syncretic, a commingling of Islamic influences with Hindu traditions. Hindus and Muslims are not divided along any cultural or social-psychological lines except in the narrow area of personal faith.

The Hindu nationalist argues that a fundamental divide between Hindus and Muslims is a basic fact of Indian history which is ignored by the secularist.[15] The Hindu nationalist would support the contention of the French anthropologist Marc Gaborieau, that Hindus and Muslims found their identity in the deepest sentiments of opposition between the two, sentiments that are traceable throughout the nine centuries of Indo-Muslim history, from the writings of the Arab traveler Al-Beruni in the eleventh century to Jinnah, the founder of Pakistan in the twentieth.[16] The Hindu nationalist is thus in basic agreement with Pakistani historians who too support the "two nations" theory and label Akbar, the syncretic Mughal monarch who is a hero to the secularist, as an apostate to Islam.

In the Hindu nationalist view, the conflict between Hindus and Muslims is squarely religious, indeed theological. Its roots lie in Islam's exclusive claim to truth and its refusal to grant equal status to Hindu beliefs and doctrines. Islam's division of people into believers and infidels and the world into arenas of peace—*dar-ul-Islam*—and of conflict—*dar-ul-harb*—which led to terrible cruelties against the Hindu infidel's person and religious shrines over hundreds of years, cannot be erased from Hindu collective memory. Moreover, the Hindu nationalist maintains, the Muslim continues to persist in intolerance, in the belief that all that is outside the Qur'an is an error if not an abomination. The Hindu nationalist avers that secularists seem to direct their arguments and appeals only toward the Hindus since they are firmly rejected by the Muslims who seek identity in their own religious tradition and personal laws even when those go against the very fundamentals of a secular state. The roots of Hindu-Muslim conflict lie in Muslim religious intolerance, Muslim failure to outgrow a medieval bigotry, and the inability to learn, in the absence of guidelines in the Qur'an, how to live in a state which is not Muslim-controlled.

To summarize: the story of Hindu-Muslim relations takes on different hues depending upon the color of the ideological lenses through which it is viewed. For the liberal historian or one with leftist leanings, the story is bathed in a roseate glow of the precolonial golden age of Hindu-Muslim amity. For these storytellers, the tale is of a commingling and flowering of a composite cultural tradition, especially in art, music, and architecture.[17] It is the story of a gradual drawing closer of Hindus and Muslims in the forms of their daily lives and of an enthusiastic participation in each other's festivals. In this vision, there is little room for conflict between the communities. Sporadic outbreaks of violence needing some explanation are almost never religious in their origin but dictated by local economic interests and political compulsions. To the conservative Hindu nationalist, on the other hand, for whom the Hindu saffron and the Muslim green do not mix to create a pale pink, the rift between the two communities is a fundamental fact of Indian history. They see Hindu-Muslim relations framed by a thousand-year-old "civilizational" conflict in which the Muslims, militarily victorious and politically ascendant for centuries, tried to impose Islamic civilization on their Hindu subjects through all means, from coercion to bribery and cajolery, and yet had only limited success. The composite civilization, according to this view, was limited to small sections of the population around the Muslim courts and to court-patronized arts like music and architecture. It also included some Hindus who adopted the Persian-inspired language and ways of life of their rulers. The vast majority of Hindus kept their civilizational core intact while they resentfully tolerated the Muslim onslaught. In this view, the outbreaks of violence between the two communities were inevitable whenever Muslim dominance was threatened; the rage of the denigrated Hindu, stored up over long periods of time, had to explode once historical circumstances sanctioned such eruptions.

Between Enemy Lines

To look critically at any aspect of Hindu-Muslim relations today is a task fraught less with difficulty than with trepidation. As political passions run high, a commitment to either the secularist or the Hindu nationalist view is considered almost mandatory. Any critique which is seen as deviating from the one or the other easily invites the epithets of "cryptofascist" from one side and "pseudosecularist" from the other. Both "crypto-" and "pseudo-" are angry words, the former connoting a base veiling of real intent, the latter alluding to a fake or malicious deception. Yet, as impotant as it is to stand up and be counted, there is still a place for standing aside and counting, something I intend to do when examining the two different views of the Hindu-Muslim past. For, ideally, the psychoanalyst is essentially an onlooker and commentator on the worlds of love and hate. Still somewhat starry-eyed after so many years in the profession, I see the psychoanalyst standing outside the fray, unmoved by the violent passions that swirl all around: his only intellectual commitment to a questioning that does not seek answers but encourages reflection, his suspicion evoked by ideals excessively noble and ideas particularly *en vogue*, his interest aroused by all that is tabooed. It is comforting for me to remember—to counteract my guilt at not being able to live up to the ideal—that an analyst is also compassionate toward ideals that are fallen short of, including his own, since I know my own emotional involvement in the issue will not always allow me the neutrality I may strive for.

Let me begin with the fallacies of the secularist position which, I believe, has underestimated the extent of the historical rift between Hindus and Muslims and has thus invited a backlash to its Panglossian view of the past. In other words, the secularist has tended to downplay the dark side of Hindu-Muslim relations in India. Scholars sympathetic to this viewpoint have pointed out that Hindu-Muslim conflicts are not only a product of the colonial period but also occurred in precolonial times and were often also communal—in the secular understanding of the term—rather than religious.[18]

In the medieval period, even the Sufis, the Islamic mystics who are so often held up as examples of "composite culture," the syncretic Muslims *par excellence*, had serious limits to their tolerance. In the question of faith they were unequivocal about the superiority of Islam and the hellish fate in store for the Hindu infidels on judgment day. As Muzaffar Alam puts it: "Indeed, in relation to Hindus, often it is difficult to distinguish between an orthodox theologian [the obstreperous *mullah* of Hindu imagination] and a liberal mystic."[19] Many a Sufi was openly hostile to the religion and social practices of the Hindus, paranoid—even at the zenith of Muslim power—that the Hindus would obliterate Islamic laws, Islam, and the Muslim community if they ever captured political power. Alam summarizes the Muslim side of the Hindu-Muslim equation thus: "An average literate Muslim believed that Islam and Hinduism belonged to two radically diverse traditions and that the twain would never meet."[20] To emphasize the sense of separate identities, of the distance between the two communities, even common social practices came to be known as *Hinduwani* and *Musalmani*.[21] Thus although Hindu and Muslim identities were not as fixed and continuous over time as the Hindu nationalist believes, neither were these identities absent as claimed by the secularist. In the medieval period, for large sections of people, Hindu and Muslim identities were intermittent rather than continuous, occasionally flowering rather than perpetually in full bloom, evoked whenever religious symbols and sentiments moved to the forefront of conscious concern, which was mostly when they were perceived to be threatened or under actual attack.

The secularist underestimation of the aversion between Hindus and Muslims and the denial of the existence of any kind of collective, cultural identities in the past derives, I believe, from the reliance of many historians and political scientists on objective rather than subjective, experiential data, which is more often mined by the anthropologist. To illustrate this, let me take the earlier example of Tipu Sultan, whose destruction of some Hindu temples and persecution of certain Hindu groups are objectively considered as motivated by his suspicion of the loyalty of these groups and of the temple priests' close ties to the Hindu house of Wodiyar which Tipu and his father had replaced. Tipu did not go on any general anti-Hindu rampage and in fact even supported some temples with donations from the state coffers.

There is another, unwritten version of these incidents which has gone into the making of what I would call the "cultural memory" (a term I prefer to "collective memory") of many Hindus. Cultural memory is the imaginative basis for a sense of cultural identity. For isn't imagination a memory of vital moments of life freed from their actual, historical context? Cultural memory, too, is a group's history freed from rootedness in time—it is as much imagination as the actual events that go into its construction. The cultural memory of Tipu's action (as of Aurangzeb's) has a markedly different flavor from what one reads in history texts. A very different realm of experience and distinctive emotion is evoked in a believing Hindu who reads or hears about Tipu forcibly circumcising Brahmins and compelling them afterward to eat cow's flesh as an unequivocal token of their loss of caste. That Hindu shares the indignation of those seventeenth-century compatriots at Tipu's destruction of the temple and their relief when they are finally rid of "the yoke of this tyrant."[22] Indeed, it would be odd to expect, as the secularist sometimes seems to do, that such a deeply religious people as the Hindus would have understood the mysterious workings of Tipu's *raison d'état* and not reacted with disgust and horror to what clearly seemed to be a brazen attack on their religious sentiments and cherished symbols of faith.

The ethnographers of the seventeenth, eighteenth, and nineteenth centuries, who were also the cultural psychologists of their eras, are preeminently the European travelers. Generally looking down upon India and its peoples from the heights of European superiority, the travelers are especially contemptuous of the Hindus, who are mostly referred to as idolators or Gentiles, whereas the Muslims, clearly identified as such, are more familiar to the Christian and thus less an object of mystery or scorn. Lacking in any knowledge of the country's religious traditions, the travelers' interest is excited by what appear to them as strange Hindu ceremonies, rituals, and customs—with an emphasis on temple courtesans, burning of widows, and orgiastic religiosity.

From the travelers, then, we can only get pointers to Hindu-Muslim relations by paying attention to casual observations and throwaway remarks that are adjunct to the European's main interest in describing to countrymen at home the political and economic situation of India and the unfamiliar manners and mores of its inhabitants. Thus, for instance, we get the following observation from the French traveler, François Bernier, who traveled in the Mughal empire between 1656 and 1668: "The tenth incarnation (of Vishnu), say the Gentiles, will have for its object the emancipation of mankind from the tyranny of the Mahometan, and it will take place at a time when according to our calculation, Anti-Christ is to appear; this is however but a popular tradition, not to be found in their sacred books."[23] Such scattered remarks, lacking the necessary context, cannot be taken as an accurate description of Hindu-Muslim relations. They do, however, make us doubt the picture of widespread amity, while pointing to the existence of many sullen Hindus resentful of Muslim rule, if not of the "Mahometans."

The exception to most other travelers is Abbé Dubois, a French missionary who spent thirty years (1792–1823) in the south of India. As a man of the cloth, the Abbé is naturally convinced of the superiority of his faith over the religions of India. Yet he also displays a compassionate understanding for the customs of the people he observed so closely for so long. Most of the time he is remarkably fair. Abbé Dubois is a natural ethnographer, with a stance toward his "field work" which would meet the approval of any graduate school of anthropology.

At first glance, Dubois's work seems to support the secularist contention that the conflict between the Hindu and Muslim was not communal but religious, no different from the quarrels between various Hindu sects. And indeed it is true that religious strife is as Indian as mango pickle. Yet when we compare the internecine strife of Hindu sects with the violence between Hindus and Muslims, the difference between the two is obvious. Here, for instance, is the Abbé's description of a "riot" he observed between the followers of Vishnu and those of Shiva:

> According to Vishnavites it is the height of all abomination to wear the lingam [the sign of Shiva]. According to their antagonists whoever is decorated with the *namam* [the sign of Vishnu] will be tormented in hell by a sort of fork similar in form to this emblem. These mutual recriminations often end in violent altercations and riots. The numerous bands of religious mendicants of both sects are specially apt to provoke strife. One may sometimes see these fanatics collected together in crowds to support their opinion of the super-excellence of their respective doctrines. They will overwhelm each other with torrents of abuse and obscene insults, and pour forth blasphemies and imprecations, on one side against Shiva, on the other Vishnu; and finally they will come to blows. Fortunately blood is seldom shed on these battle fields. They content themselves with dealing each other buffets with their fists, knocking off each other's turbans, and much tearing of garments. Having thus given vent to their feelings, the combatants separate by mutual consent.

That these religious dissensions do not set the whole country ablaze, occasion those crimes of all kinds which were for centuries the

result of religious fanaticism in Europe and elsewhere, is due no doubt
to the naturally mild and timid character of the Hindus, and especially
to the fact that the greater number compound with their consciences
and pay equal honor to Vishnu and Shiva. Being thus free from any bias
towards either party, the latter serve as arbitrators in these religious
combats and often check incipient quarrels.[24]

The description of this riot reveals a ritualized, gamelike quality which
combines passion with restraint. It is a ritualization of antagonisms, what Erik
Erikson called "a creative formalization" which helps to avoid both impulsive
excess and compulsive self-restrictions.[25] The Vaishnavites and the Shaivites
engage each other in both interplay and combat, practicing "a form of war
which can occur only among those who are at peace." In contrast, the Hindu-
Muslim conflicts have no such playlike quality, pervaded as they are by
deathly intent, with the burning down of houses, demolition of temples,
mosques, and shrines.[26] Their vocabulary is of mortal enmity, victory, and
defeat, a combat that must lead to humiliation and grievous wounds to the
collective self of one group or the other.

I have already mentioned that the Hindu nationalist may well be overestimating (in contrast to the secularist underestimation) the existence and
strength of overarching Hindu and Muslim religious identities in India's precolonial past. The Hindu nationalist is, I believe, also overestimating the role
of doctrinal differences between Islam and Hindu beliefs for the difficulties
in the relations between the two communities. To me the Hindu-Muslim rift
appears as much the consequence of a collision between two collective nar-
cissisms, between two equally grandiose group selves, each convinced of its
civilizational superiority, as of differences in matters of faith. Abbé Dubois
brings out clearly the injuries to group narcissism, the wounds to collective
vanity sustained in the Hindu-Muslim encounter:

The Brahmins in particular cherish an undying hatred against the Ma-
homedans. The reason for this is that the latter think so lightly of the
pretensions of these so-called gods of earth; and, above all, the Ma-
homedans do not scruple to display hearty contempt for their ceremonies and customs generally. Besides, the haughty Mussulmans can vie
with them in pride and insolence. Yet there is this difference: the arro-
gance of a Mussulman is based only on the political authority with
which he is invested, or on the eminence of the rank he occupies;
whereas the Brahmin's superiority is inherent in himself, and it remains
intact, no matter what his condition in life may be. Rich or poor, unfor-

tunate or prosperous, he always goes on the principle ingrained in him that he is the most able, the most excellent, and the most perfect of all created beings, that all the rest of mankind are infinitely beneath him, and that there is nothing in the world so sublime or so admirable as his customs and practices.[27]

The Hindu nationalist may also be overestimating the depth of the Hindu's historical aversion to the Muslim, which was perhaps more prevalent in the upper castes where Muslim religious intolerance came up against the Brahminical conviction of Hindu superiority. Dubois remarks:

> But if Brahmins cannot with any justice be accused of intolerance in the matter of religion, the same can certainly not be said in regard to their civil usage and customs. On these points they are utterly unreasonable. . . . Though they have had to submit to various conquerors who have proved themselves to be their superiors in courage and bravery, yet in spite of this, they have always considered themselves infinitely their superior in the matter of civilization.
>
> The Mahomedans, who can tolerate no laws, no customs, and no religion but their own, used every advantage which conquest gave them in a vain attempt to force their religion on the people who had succumbed to them almost without resistance. But these same Hindus, who did not dare to complain when they saw their wives, their children, and everything they held most dear carried off by these fierce conquerors, their country devastated by fire and sword, their temples destroyed, their idols demolished, these same Hindus I say, only displayed some sparks of energy when it came to changing their customs for those of their oppressors.[28]

What excited the Hindus' hostility was as much the Muslim assault on their lifestyle as on their idols. As we shall see later, the Hindu's shocked disgust, for example, at the Muslim eating of beef, then as now, is a far more potent factor in Hindu-Muslim relations than Islam's reputed intolerance.

The Hindu nationalist, I believe, also overemphasizes the impact of ten centuries of Muslim domination. The explanation for the Hindu's negative sentiments toward the Muslim as lying in a subjugated people's "natural" resentment is not wholly convincing if we remember that such aversion was negligible in the case of the British. In spite of the fact that the *raj* was economically exploitative, funneling wealth out of the country, whereas during the Muslim rule wealth stayed within, the latter evokes a hostility not due to the former. Political subjugation and economic exploitation, it seems, played less of a role in determining the Hindu reaction because the Hindu collective identity, however nebulous, was crystallized around shared religious symbols rather than based on political or economic structures. Muslims were perceived to be outragers of Hindu religious sentiment and mockers of their faith whereas the British were, at worst, indifferent. Granted that the British too ate beef—a practice deeply repugnant to most Hindus—but they were too few and carried out their private lives holed up in bungalows and barracks which were shielded from public scrutiny by high walls and thick hedges. In contrast, the Muslim lived cheek and jowl with the Hindu. This proximity created the potential for the emergence of new cultural and social forms but also occasioned simmering resentment and nagging friction. The British beef-eater was remote, almost abstract. The Muslim butcher in his blood-flecked undervest and *lungi*, wielding a huge carving knife, was a very visible part of a town's life, a figure of awe and dread for the Hindu child and of a fear-tinged repulsion for the adult. The Englishman remained a stranger, the Muslim became the Other.

Looking at the Hindu-Muslim encounter as decisively colored by the facts of dominance and subordination, by aggression and resistance, by the zero-sum game of winners and losers, the Hindu nationalist pays homage to the influential paradigm in contemporary historical, anthropological, and political science writing which considers power as the main axis around which all relations between groups are structured. The impressive work that has resulted through the emphasis on power, especially on the inequality of colonial and imperial relations, has been invaluable. But as Raymond Grew points out, this very emphasis also tends to obscure and often ideologize the processes of assimilation, transformation, reassertion, and re-creation, which too are inherent in all cultural encounters.[29] The Hindu-Muslim encounter has been no exception.

The gulf between the two opposing views of the Hindu-Muslim encounter is not a matter solely of interest to scholars and political propagandists but is reflected in and vitally influences many facets of contemporary consciousness. Much of the Indian heritage—monuments, art, music, legends, history—which people of an earlier generation were accustomed to regard as noncontroversial has suddenly become hotly contested. As an example, let me take the legend of the founding of Hyderabad. For those subscribing to the syncretic school, this legend is the narrative embodiment of an essential Hindu-Muslim amity in the past. The story itself is a *mythos*, seeking to convince through the power of aesthetics and symbolism, and is a counterpoint to the *logos* of formal thought on Hindu-Muslim relations which is routinely employed by the social scientist. The tale goes thus:

> Sultan Mohammed Quli Qutub Shah (1580–1612) was the grandson of Sultan Quli Qutub Shah, founder of the Qutub Shahi dynasty. In 1579, when still a prince and just fourteen years old, he fell in love with Bhagmati, a commoner [and a Hindu], an extraordinarily talented and beautiful dancer. She lived across the river Musi in the village of Chichalam, some distance away from the royal fortress at Golconda. Every evening when dusk fell, the prince stole away from the palace grounds to meet his beloved across the river. One day a terrible storm broke and the river was in spate. Fearing that his lover might drown, the prince braved the turbulent rising waters and saved Bhagmati. Compelled to accept his son's choice, the king, Sultan Ibrahim, had a large stone bridge built across the Musi to enable Mohammed Quli to court the dancer. Known today as the Purana Pul ["old bridge"], it stands mute witness to this story. On his accession to the throne, Mohammed Quli married Bhagmati and in her honor built a splendid new city on the site of the village Chichalam. He called the city "Bhagnagar" or the "City of Good Fortune." Bhagmati later took the name of Hyder Mahal and Mohammed Quli renamed the city as Hyderabad.[30]

It is not surprising that, whereas history discerns the origins of Hyderabad in the mundane facts of congestion and lack of water in the old fortress capital of Golconda, legend attributes the founding of the city to the sublimity of a prince's love for a commoner. What is more relevant to our purpose, however, is the way Hindu nationalists interpret the legend today. They see in the tale yet another illustration of the fundamental Hindu-Muslim divide. "All the story tells us," says a militant Hindu, active in the campaign to have Hyderabad revert back to its original name of Bhagnagar, "is that the Mussulman has always fucked our women whenever he has wanted to, as he has fucked us over the centuries. If he deigned to take one of our women into his harem, he could not tolerate her remaining a Hindu but forced her to convert to Islam. Where are the stories of Hindu princes marrying Muslim wives?" This particular interpretation of the legend is not about how a youth's erotic obsession for a girl flowered into the deep love of a mature man, or about an era of close Hindu-Muslim relations which permitted, even when they did not encourage, love across religious persuasions. For the Hindu nationalist, the legend is about Hindu defeat and a collective shame wherein the community's most beautiful and accomplished women had to be ceded to the Muslim conqueror.

Finally, what is the truth? As far as I can see the truth is that there are two overarching histories of Hindu-Muslim relations—with many local variations—which have been used by varying political interests and ideologies and have been jostling for position for many centuries. In times of heightened conflict between the two communities, the Hindu nationalist history that supports the version of conflict between the two assumes preeminence and organizes cultural memory in one particular direction. In times of relative peace, the focus shifts back to the history emphasizing commonalities and shared pieces of the past. Many of the cultural memories which were appropriate during the conflict will retreat, fade, or take on new meaning, while others that incorporate the peaceful coexistence of Hindus and Muslims will resurface. And so it goes, on and on.

TWO

The Riot

M y first personal experience of Hindu-Muslim violence was at the time of the partition of the country in 1947, when ferocious riots between the two communities engulfed many parts of the subcontinent, especially in the north. I was nine years old at the time and we lived in Rohtak, a small town some fifty miles west of Delhi, where my father was an additional district magistrate, "the ADM Sahib." As the killings and looting raged uncontrolled in the villages and towns of Punjab, more and more members of his extended family poured into Rohtak as refugees from the cities of Lahore, Lyallpur, and Sialkot, where they had lived for many generations and which now lay in the freshly created state of Pakistan. The rooms and verandas of our house became sprawling dormitories, with mats and durries spread close to each other on the floor as uncles, aunts, and cousins of varying degree of kinship lived and slept in what for a child was an excitingly intimate confusion. The kitchen, over which my mother had willingly abdicated all control, hummed the whole day with the purposeful activity of women, and there was not a time of day when a few bodies were not seen huddled in nooks and corners in various stages of sleep.

With the loss of their homes and places of work, with the snapping of long-standing friendships and other social ties, there was little for the refugees to do in our house except seek comfort from the sharing of each other's riot experiences. This they did in groups which continuously changed in their membership as they shifted from one room of the house to another. As a small boy, yet privileged as the son of a father who gave them food and shelter, I could sit in on any group of adults, though at its edge, without being shooed away and told to go and play with other children. I became aware of their bitterness about the leaders of a newly independent India, Nehru and especially Gandhi by whom they felt most betrayed. Gandhi was the pet ob-

ject of my grandmother's aversion, and many of my uncles and aunts shame-
lessly encouraged her as she held forth in her toothless, gummy voice, surprisingly similar to the Mahatma's own, on Gandhi's many affronts to Hindu
sentiment and advanced salacious speculations on the reasons for his love of
the "Mussulman."

It was also the first time I became aware of the Hindu hate of the
Mussulman—the destroyer of temples, devourer of cow flesh, defiler of
Hindu womanhood, rapers and killers all! Mussulmans were little better than
animals, dirty and without self-control, who indulged all the demands of the
senses, especially the violence of the body and pleasures of the flesh. Up to
this time I had known Muslims as occasional colleagues of my father, some
boys in school and, especially, as indulgent servants. In Sargodha, where my
father was posted before he was transferred to Rohtak, I was particularly fond
of Imtiaz, his Muslim orderly, who took me on forbidden bicycle rides to the
bazaar. Once, seeing him get his forearm covered with an elaborate tattoo, I
too had insisted on one—to the subsequent shocked disapproval of my parents. Then there was Fatima, a teenage girl who looked after me from the
ages of four to seven, and who was almost on par with my mother as the
object of my first desires and longings. Fatima was a patient and very often a
willing participant in the games I invented for both of us. She was a valiant
liar on my behalf whenever one of my undertakings ended disastrously. Half
girl, half woman, Fatima delightfully forgot to be consistently one or the
other when she was with me. Hitching up her *salwar,* she would scamper up a
guava tree to pluck the best fruit from the top branches. Her maternal persona taking over once she was back on ground, she would clean the guavas
for me and hold the salt in the open palm of her hand while I ate. Fatima was
an indispensable assistant on our fishing expeditions to the small pond that
lay in the grounds of the house. She helped me make the fishing rod from a
twig, a piece of string, and a bent pin. She kneaded the dough we brought
and made it into small pellets which were used as bait. In spite of my never
catching any fish she did not destroy my illusion that there were indeed some
lurking under the scummy green film that covered the pond.

It is not as if I were unaware that the Muslims were somehow different,
although I do not recollect ever hearing the statement, "He [or she] is a Mussulman," as a marker of a person's identity in our home. I knew Imtiaz and
Fatima could not enter the kitchen where Chet Ram, the Brahman cook, held
sway, because they were Muslims. The Muslim parts of Sargodha were subtly
different from the Hindu *mohalla*s concentrated around the bazaar. In the
early evening, the cooking smells wafting out into the alleys were more

pungent—the odor of mutton fried with onion, garlic, and ginger paste, with coriander and cumin, seemed embedded in the very walls of the houses. Old men with henna-dyed beards sat out on stringed cots, smoking their hookahs and murmuring their incessant gossip. The women, covered from head to toe in flowing white and black veils, glided silently through the alleys, followed by small children scurrying to keep up. There were also fewer stray dogs in the alleys, the ritually unclean animal being far less tolerated by the Muslim than by the indifferent Hindu.

As a little child, I had registered the differences but never felt the need to either evaluate or explain them to myself. It was only now, in Rohtak, that the family's "war stories" from the riot-torn towns of Pakistan began to retrospectively shape my early observations in the direction of prejudice. Two of these I recount below. For a time these stories threatened to become the core of my memory of "the Muslim" although, in the end, I like to believe, they did not overlay the child's love for Imtiaz and Fatima, did not replace it with fear, anger, and aversion. When I was carrying out this study in a Muslim locality in Hyderabad and engaging groups of Muslims in conversation, I became aware that within myself "the Muslim" was still somewhat of a stranger. The strangeness was not due to my ignorance of him but to my being singularly affected by someone I did not know. The ambivalence of fear and fascination from my past with which I regarded Muslims had not vanished; I was not indifferent to the subjects of my study. I became aware that my first impulse was to defend against the threat the Muslims posed to my boundaries by strengthening and fortifying them as a Hindu. Then, in a kind of reaction formation, my tendency was to move in the opposite direction by consistently placing a more positive, "humane" gloss on Muslim statements and actions than on Hindu ones. Ambivalence, however, also has a positive aspect. It prevents the crystallization of ideological convictions and an approach to the study with preconceived notions firmly in place. Convictions, as Nietzsche remarked, are more damaging to truth than lies.

The Story of a Cousin Told by His Elder Brother

Sohan Lal killed himself on the way to Rohtak. He threw himself in front of a train. I could not stop him. We had made all the arrangements for the escape from Lyallpur. A Muslim truck driver was ready to drive the three hundred miles to the border for six hundred rupees. Sohan Lal had been married for only five months. He had a very pretty wife.

On the day of our departure we went out to make the final arrangements with the truck driver. The house was attacked in our absence. When we came back we hid on the roof of a Hindu neighbor's vacant house. We watched five husky Muslims in our courtyard. They had long butcher's knives stuck in their *lungis*. They were methodically looting the house. The corpse of our youngest brother—we were three—lay in the courtyard, the head completely severed from the trunk. One of the Muslims sat on a chair in front of the corpse, directing the looters. They were bringing out the packed trunks from inside the house and throwing them in front of him on the ground. The ground was cluttered with wedding *sarees* and colored silk blouses. I can still see the shining brass pots lying on their side reflecting the rays of the afternoon sun. We could not move. I was transfixed by the sight of the leader's hairy torso of which every inch was covered by a thick black fur. Then two of the Muslims went inside the house and brought out Sohan Lal's wife and the leader pulled her to him. She sat on the man's lap, naked to the waist, her petticoat ripped open, and the Muslim's hairy hand, like a giant black spider, covered her thigh. After laying her on the ground next to our brother's corpse, where drops of blood still oozed from the severed neck, they raped her in turn. I was holding Sohan Lal fast, my palm covering his mouth. If he had made the slightest sound the Muslims would have discovered us. But I do not think Sohan Lal would have done anything. His legs were buckling under him and I had to hold him up. After they finished, they ripped open her belly. Sohan Lal never said a word after it was all over and the Muslims had gone. In the days it took us to cross the border he remained mute. I tried my best to make him talk, to make him shed some of his grief in tears but his soul remained far away. He killed himself just before we reached Rohtak.

The Cousin from Lahore

We did try to retaliate, at least the younger Sangh [Rashtriya Swayam Sevak Sangh] members like me. And of course the Sikhs. A police inspector told me of going to a Sikh village where there was a reported massacre of the Muslims. As the police entered the village they passed under a kind of welcoming arch which was a rope strung out between the poles. To this rope, attached with short pieces of string, were the circumcised penises of all the Muslim men who had lived in the village, hanging there as if they were small eels drying in the sun. In our own neighborhood there were three Muslim houses. Two of the families went away, leaving only Gul Mohammed behind. He was silversmith, a quiet graying man who kept to himself and did not really have any friend among his Hindu neighbors, although he had lived in the same street for over fifteen years. We knew him and his family—a wife and three young children—cursorily, nodding to him as we passed by his shop located on the ground floor of his house. In his faded, embroidered skull cap, often working late into the night, his head bent down in concentration as he fashioned silver bracelets or ornamental anklets with delicate strokes of a hammer, he was a familiar figure to all of us. The young men from our street who went out during the riots to join Hindu mobs operating in other parts of the city, averted their eyes when they passed by his shop. They had left Gul Mohammed alone, not because of any particular affection for him but because of the established pattern among the rioters, both Hindu and Muslim. A mob always foraged wide from its home base, killing and plundering in other distant parts of the town, leaving people of the other community living in its own area unharmed. It is easier to kill men who are strangers, to obliterate faces which have not smiled on one in recognition. It is easier to burn houses which have never welcomed one as a guest. So we kept inside our houses when a Hindu mob from Anarkali came to our alley for Gul Mohammed. Later, I was told they broke open the door and one by one, Gul Mohammed's family was dragged out into the alley where they were trussed up with ropes and left lying on the ground. From the open windows of the house, string cots, low wooden stools, and sleeping mattresses were thrown out onto the ground where they were gathered into a pile. The doors and window shutters of the house were chopped into kindling and added to the heap which was set on fire. One by one, the children were picked up and thrown into the burning pyre. Gul Mohammed's wife was the last one to be burnt alive, having been first forced to watch her husband and children die in the agony of the flames. The shop was then broken into and methodically stripped of the silverware. Within an hour our alley was silent again, only a charred and still smoking heap left to mark the end of Gul Mohammed's family. Whenever possible, this is the way Hindu mobs preferred to kill Muslims—by burning them alive. A Muslim who is burnt and not buried after death is automatically consigned to hell fire.

Even as I retell the stories of my relatives from memory, I know I cannot trust that they adhere strictly to facts. I am, of course, aware of the small embellishments I have made for the purposes of making the narratives more aesthetically compelling. I wonder if in the original stories there were details from other accounts of riots, incorporated by the teller to increase the emotional impact of his or her own story. In their first versions, some of the more gruesome details were prefaced by "I am told," a qualification which disappeared in the retellings. My later, adult experience of riot accounts has taught me that the *talk* of atrocities which one was told about (and then even personally witnessed) is much more than their actual occurrence. The importance of the rhetorics of violence, as the British psychologist Peter Marsh has observed, is not necessarily that they illuminate actual action but that they substitute for it.[1]

I am also unsure how much I can trust my own memory not to make additions from its store of images, picked up from narratives of riots, even as I tell the tale. The truth of these stories, then, lies in the archetypal material they contain rather than in the factual veracity of particular details. The riots brought to the surface (as they continue to do every time they occur in a fresh edition), both at the level of action and of imagination, certain primitive fantasies of bodily violence which are our heritage from infancy and childhood. Prominent among these fantasies are those relating to sexual mutilation—the cutting off of male genitals and the sadistic fury directed against female breasts which are hit repeatedly by iron rods, stabbed with knives, and lopped off by scythes and swords. At one level, the castration of males and the cutting off of female breasts incorporate the more or less conscious wish to wipe the hated enemy off the face of the earth by eliminating the means of its reproduction and the nurturing of its infants. At another, more unconscious level, in the deep regression and the breakdown of many normal defenses occasioned by the widespread violence and the fear of one's own imminent death, the castration of the enemy may be viewed as a counterphobic acting out of what psychoanalysis considers as one of the chief male anxieties: that is, it is a doing unto others—castration—what one fears may be done to one's self. The mutilation of the breast may be similarly derived from the upsurge of a pervasive infantile fantasy—the fantasy of violent revenge on a bad, withholding breast, a part of the mother whose absence gives rise to feelings of disintegration and murderous rage.

Sexual violence undoubtedly occurred during the partition, although far below the level enshrined in collective memory. On a more sociological level, the chief reason for the preponderance of specifically sexual violence in the partition riots in the north is that, as compared to many other parts of the country, the undivided Punjab was (and continues to be) a rather violent society. Its high murder rate is only one indication of a cultural endorsement of the use of physical force to attain socially approved ends such as the defense of one's land or of personal and family honor. There is now empirical evidence to suggest that the greater the legitimation of violence in some approved areas of life, the more is the likelihood that force will also be used in other spheres where it may not be approved. In this so-called cultural spill-over effect there is a strong association between the level of nonsexual violence and rape, rape being partly a spillover from cultural norms condoning violent behavior in other areas of life.[2] Given this violent tradition and its associated cultural norms, the riot situation further undermined, if did not completely sweep away, the already weak norms curbing male aggression. It is then quite understandable that sexual violence during the partition riots could reach levels of brutality which have been rarely approached in subsequent riots in other parts of the country.

It is only now that I can reflect more composedly, even tranquilly, to give a psychological gloss to the stories of the riots. At the time I heard them, their fearful images coursed unimpeded through my mind which reverberated wildly with their narrators' flushes of emotion. There was a frantic tone to the stories, an underlying hysteria I felt as a child but could only name as an adult. After all, my uncles, aunts, and cousins had not yet recovered from the trauma of what had befallen them. The partition horrors stalked their dreams. They were still not free of the fear of losing their lives, a fear that had clutched them for weeks. They had lost their homeland, where they had been born and lived, which constitutes such an important, albeit unconscious, facet of our identity. With the loss of their homes, their sense of personal identity was tottering—had become "diffused" in Eriksonian terms[3]—while they had yet to begin the process of adapting this fragmenting identity to a new homeland.

It is sobering to think of hundreds of thousands of children over many parts of the subcontinent, Hindu and Muslim, who have listened to stories from their parents and other family elders during the partition and other subsequent riots, on the fierceness of an implacable enemy. This is a primary channel through which historical enmity is transmitted from one generation to the next as the child, ignoring the surface interpretations and rationalizations, hears the note of helpless fury and impotence in the accounts of beloved adults and fantasizes scenarios of revenge against those who have humiliated family and kin.[4] The fantasies, which can later turn from dimly conscious images to concrete actions during communal conflagrations, are not only a vindication of the parents and a repayment of the debt owed them but also a validation of the child-in-the-man's greater strength and success in overpowering those who had shamed his family in the distant past. Given the strong family and kinship ties all over the country, a Hindu's enmity toward the Muslim (and vice versa) is often experienced by the individual as a part of the loyalty due to or (in the case of a more conflictful parent-child relationship) imposed by the parents. Later, as the child grows up, the parental message may be amplified by the input of one or more teachers. As Rajesh, one of the subjects of this study who we will encounter at some length later, remarked: "We had a history teacher in school. He was the type who loved his subject. He would keep the text book aside and teach us the lesson extempore—like stories. When he used to tell us about the inhuman atrocities committed by Muslim invaders on the Hindus, I remember I used to get so angry that I felt like walking out of the class and beating up a few Muslim boys."

Leaving aside the stories, I am uncertain whether even my direct childhood memories of the riots, with their vivid images which carry such an intense charge of *noesis*, the certainty of knowing, can be completely trusted to represent reality or are even wholly mine. For instance, I "remember" going with my father to the railway station one night. Was it Rohtak? Hindu and Sikh refugees from Pakistan were camped on the station platform. Many had moaned in their sleep and a couple had woken up screaming (I now imagine) to escape from their persistent nightmares. We had walked through the sea of uneasy sleepers, their faces discolored by the dim violet glow of the neon tubes hanging high above the platform. Sitting silently among empty canisters and tattered bedrolls, shrinking at our approach, the children did not cry and rarely whimpered, their large dark eyes full of a bewildered hurt and (again I imagine) the memories of stabbed and hacked bodies lying in the streets of towns and villages which now belonged to Pakistan. One particular image has become permanently etched: a four-year-old boy with a running nose, the yellow-green mucous, a thin plaster of salted sweat on the upper lip, dense with buzzing flies which the child did not lift up his hand to drive away, afraid perhaps of giving offense to even the smallest of living creatures.

I never personally witnessed the kinds of violence described in the family stories during the few days of rioting in Rohtak. For we lived at the outskirts of the town, in Civil Lines, where the spacious bungalows of the *sahibs* of the Raj and a few elite non-officials were located. The Civil Lines families went rarely into town, preferring the company of each other. Our social life was focused on the Rohtak Club and was carried out in its high-ceilinged rooms with their covered padded chairs, the wooden dance floor, and books on big game hunting and mores of obscure Indian tribes lying unread on the shelves of teak bookcases. Sometimes in the evening, when children were not allowed in, I had watched my father and his friends sitting outside on the lawn from behind the cactus hedge surrounding the club. In their white drill trousers and their cotton bush shirts, they looked fresh and cool, radiating an aura of peace and quiet authority which made me feel safe and quietly sleepy. A part of this effect was achieved through the sensory background of their setting—the settling dusk, the smell of freshly watered grass, the low murmurs of waiters gliding between the clubhouse and the widely spaced bridge tables bearing iced lemon and orange squashes. And as they sat there, the upright garden lamps transforming the lawn into a dull yellow island surrounded by the brilliant Indian darkness from which only moths and fireflies ventured in as intruders, the silence disturbed only by the occasional dream cry of a peacock, they had looked remote from the dust, the color, and the noise of the town they administered.

I remember well the night the riot started. From the terrace, where most of the family gathered on hearing a continuous, muffled roar break the stillness of the night, I counted at least twenty separate fires within the span of an hour as Muslim homes and shops were burnt on that first night. By midnight, the night had the shimmering glow of a slow-burning coal fire, the overcast sky beginning to have the ragged crimson edge of an uneven and an unnatural dawn. Although on the following days the sounds of the riot coming from the town were blended into a low-pitched buzzing, not unlike the one near a beehive, I sometimes imagined I could distinguish the distant shouts of the mobs roaming the bazaars from the panic-filled screams of their victims.

We had enough company that night. The roof terraces of our neighboring bungalows were crowded with whole families come up to watch the distant fires. Angry cries of babies awoken from sleep mingled with excited shouts of discovery as fresh fires were sighted. There were animated exchanges across the roofs as to the exact location of a new fire and the possible reactions of the Muslims. On the whole, the onlookers were in a gay mood; there was feeling of respite from the petty concerns of daily life, a kind of relaxation which comes from the release of long pent-up tensions. "This is a lesson the Muslims needed to be taught! We should have put them in their places long ago!" was the general consensus.

Although the night air began to be permeated by the acrid smell of smoke, the fires were far away and the possibility of any danger to our own homes and lives remote. At the most, the distant threat gave all of us a tingling sense of excitement which heightened the gaiety of what was fast turning into a festive occasion.

For the children, and perhaps for the adults too, that first night of the riot thus had a quality akin to the day of the kite-flying festival at the onset of spring, when people throng the roofs and the clear blue of the sky is profusely dotted with kites in all their bright colors; the town resounding to the battle cries of children as the men compete against each other, trying to cut the string holding a rival kite aloft with their own. The duels taking place in the town that night did not use paper kites as weapons, and the battle cries we heard so faintly were no mere expression of childish exuberance but declarations of deadly intent. Yet, in the safety of our house and surrounded by the family, an uncanny impression of the riot as a macabre festival persisted throughout the hours I spent on the roof.

When the riots were brought under control after three days, I remember that my father gave in to my persistence and promised to take me into the town the next morning to see their aftermath. I remember waking up early that day and looking out at the speckled dawn as the sun struggled with the first clouds of the season. The monsoon was a few days away and, my elbows resting on the window sill of my parents' bedroom, I watched its forerunners, dark fluffy clouds racing across the sky as imperious heralds. The morning had been different from others, smelling not only of the sun's warmth but also of budding grass shoots and the dark, far away thunder. The walk through Rohtak's bazaars with my father was disappointing. I had expected to find images from the stories I had heard take concrete form. I expected to see smouldering heaps, amputated limbs, cut-off breasts—which I pictured as pale fleshy balls without a trace of blood. The reality was oddly disappointing. Except for an occasional house with charred doors, missing windows, and smoke scars on its front, the bazaars presented the unchanging vista of a provincial town awakening to another day. There were the men vigorously (and loudly) chewing on marigossa twigs to clean their teeth and clearing their throats with much hawking and spitting. Others murmured their prayers as they bathed under the cool streams of water from public hydrants. The women hissed encouragement over naked babies held up above the gutter. Older children squatted by themselves, with that faraway look which bespeaks of an inward absorption in the working of one's bowels, a trance occasionally broken as they bent down to contemplate their own dirt.

Almost twenty years later, in 1969, when I was again a witness to another Hindu-Muslim riot, this time in Ahmedabad in the western state of Gujarat, I was surprised to hear essentially the same rumors I had heard as a child in Rohtak. Thus we heard (and in Rohtak believed) that milk vendors had been bribed by the Muslims to poison the milk in the morning. Four children were said to be lying unconscious and two dogs had died after having drunk of the poisoned milk. Apparently, most of the servants in Civil Lines who went into the town frequently had personally seen the dogs in their death throes. Women had hurried to empty out the pails of milk; sticky patches of white soon spread to plaster the cobbled stones of the streets. We heard that Muslims had broken into grocery shops in the night and mixed powdered glass with the salt. A police van with a loudspeaker was said to be driving around the town, warning people not to buy salt. Both in Rohtak and Ahmedabad there was talk of large stocks of weapons, acid, and other materials needed for manufacturing bombs, cached in the underground cellars of mosques; of prior Muslim preparations for a slaughter of the Hindus being forestalled by the riot. In Ahmedabad there was the additional rumor of armed Pakistani agents seen parachuting into the city at night. Its Rohtak counterpart was the imminent attack by thousands of armed Meo tribesmen making a detour to the town on their way to Pakistan.

The fact that rumors during a riot take such dramatic and fanciful turns is not surprising. In a study of the ratio of rumors to actual events such as killing, rape, beating, harassment, property violation, and inconvenience among the Asians expelled from Uganda by Idi Amin, the relationship was strikingly linear.[5] That is, the more threatening and dramatic the experience, the more likely it was to be a wellspring of rumor. At the high point of a riot, the content of the rumors is at its most threatening and the speed at which they circulate at its highest. For it is at this particular time when three of the four conditions for the generation and transmission of rumors—personal anxiety, general uncertainty, and topical importance—are at their highest level. The fourth condition, credulity, is no longer in operation since, at high levels of anxiety, disbelief in rumor is suspended, that is, rumors will be believed regardless how farfetched.[6]

Rumors, of course, also serve some less conscious purposes. Deriving from and reinforcing the paranoid potential which lies buried in all of us, they were the conversational food which helped in the growth of a collective Hindu body. They sharpened our awareness of our own kind and many, who though they lived in the same bazaar were relative strangers earlier, became brothers overnight. They made misers discover a forgotten generosity as they offered to share food with those who had none; neighbors who had little use for each other now inquired daily about each other's well-being. There is little doubt that rumors are the fuel and riots the fire in which a heightened sense of community is also forged. If I remember the Rohtak riots so vividly, it is not only because I was an impressionable child but also because of the deep sense of communion I felt with my family and the wider, although vague, entity of "the Hindus." The riots generated emotions which expanded my boundaries. They gave rise to exhilarating feelings of closeness and belonging to something beyond myself which I desperately wanted to

keep. My memory of the Rohtak riots, I recognize, is not free from a shame-
faced nostalgia for a shining flower which sprang from the mean soil of de-
caying corpses and ashes left behind by arsonists' fires.

In undermining our familiar controls over mental life, a riot is often experienced as a midwife for unfamiliar, disturbing fantasies and complex emotions, such as both disgust and overwhelming sexual attraction for a member
of the enemy community. The overcharged atmosphere of violence breathed
day in and day out by a person lifts the lid on the cauldron of instinctual
drives as civilized sensibility threatens to collapse before the press of instinctuality in both its sexual and violent aspects. Accounts of sexual violence during a riot, for instance, not only evoke the publicly acceptable reaction of
horror but may also release the more hidden emotion of a shameful excitement which bespeaks instinctual desire in its rawer form. Besides the expression of moral outrage, riot violence can be subjectively used for an unwanted
but wished for vicarious satisfaction of sadistic impulses, for the fulfillment of
one's urge to utterly subjugate another human being, to reduce his or her
consciousness to a reactivity of the flesh alone.

In fiction, this complex flow of subjectivity during a riot has been bril-
liantly captured by the Hindi writer Krishan Baldev Vaid in his novel *Guzra
hua Zamana* ("A bygone era"). Biru, the teenaged hero of the novel, together
with his parents, his sister Devi, and Kumari, the young wife of a neighbor,
who Biru has always lusted after with the innocence and ancient knowledge
of a boy on the verge of manhood, has been given shelter by a Muslim friend,
Bakka, during the partition riots in a small town in Punjab. As the marauding
Muslim mob, consisting of many men Biru knows well, including Bakka himself, roams the streets at night in an orgy of looting, killing, and rape, the
Hindu family cowers in the small dark room and a terrified Biru's thoughts
flow in a full, barely controllable stream.

> Even if I survive it will be as a cripple. Before pushing us out, Bakka will
> first cut an ear off everyone. Devi and Kumari will also have a breast
> chopped off. Perhaps he will also break one of my legs. What if all the
> others are killed and I survive! I will commit suicide. I know how to.
> Somewhere here there must be a rope. What if I am killed and the
> others live? Mother will surely kill herself. Or she will become mad.
> She will go around asking, have you seen my Biru? My innocent, naive
> Biru? What will probably happen is that we will all die and only Kumari
> will be left alive. Bakka will take her as his wife. Or as his slave. He will
> change her name. Sakina or Hafiza. I like Muslim names. Also Muslim

women. When Bakka comes to kill me I will say, don't kill me I like Muslim names and Muslim women. He will be so surprised by my courage that his uplifted hand will remain suspended in air. I'll say, I am half a Muslim. When I hear the call for prayers from the mosque I shiver all over. He will think I am making fun of Islam but I am really telling the truth. . . .

The killer will agree that I am a Muslim at heart. But this will not stop him from striking. If I was in love with a Muslim girl would I have converted for her sake? I certainly would have become a Muslim if she had asked. Lovers have faith not religion. . . .

The accounting will start once it is morning. The counting of corpses. How many Hindus, how many Sikhs. There must be a few Muslims too. The intention of killing ten of us for every one of them. On the other side (the Muslims would say) so many of ours were killed, why so few of them here? There they took out processions of our naked women, why has that not happened here? Strip off the clothes of their women! Tear apart their bodies too. In front of their men. And then parade them in the bazaar! In front of their impotent men! At least they will learn to fear God! There, we hear, they cut off the breasts of our women, their hair too. We also will not let them get away intact. Chop one off everyone! Shave their heads! And then kick them in the arse! These are the ones who would not let us touch them. They would not eat from our hands. Now force them to eat everything. Stuff it into their mouths! And say, go to your Hindustan! Why are so few orphans here? Why is the sound of the weeping of widows so low? Why are the heaps of rubble so small? Do not rest till all these accounts are settled. Avenge blood with blood! For a hurled brick, retaliate with a stone! Take vengeance on the son for the deeds of the father! . . .

And this cycle will continue, for centuries. It is better if it remains dark. Because the darkness of the day will be unbearable. Because when morning comes no one will be ashamed. No one will embrace. No one will console.[7]

Territory and Passion

The partition violence is commonly agreed to have been the most momentous event in the shaping of Hindu-Muslim relations in independent India. It is not as commonly recognized that it may not have been the memories of this violence which have been passed down through the generations—traumatic as the violence was in its scale and intensity—but the *division* of the country into two states of India and Pakistan which has had the stronger psychological impact on many Hindus. The partition of India sharpened, if not gave birth to, the distinction between the secularist and the nationalist Hindu. As often happens, even for the same set of memories, the lessons drawn were quite contradictory. The secularist looked confidently to the country's future polity once this regrettable business of dividing the country was over. One of the most respected political figures of the post-independence era, Jai Prakash Narain, argued that it had been like two brothers fighting for separation. Once the separation had taken place and the parental assets were divided, the brothers would live in amity and fraternal harmony.[8] The secularist was convinced that the burning embers of the partition conflagration were permanently extinguished. Its memories were gone forever and perhaps existed only in the nightmares of an older generation which would soon disappear. "It can never happen again," was the common refrain in the first twenty years after independence. The gates to religious violence were securely locked and the riots which took place occasionally were regarded like the fall of small pebbles in the aftermath of the big landslide. Men of goodwill among both Hindus and Muslims echoed the poet Iqbal's famous line, "Religion does not teach mutual enmity." Others maintained that it was only because of the machinations of the British that the partition riots took the gruesome turn that they did.

Most of all, the secularist pinned hopes about the end of Hindu-Muslim conflict on economic development. The position taken by Nehru, which for many years produced a remarkable consensus within India's political class and the Westernized intelligentsia fascinated by Marxism, was that industrialization of the country and the spread of the "scientific temper" through modern education would undermine the religious outlook of the people and consolidate secular values. Implied in this "modernity project"—a catch-all term for political democracy, scientific rationality, and philosophical individualism—were the notions that the tasks of economic development would absorb all the energies of the people, and any conflicts which arose as a consequence of this enterprise would be taken care of by the democratic processes.

For the Hindu nationalist, politically weak till the remarkable ascent of the Bharatiya Janata Party (BJP) and its Hindutva movement in the last few years, the partition, with Jinnah's Muslim League successfully insisting on a separate state for the Muslims, was the final proof that Hindus and Muslims were really two different nations as Jinnah had claimed. There was a basic opposition between Islam and Indian nationalism, and, given the right circumstances, Indian Muslims will want yet another separate state for themselves. As we shall see later, "They [the Muslims] want to create another Pakistan" is an emotionally powerful appeal in contemporary Hindu nationalist discourse.

There was, of course, a third Hindu, probably in a large majority till at least a few years ago. This was the indifferent Hindu for whom the Hindu-Muslim problem and the national identity question were simply not salient. Such Hindus continued to live in their faith with a traditional indifference—often confused with tolerance—toward the Other sharing their space, whether the Other was the Mussulman or the Isai (Christian).

National identities, we are told by political scientists, can be based on several defining principles of collective belonging: territory (e.g., Switzerland), ethnicity (e.g., Japan), religion (e.g., Pakistan), and ideology (e.g., the United States).[9] Although territory is invariably a part of the idea of the nation-state, it does not have to be the defining principle in all cases. For instance, the notions of ethnicity in Germany or religion in Iran evoke greater political passions than territory. In India, the political scientist Ashutosh Varshney suggests, for both the secularist and the Hindu nationalist the defining principle in the idea of national identity is territory; "national unity" and "territorial integrity" are thus highly charged phrases in the Indian political discourse.[10] In the secular imagination, the territorial notion of India, emphasized for twenty-five hundred years since the times of the Mahabharata, is of a land stretching from the Himalayas in the north to Kanya Kumari (Cape Comorin) in the south, from the Arabian Sea in the west to the Bay of Bengal in the east. These boundaries are coterminous with the "sacred geography" of the Hindu nationalist whose hallowed pilgrimage sites mark off essentially the same boundaries of the country, although the Hindu nationalist would go back much further into mythic history than two and a half millennia to date the origin of these sites. Varshney remarks:

> Since the territorial principle is drawn from a belief in ancient heritage, encapsulated in the notion of "sacred geography," and it also figures in both imaginations [secularist and nationalist], it has acquired political hegemony over time. It is the only thing common between the two competing nationalist imaginations. Therefore, just as America's most passionate political moments concern freedom and equality, India's most explosive moments concern its "sacred geography", the 1947 par-

tition being the most obvious example. Whenever the threat of another break-up, another "partition", looms large, the moment unleashes remarkable passions in politics. Politics based on this imagination is quite different from what was seen when Malaysia and Singapore split from each other, or when the Czech and Slovak republics separated. Territory not being such an inalienable part of their national identity, these territorial divorces were not desecrations. In India, they become desecrations of the sacred geography.[11]

Later we shall look in some detail at the psychological processes involved in the arousal of political passions around the issue of territorial integrity which, the Hindu revivalist seeks to convince the indifferent Hindu, is under grave threat from all Indian Muslims and not only from those clamoring for secession in Kashmir.

Profile of a Riot

As I now look back at the partition riots, I am aware that perhaps there are very few people who reflect on the past with the professional historian's perspective. For most of us, as the sociologists Howard Schuman and J. Scott have remarked, it is only the intersection of personal and national history that provides the most vital and remembered connection to the times we have lived through.[12] If the partition is a significant source of collective memory it is not only because the origin of a nation is emotionally a particularly charged time. As Maurice Halbwachs has observed, not all emotion-provoking events are memorable, only those which require considerable psychological adaptation.[13] The partition events were not only unique and provoked strong emotional reactions but also required profound changes in behavior and beliefs of those affected by them.

Yet the memory of the deep experiences of those days grows dim as I write, like a dream which loses its experiential charge even as it is recollected and retold. Recollections of all I have heard and read about other Hindu-Muslim riots come rushing in to make my unique event part of a category, with the dulling of individual detail and highlighting of similarities which mark the birth of a category.

As a category, communal riots in India differ from other kinds of riots—student riots, caste riots, language riots, agricultural and labor rioting—in that they are the most violent and most difficult to control. They are the most virulent because the particular conflict, generally a blend of religious, political, and economic aims becomes imbued with religious ultimacy. In other words, the issues at stake become life and death issues through an arsenal of ideational and ritual symbols. Moreover, as we saw in the last chapter, both Hindu and Muslim religious cultures have a long tradition in specifying "the enemy" and, as in other religious cultures, their violent champions have an acceptable, even admired rationale for the violence unleashed in "defense." Communal riots also differ from other riots in that they rarely remain confined to one location so that within a few days or (given the speed and reach of modern communications) hours, they can engulf many parts of the country.

Leaving aside the difficult and contested question of their ultimate cause, the eruption of a riot is always expected and yet takes everyone by surprise. By eruption I do not mean that a riot is spontaneous and involves no degree of planning or preparation, but only that it generally takes place after a considerable degree of tension between the two communities has been built up. To change the metaphor, the riot is then the bursting of a boil, the eruption of pus, of "bad blood" between Hindus and Muslims which has accumulated over a few days or even weeks in a particular location. In some cities and towns—Ahmedabad and Hyderabad come immediately to mind —where the boil is a festering sore, the tension never really disappears but remains at an uncomfortable level which is below that of violent eruption.

Besides the ultimate cause, then, a riot has a period of *immediate tension* and a *precipitating incident* which have received much less attention than the more glamorous search for "ultimate" causes. The buildup of immediate tension occurs when religious identities come to the forefront because of a perceived threat to this particular social identity. The threat, a collective distortion of the meaning of a real event, makes members of the community demonstratively act through words and actions as Hindus, or as Muslims. In turn, the demonstration of this religious identity threatens members of the other community who, too, begin to mobilize their identity around their religious affiliation. Thus begins a spiral of perceived (or misperceived) threats and active counter postures which raises the tension between Hindus and Muslims. To give examples from some major riots: The recent demolition of Babri mosque was perceived as a threat to Muslim religious identity—a chain of mental associations leading from the razing of an unused mosque to the disappearance of Islam in India—which was then openly demonstrated against and, in turn, reacted to by a further consolidation and demonstration of a militant Hindu identity. The 1969 riot in Ahmedabad was preceded by a period of tension when members of the Rashtriya Swayam Sevak Sangh (RSS) began a campaign demanding the "Indianization" of Muslims and thus initiating a similar chain of mental associations and actual events. We saw that the threat to Hindus is generally around the issue of the country's territorial integrity which the Muslim seems to threaten either through a demonstrative identification with pan-Islamic causes or in the demand for a separate cultural identity, expressed through the insistence on maintaining Islamic personal law or in demanding a greater role for Urdu. Here the Hindu distortion of the threat takes place through an associative chain where such Muslim actions are imagined as precursors to a separate Muslim enclave, the creation of another Pakistan and, ultimately, the dreaded revival of medieval Muslim rule. For instance, the immediate tension which led to the Ranchi riots in 1967 was initiated by the state government's plan to raise the official status of Urdu which was perceived by the Hindus as a step down the road of Muslim separatism.

"Tension" of course, is too general a term to convey more than the most superficial of meanings. We need to further explore the contents and processes of this "tension" in our specific context of Hindu-Muslim rioting. What happens in the period of tension is that individuals increasingly think of themselves as Hindus or Muslims. In the more psychological language of the "social identification" theory, associated with Henri Tajfel and his co-workers, when group salience becomes high, an individual thinks and behaves in conformity with the stereotypical characteristics of the category "Hindu" (or "Muslim") rather than according to his or her individual personality dispositions.[14] In a period of rising social tension, social identity dominates, if it does not altogether replace, personal identity as individuals perceive members of the Other group purely in terms of the former. As Hindus and Muslims increasingly see each other as stereotypes, there follows an inevitable homogenization and depersonalization. Individual Hindu or Muslims become interchangeable, perceiving each other in terms of shared category characteristics rather than their personal, idiosyncratic natures. Conversations couched in terms of group categories increase markedly: "Look at what the Hindus are doing!" "The Muslims have crossed all limits!" The stereotypes attributed to one's own and the adversarial group, we shall see later, take their shape from popular history, orally transmitted through generations.

The immediate tension at the eve of the riot is not merely a matter of cognitive functioning according to a social identity. The tension is also constituted of strong affects and emotions, "raw passions" if one will. The somewhat bloodless formulations of social identity theory are not completely sufficient to explain a process which will end up being so bloody. Here we need to add psychoanalytic insights on the intertwining of the individual and the group from earliest childhood onward and a revival of the associated emotions in the current situation.

In the first years of life, it is only gradually that the child learns to integrate dichotomous "good" and "bad" images of the self—the angry and the loving baby—as well as opposing representations of caretakers who both gratify and frustrate. The child also learns that to have hostile impulses directed toward those on whom it depends is dangerous to its own well-being and that these negative feelings must be disowned. One of the main ways of disowning "bad," hateful representations is to externalize them, first on to inanimate objects or animals and then to people and other groups. In a given cultural group, mothers and other adults usually offer the same targets of externalization, or "reservoirs," as the psychiatrist Vamik Volkan calls them.[15] The Hindu (and associated cultural symbols) is thus an emotionally charged target of externalization for the Muslim's own "bad" representations and angry feelings (and vice versa) from an early period of life, a convenient reservoir also for the subsequent rages which grow out of thwarted needs and private hurts. Together with this creation of the enemy, which is "neither 'merely' real nor 'merely' projection,"[16] there is also a process of identification with one's group taking place. The child is assimilating within itself images of family and group members, thus coming to resemble them more and more while increasing its emotional investment in the group's shared symbols and traditions.

In the period of immediate tension, when the salience of one's religious-cultural group increases markedly, the feelings of love connected with the early identifications revive, as do the hate and rage associated with the targets of externalization. Since the enemy is also a reservoir of our own unwanted selves and negative feelings, it is important it be kept at a psychological distance. Consciously, the enemy should never be like us. Even minor differences between "us" and "them" are therefore exaggerated as unbridgeable chasms in what Freud called the "narcissism of minor differences"[17] which evoke stronger hostility and hate than do wide disparities. There is a special quality to the enmity I feel for a person who resembles me most but is not me. Next to my brother, it is my neighbor the Ten Commandments enjoin me to love as I do myself, precisely because my neighbor is the one I am most likely to consider as a rival. The stereotyping of the enemy group involves a progressive devaluation which can extend to the point of dehumanization where "'they" come close to the child's earliest, nonhuman targets of externalization. Making the enemy nonhuman is to avoid feeling guilt about destroying "it" in the riot that is imminent.

To summarize: the heightened salience of social identity, fueled by a revival of strong childhood emotions that arise from the intertwining of the self and the cultural group, together with the fact that the groups involved are religious ones, thus imbuing the conflict with religious ultimacy, are the distinctive markers of the tension immediately preceding a riot.

Among the various precipitating incidents, there are two which occur with such regularity in reports of riots that they may fairly be called archetypes. One of them has to do with Muslim violence toward the cow while the other pertains to disputes over religious processions. Whereas riots around the former are specific to India, riots provoked by religious processions have been common in the history of religious violence.[18] Both incidents are archetypal in the sense that, irrespective of their factual veracity in a particular case, they are perceived as legitimate causes for violence to begin—shots from the starter's gun, so to speak. There is thus an unarticulated expectation that an incident around a cow or a religious procession should belong to the account of a Hindu-Muslim riot even if such an incident did not actually take place. Historically speaking, this expectation is not unjustified. Consider, for instance, the precipitating incidents of communal riots in the Punjab in a single year in the last century.

In 1886, riots occurred in Ambala, Ludhiana, Hoshiarpur, and Delhi. In Ambala, the precipitating incident was a change, insisted upon by the Muslims, in the route of the Hindu procession on the festival of Bawan Sawadasi. It was also widely rumored that the Muslims intended to bring large quantities of beef into the city the next day on the occasion of Eid. In Ludhiana, the riot began with the report that a cow had been sacrificed in a Muslim's house. In Hoshiarpur, the Muharram procession of the Muslims had passed a major part of its route when a bull suddenly appeared amidst it. The processionists were already involved in an argument with the Hindus over the entanglement of the *tazia* in branches of a *pipal* tree, held sacred by the Hindus, which the Muslims wanted to cut. The Hindus objected to the Muslims' beating of the bull and the riot was on. In Delhi, the riots began with the clash between Muslim and Hindu processions whose routes crossed each other.[19] It is not surprising to read eighty years later that one of the worst riots of post-independence India, the 1969 riot in Ahmedabad, was set off by a Muslim vegetable seller who hit a cow which had stopped at its stand for a munch. Fisticuffs with the Hindu cowherd followed and "the treatment of the cow (which was not seriously injured), greatly magnified out of all proportion, spread through the city and touched off further incidents. The rioting continued in various parts of Gujarat for some ten days."[20]

The precipitating incident is immediately followed by the aggrieved group taking out a procession—when the procession itself is not the incident. A procession is necessary for the creation of what I call a "physical" group. A physical group is a group represented in the bodies of its members rather than in their minds, a necessary shift for a group to become an instrument of actual violence. For if we reflect on our own experiences of various groups we become immediately aware of a significant difference between, say, my experience of my cultural identity as a Hindu and my psychic processes when I am taking part in a religious assembly. In other words, belonging to a relatively abstract entity, the Hindus, touches a very different chord of the self than the one touched by being a member of a physical group, such as a tightly packed congregation in a Hindu temple. The self-experience of the latter is determined more by concrete, bodily communication and physical sensations in the press of other bodies. The self-experience of the cultural-group identity, on the other hand, is evoked more, and differently, by shared cultural symbols and history—heavily mythological—which is shaped by the group's hopes and fears and distorted by its ambitions and ideals.

[margin note: mob mentality]

The information I receive sensorially and sensually, linguistically and subliminally in a physical group and which influences the experience of my self at that particular moment, is of another order, and is processed differently, than the information received as member of a cultural group. In a crowd—an example of a physical group—the very nature of the situation with many people in close bodily contact brings a considerable sensual stimulation through channels of touch, vision, hearing, and smell which are simultaneous and are intensified by the multiplicity of their sources.[21] There is also a communication of body heat, muscle tensions, and sometimes, of body rhythms. The individual is practically wrapped up in the crowd and gets continuous sensual pounding through all avenues that one's body can afford. The consequence is a blurring of the body image and of the ego, a kind of self-transcendence that is reacted to by panic or exhilaration as individuality disappears and the "integrity," "autonomy," and "independence" of the ego seem to be wishful illusions and mere hypothetical constructs. That the physical and cultural groups sometimes coincide and that it is the endeavor of those who use and manipulate symbols of cultural identity to bring the cultural group closer to the psychological state of a physical group is a subject which I will not pursue here.

[margin note: The individual becomes one with the group through overwhelming physical sensations.]

I do not find the argument convincing that, as personal identity disappears in a crowd, the residue is some regressed, primitive state where the violent side of human nature is unleashed, as has been postulated in both the Freudian and the Jungian traditions. Such formulations need to be relativized and seen in the context and framework of a particular place and period in history—Europe between the two World Wars—when extremist ideologues of the Left and Right were creating mass movements imbued with messianic fervor. Building on the classical notions of crowds described by Gustave Le Bon (whose own ideas, in turn, were framed by the dread the French upper class felt in relation to the revolutionary masses), Freud's reflections on the psychology of crowds as well as Jung's observations on mass psychology were not free of the ideological concerns of their time, namely the liberal fear of the loss of individual autonomy in a collectivity and the socialist concern about how to make the desired collectivities more tolerable and tolerant.

Identity in a crowd only gets refocused.[22] This refocusing is certainly dramatic and full of affect since a crowd amplifies all emotions, heightening a feeling of well-being into exaltation, fear into panic. The loss of personal identity in a crowd, however, makes individuals act in terms of the crowd's identity, for instance, according to the behavior "expected" of an anti-Hindu or anti-Muslim mob. The individual is not operating at some deeply regressed, primitive level of the psyche but according to the norms of the particular group. The violent acts are thus not random but represent the expression and adaptation to a novel situation of a historical tradition of anti-Hindu or anti-Muslim mob violence.

It is paradoxical that religious processions, presumably with spiritual aims, perhaps produce the most physical of all groups. Rhythms of religious ritual are particularly effective in breaking down social barriers between the participants. They produce a maximum of mutual activation of the participants and a readiness for action, often violent. This is why violence, when Muslim initiated, often begins at the end of Friday afternoon prayers when congregants, who have turned into a congregation, stream out of the mosque into the street in a protesting procession. Processions at Muharram for the Muslims and Dussehra (and increasingly Ganesh Chaturthi) for the Hindus are almost a certain recipe for violence when they are preceded by a period of tension between the communities and when a precipitating incident has just occurred.

Whereas internally a procession must transform itself into a physical group, externally it should demonstrate the community's strength. As the political scientist Sarah Moore points out, the success of the procession depends not only upon the number of people taking part but also on the route it takes.[23] Routes are valued differently. To take a procession near or through an area inhabited by the adversary is more valued than taking a route which avoids potential confrontations. A procession which can pass through known trouble spots and major traffic arteries is considered more successful than one which slinks through back alleys. The number of chaperoning policemen, protecting processions which are going to cause the very trouble the police are trying to prevent, is another indicator of success.

Normally, the first two to three days of a major riot are the most violent, when the majority of the casualties take place. As the police regain control of the situation, the riot settles down to a low-level intensity of violence. Isolated incidents of stabbing, looting, and arson take place in the narrow alleys and twisting bylanes rather than in the major bazaars. Gradually, peace returns, although some kind of curfew and orders prohibiting the gathering of more than five persons may remain in force for many weeks. The official end of the riot is marked by the state appointing a commission of inquiry headed by a retired judge who is asked to determine the sequence of events leading to the riot, name those who were responsible, tally the losses, and offer suggestions to prevent future riots. The sole result of such an inquiry, besides offering temporary employment to the judge, is the transfer of a few hapless police officers who are held culpable for not having taken adequate precautions. Police officers, of course only the dishonest, have long since calculated the monetary value of this occupational risk and have made it a part of the compensation they feel entitled to, above and beyond the miserly salary they are paid by the state.

[handwritten marginal note: R we in L. field?]

Hyderabad: December 1990

The Hyderabad riot of December 1990, the central event of my study, occurred after a period of relative peace between the Hindus and Muslims, the last riot in the city having taken place in 1984. Before that, riots had been an annual feature since 1978, the year of the first major communal conflagration since 1948 when Hyderabad became a part of independent India.

The 1978 riot was triggered by the rape of a Muslim woman, Rameeza Bi, and the murder of her husband, Ahmed Hussain, in the Nallakunta police station. In the beginning the mobs protesting police brutality included Hindus, but soon the situation took a turn where the two communities became pitted against each other. The incident sparking off the antagonistic postures was, as usual, the tiniest of sparks: some Hindus beat up a Muslim boy, the Muslims retaliated, the Hindus retaliated against the retaliation, and so on in an ever increasing escalation. The riots were centered around Subzimandi, the central vegetable market, which is also one of the two locations of this study. Given the general propensity of the students of Hindu-Muslim relations to explain the violence between the two in economic terms, the hidden agenda of these riots is said to be an economic offensive by the Muslims designed to recapture Subzimandi from Hindu traders.[24] Destitute for almost three decades, most of the wealthier members of their community having migrated to Pakistan or other countries, the Muslims of the old city had suddenly come into money through remittances from the Arab countries of the Gulf, where the economic boom in the late seventies had created a big market for Muslim labor from Hyderabad. After having suffered a rapid economic decline within a decade of Hyderabad's integration with India, the Muslims again sought to regain control of the city's vegetable trade which they had lost to the Hindus.

After 1978, there was at least a riot a year, sometimes more, usually at the time of major religious festivals. The tension in the city is especially palpable during Ganesh Chaturthi of the Hindus, when clay idols of the god are taken out in procession through the streets to be immersed in the Musi river, and Muharram of the Muslims, when the Shias march through the city bewailing the martyrdom of Hussein, the Prophet's grandson. The riots also erupted on many other pretexts: Hindu shopkeepers refusing to close their shops in the strikes called by the Majlis (to protest against the takeover of the *kaaba* [shrine] in Mecca by a man claiming to be the Mehdi), the burning of the Al Aqsa mosque in Jerusalem, the removal of a chief minister perceived as sympathetic to one community. Between 1978 and 1984, over four hundred people lost their lives and thousands more were injured in the communal riots. A common thread in some of these riots (as in riots elsewhere) is the assumption of the state's role by the mobs of one or the other community. Like the sixteenth-century Catholic-Protestant riots in France described by Natalie Davis, the Hindu or Muslim mob perceives itself as doing what the state should have done in the first place; it is helping the political authorities get over their failure in fulfilling their duties, thus providing itself a certain legitimacy.[25]

Coming back to the 1990 violence, the countdown for the Hyderabad riot began when L. K. Advani, the president of the BJP, began his *rath yatra* ("chariot pilgrimage") from the temple of Somnath on the west coast to Ayodhya in the Hindu heartland of the north. The stated purpose of the *yatra*, which was to take Advani through a large part of the country in thirty days and over ten thousand kilometers, was the construction of the Rama temple at the legendary birth site of the god where stood a mosque constructed in 1528 by founder of the Mughal dynasty. The Toyota van in

which the BJP leader traveled was decorated to make it resemble the chariot
of the legendary hero Arjuna, as shown in the immensely popular television
serial of the Mahabharata. Advani's chariot aroused intense fervor among the
Hindus. Crowds thronged the roads to catch a glimpse of the *rath*, showered
flower petals on the cavalcade as it passed through their villages and towns,
and the vehicle itself became a new object of worship as women offered ritual
prayer with coconut, burning incense, and sandalwood paste at each of its
stops. In a darker, more somber aftermath, there were incidents of violence
between Hindus and Muslims at many places in the wake of the *rath yatra*.

Like a pond choked with lotus stalks during the monsoon, this religious-
political exercise was replete with symbols. The symbolism began with the
"chariot": a large lotus, the symbol of the BJP, was painted on the front grill of
the Toyota. The lotus is one of the most Hindu of the universal symbols and
is ubiquitous in India's religious iconography. Various lotuses are associated
with different gods and goddesses; for example, the eight-petaled lotus is the
dwelling place of Brahma. The lotus on the van—the chariot—was therefore highly significant. In the Hindu mind, influenced by tales from the Mahabharata and the visuals of popular poster and calendar art, the chariot is
the vehicle of gods and mythical heroes going to war. Above all, the chariot
is associated with Arjuna, with Lord Krishna as his charioteer, as he prepares
for a just, *dharmic* war against an evil though intimately related foe, the Kau-
ravas. Arjuna's horses were white, signifying his purity; Advani's Toyota-
chariot, which the newspapers were soon to call the "juggernaut of Hindutva," was also white.

Somnath, the starting point of the *yatra* and the location of an ancient
Shiva temple, is also the greatest symbol of Hindu defeat and humiliation at
hands of the Muslims. The legend of Somnath, which has entered Hindu
folklore over large parts of the country, tells us that in the eleventh century
Somnath was the richest and the most magnificent temple of Hindu India.
One thousand Brahmins were appointed to perform the daily worship of the
emblem of Shiva, a thirteen-and-a-half foot *lingam*, four-and-a-half feet in cir-
cumference. Three hundred men and women were employed to sing and
dance before the *lingam* every day and the temple treasury possessed vast
riches in gold, silver, and precious gems, accumulated over the centuries.
Mahmud, the sultan of the central Asian kingdom of Ghazni, who swept over
north India almost every year like a monsoon of fire and was famed far and
wide as the great destroyer of temples and a scourge of the Hindus, came to
know of the Hindu belief that he could destroy so many of their temples only
because the deities of those temples had forfeited Somnath's support. With a
view to strike at the very root of the Hindus' faith in their gods, and tempted

by the prospect of plundering the temple's treasures, Mahmud marched to Somnath. The Hindus were complacent in their belief that Shiva had drawn Mahmud to Somnath only to punish the sultan for his depredations. Hoping for a manifestation of Shiva's divine wrath, the Hindu resistance to Mahmud was unorganized and offered much too late. Hundreds of thousands of Hindus perished in the ensuing slaughter, according to legend—fifty thousand, according to nationalist historians. The temple was razed to the ground. The Shiva *lingam* was broken to pieces and together with the temple's plundered treasure transported to Ghazni where its fragments were fashioned into steps at the gate of the chief mosque. The Hindu historian, acknowledging Mahmud's skill as a general and the fact that Muslim chroniclers regard him as one of the most illustrious kings and great champion of Islam, adds: "By his ruthless destruction of temples and images he violated the most sacred and cherished sentiments of the Indian people, and his championship of Islam therefore merely served to degrade it in their eyes such as nothing else could."[26] Somnath and Mahmud of Ghazni have become intimately associated over the following centuries. Today, among Hindus, the name of the temple conjures up less the image of Shiva than the memory of one of the most rapacious and cruel of Muslim invaders. In choosing to start the *rath yatra* from Somnath, the symbolic reverberations of the act were well calculated; the righteous Hindu chariot was setting forth to avenge ancient humiliations, to right old historical wrongs.

For the Hindus, Somnath is indeed what Volkan calls a "chosen trauma," just as the demolition of the Babri mosque at Ayodhya in December 1992 fairly bids to become one of the chosen traumas of the Indian Muslim.[27] The term "chosen trauma" refers to an event which causes a community to feel helpless and victimized by another and whose mental representation becomes embedded in the group's collective identity. Chosen trauma does not mean that either the Hindus or the Muslims chose to become victims but only that they have "chosen" to mythologize, psychologically internalize, and thus constantly dwell upon a particular event from their history. A chosen trauma is reactivated again and again to strengthen a group's cohesiveness through "memories" of its persecution, victimization, and yet its eventual survival. In the late nineteenth century, Swami Vivekananda had "remembered" Somnath thus: "Mark how these temples bear the marks of a hundred attacks and hundred regenerations continually springing up out of the ruins rejuvenated and strong as ever."[28] At the beginning of the last decade of the twentieth century, Advani was to summon up the Hindu chosen trauma again from the depths of cultural memory.

If the *yatra* began in Somnath it was symbolically symmetrical for it to end in Ayodhya, the birthplace and capital of the kingdom of Lord Rama and thus the site of the Hindu's chosen glory. For many Hindus, the story of Rama is the most resplendent moment of India's history. The revival of its memory, commemorated annually in the Ram Lila, makes the collective chest swell with pride. The chosen glory, too, is psychologically internalized and is as salient for a group's cultural identity as its chosen trauma; both constitute landmarks on the terrain of a group's cultural memory.

Advani's cavalcade, of symbols as much as of people, came to a halt when on 23 October he was arrested in Bihar before he could start on the last lap of his journey to Ayodhya, where the BJP and its allied organizations, the *sangh parivar*, had promised to start the construction of the Rama temple on 9 November. The already high political passions were now nearing the point of explosion. The spark was provided by the chief minister of Uttar Pradesh, Mulayam Singh Yadav, who had vowed that to prevent the construction of the temple he would not "let even a bird enter Ayodhya." The well-oiled machine of the *sangh parivar*, however, had succeeded in smuggling in thousands of *kar-sevaks* from all over the country for the task of construction. On 9 November, Yadav ordered the police to open fire on the *kar-sevaks* who had broken through the police barriers and were intent on the demolition of the Babri mosque as a prelude to building of the temple. Scores of *kar-sevaks* died in the police attack. Their bodies were cremated on the banks of the river Saryu and the ashes taken back by the BJP workers to the villages and towns in different parts of the country from which the dead men hailed. There they were eulogized as martyrs to the Hindu cause. Soon, Hindu-Muslim riots erupted in many parts of the country.

In Hyderabad, more than a thousand miles to the south of Ayodhya, the riots began with the killing of Sardar, a Muslim auto-rickshaw driver, by two Hindus. Although the murder was later linked to a land dispute between two rival gangs, at the time of the killing it was framed in the context of rising Hindu-Muslim tensions in the city. Muslims retaliated by stabbing four Hindus in different parts of the walled city. Then Majid Khan, an influential local leader of Subzimandi who lives and flourishes in the shaded space formed by the intersection of crime and politics, was attacked with a sword by some BJP workers and the rumor spread that he had died. Muslim mobs came out into the alleys and streets of the walled city, to be followed by Hindu mobs in their areas of strength, and the 1990 riot was on. It was to last for ten weeks, claim more than three hundred lives and thousands of wounded. One of the wounded was the two-year-old girl in the photograph.

THREE

The Warriors

. . . In my heart there are furies and sorrows.
                    —Quevodo

M ajid Khan survived the attack. When I met him two-and-a-half years later, he was especially keen to show me the scar from the sword blow which had split his balding head in the middle. The thick ragged scar, many shades darker than the nut-brown scalp it traversed before meandering down into the fringe of wispy black hair at the back of his neck, was displayed as a proud badge of honor, a battlefield decoration from an old war. The murderous assault had made him, as Majid Khan put it, "the hero of Hyderabad." "Thousands of people gathered at the hospital when they heard the news about the attack," he recollected with pride as he looked in the direction of two young men in the room for their choral confirmation. "Thousands every day," the men obligingly responded. "Nothing united the Muslim nation of this city as much as that cowardly blow," said Majid Khan. "Absolutely true. Hyderabad has never seen anything like it before," both the men confirmed, this time with greater enthusiasm as they warmed up to their roles.

I took the men, in their early thirties, to be his *chamchas* ("spoons"), the fawning, all-purpose factotums who hang around politicians and film stars, catering to their physical and especially to their narcissistic needs. Majid Khan was not yet a political star of the kind who would be surrounded by a whole group, by what I would call a *katori* ("cup"), the modest local version of the *coterie*, which has traditionally built up around prime ministers.

Majid Khan's political fortunes have nonetheless soared since the riots, and the visiting card he gave me was testimony to his importance in the Majlis. Printed in English, his name in cursive red letters riding many lines of different-sized letters in green, like the miniature flag of a new Islamic nation, the card informed me that Abdul Majid Khan was a council member of the All India Majlis-e-Itehad-ul-Muslimeen, a director of Sarussalam Urban Co-operative Bank, had two telephone numbers and a residential address in Karwan Sahu, the part of the city where he owned a house and an eatery (which may be called a restaurant but which is respectfully referred to as a hotel).

I think we took him by surprise when we walked unannounced into the anteroom of his house around eleven in the morning of a hot, late April day. If he was inconvenienced by our intrusion, his deep-set eyes in a dark round face did not betray annoyance. Interrupting his conversation with the *cham-chas* to greet us warmly, he inquired about Sahba's health and expressed his great pleasure in seeing her again, before turning to me in courteous regard. A middle-aged, barrel-chested man of medium height, with a short thick neck that took its function of joining the head to the trunk more seriously than of separating the two, Majid Khan, even in his undervest and the crumpled green-and-black checked *lungi*, dominated the room with a miasma of raw power. One of the walls of the room was covered with mounted black-and-white photographs which showed him garlanding state and national politicians and being garlanded in turn by more local ones. As expected, the tall, cadaverous leader of the party, Sultan Owaisi, was a gravely benign presence in most of the photographs. Another wall was fully papered over by a colored, grainy photograph of a wooden Swiss chalet standing at the edge of an icy cool stream and outlined against an impossibly blue sky, the color of the sky highlighted by two fluffy light grey clouds. Spring trees cast dark velvet shadows on sun-dappled grass. Plump European cows with silky sheens and pink udders grazed in the gently rolling meadow. Outside, the morning was steadily getting hotter. The temperature had crossed the hundred degree mark, yet the broiling sun had only begun its inexorable ascent.

Majid Khan's slight discomfort, as we exchanged further courtesies while he inquired about the purpose of my visit, was not due to the heat or the sheen of perspiration on his bald scalp that periodically coalesced into large drops of sweat which then trickled down his forehead. He seemed to be more bothered by the informality of his attire and our meeting place. For someone aspiring to be a political figure of more than local significance, Majid Khan naturally wanted to present himself in more appropriate surroundings and suitably dressed for the role. Excusing himself, he asked one of his men to take us to the party office located about a hundred yards from his house above his restaurant where we were to wait for him.

The office itself was sparkling new but looked bare and unused. Along one wall, painted in what I have come to regard as Hyderabad blue, there was a brown plastic-covered sofa. The only other furniture was a table with a formica top and a white plastic cane chair. The sofa, the table, and the chair were covered with a fine layer of dust. There were no cupboards, boxes of files, pens, pencils, paper clips, note pads, or other paraphernalia which be-speak of an office where work is done. We were asked by our companion to step into the adjoining room which was more luxuriously, even garishly ap-pointed, in a lower-class fantasy of aristocratic splendor as shaped by Hindi cinema. The peach-colored plush-covered sofa could easily seat six while the divan, with two cylindrical pillows encased in dark pink satin covers and in an exultant floral design, was equally spacious. A gleaming new Mirzapur carpet in loud blue with an intricate dark red Persian motif covered the full area of the floor. Majid's man politely asked us if we would care to look at the *sahib's* photographs, an offer we accepted with equal politeness. The man came back after a few minutes, carrying two bulging cardboard shoe boxes and followed by a younger man, the *chamcha's chamcha*, bearing two bottles of cold lemonade. As we sipped the oversweet lemonade, we were taken on a photographic tour of Majid Khan's life which highlighted his political career and the social status he had achieved. There was genuine awe and admiration in the *chamcha's* voice as he pointed out the burly figure of his patron in var-ious situations: here he is in the welcoming committee receiving the former Chief Minister Sahib, there he is next to Sultan Sahib in the reception for the Governor Sahib, there he is in the front of the group garlanding Sultan Sahib at the opening ceremony of the bank.

As we murmured our involvement with subdued "oohs!" "ahs!" and in-creasing "uh-huhs!" Majid Khan came into the room followed by one of the young men we had earlier met at his home. Majid Khan was now clad in the politician's uniform of fresh, lightly starched white kurta-pyjamas and matching white leather sandals. He apologized elaborately for keeping us waiting and then took out a remote control device from his pocket with which he tried to switch on the vertical fan standing next to the divan. The blades completed one full circle before coming to a halt. The remote control button was pressed again and the fan made another effort. This was repeated a couple of times before an almost imperceptible nod to the *chamcha* gal-vanized him to switch on the fan manually. During the play with the fan, Majid Khan kept on talking to the young man about how everything was now sorted out with the police and that there was no longer any cause for concern. I had the distinct feeling that this conversation had already taken place earlier in the house and on the way to the office. It seemed to me that the highlights were now being repeated for our benefit; Majid Khan was in-troducing himself. Without appearing to be overtly boastful, he was convey-ing through the conversation the extent of his power, the breadth of his concern, and the degree of his importance in the life of his community and the *mohalla* where he lived. Someone, it seems, had reported to the police that a bomb and a revolver were hidden in a house in the neighborhood. A police party came to Karwan in the evening, took away everyone in the house to the police station for questioning, and some of the men were roughed up. A young man, who worked in a factory, was the only member of the family who was not at home at the time of the police raid. He came running to Majid Khan for help. Majid went to the police station and arranged for the release of the young man's family, a task made easier by the fact that the house search had not yielded any weapon. After the young man left, Majid Khan proceeded to deliver a lengthy monologue on the ever increasing *zulm*, the oppression of the Muslims, by the police. The *chamcha* took up the narrative by telling us of other incidents where Majid Khan had also starred as the helper and savior of the oppressed poor, fearlessly confronting police highhandedness, facing down armed policemen who were ready to fire into Muslim crowds during a riot.

For me, it was difficult to reconcile the image of this courteous, confident man whose zeal in the service of his community could not be a total pretense, with the one projected by Hyderabad's English language newspapers and the police for whom Majid Khan was a well-known *goonda*. Most of the urban elite know the *goonda* in his caricatured form from Hindi movies as the villainous, dark-skinned, usually unshaven, solidly muscled tough in tight sweatshirts and jeans (or in a check *lungi*, if Muslim), with a knotted scarf around the neck and a gold chain nestling in the chest fur. The Hyderabad police have a special name for them. In their records such men are listed as "rowdies"; a rowdy, the Oxford English Dictionary informs us, is a "rough, disorderly person; one addicted to quarrelling, fighting or disturbing the peace." Although the word itself is of American origin, today a rowdy conjures up more the image of a British soccer fan wreaking mayhem in a European football stadium than a knife-wielding tough in the back alleys of Hyderabad. The police also call them "history sheeters," which refers to the sheets of paper in police files where, year after year, a history of their unlawful activities is carefully recorded from the surveillance and surmise of plainclothes officers, together with the noting of arrest records and any subsequent trial verdicts.

In the *mohalla*s where Majid Khan and others of his kind live, there are not too many who would go along with their characterization as *goonda*s by the police and upper middle-class sentiment. Unsurprisingly, the men do not have a name for themselves, although they would prefer a descriptive phrase such as "friend of the poor" or "protector of the oppressed." A name would categorize them, separate them from the rest of the community, take them out of the ocean in which they swim as big fish but nonetheless constitute a vital part of the ocean's ecology. The only name they are not reluctant to accept and which is also acceptable to others, including the police, is *pehlwan*. Specifically, *pehlwan* is a wrestler, but generally it may also mean a "strong man"; the purpose for which the strength is employed is left ambiguous and open to the interpretation of different groups. So let me call them *pehlwans* (rather than *goondas*, hooligans, rowdies, history sheeters), whether or not they have actually trained as wrestlers or bodybuilders, although a surprisingly large number have done so. Indeed, it is the culture of traditional Indian wrestling, which I will discuss later, which has had a profound influence in the formation of their personalities and which constitutes the most distinctive marker of their identities.

Strictly speaking, then, Majid Kahn is not a *pehlwan* although he went through a few years of training as a wrestler, the *taleem*, as a boy. His younger brother is the well-known Mumtaz *pehlwan* and many of the young men who hang around him, *his* men, are aspiring *pehlwans* who follow the wrestler's daily regimen. He is, though, a great admirer of the whole wrestling ethos, which he feels builds character and prevents young men from going astray. He feels distressed that traditional wrestling is coming to an end in Hyderabad, and young men are drawn more to such imports as judo and karate. The Japanese martial arts are just that, arts to be picked up without the necessity of being steeped in and internalizing the culture which underlies them. The reasons for the decline of wrestling are many. Primarily, economic deterioration makes it difficult for a family to let one of their sons turn into a *pehlwan*, since he would then need an expensive diet of pistachios, almonds, choice cuts of meat, and liters of milk every day. Then the Hindu-Muslim tensions have led the police to ban wrestling matches in the city, since a bout between a Hindu and a Muslim wrestler can easily ignite a riot between the two communities. "Only ten percent of the *pehlwans* are involved in violence," Majid said. "In fact becoming a *pehlwan* improves the character and disposition of many young men who are otherwise inclined to be violent and intemperate. When four people respectfully salute you as *pehlwan* as you walk down the street, you hold your head high and wouldn't do anything to lose that respect."

Majid describes his own role in the riots primarily in terms of a peacemaker, an older mentor with some influence on young hotheads of the Muslim community, especially in Karwan. He is generally successful in calming violent passions and excited crowds. "It is not so easy to control these boys," he says in mock sorrow as he indulgently smiles at the adoring young *cham-cha*. "Without any provocation, these young men are taken in by the police during a riot who register murder cases against them. Released on bail, they come out swaggering, as if they really are killers and have become equal to the *pehlwans*. The police have notarized them as killers and what better credentials can they have?" Majid Khan believes a major part of his role during the riot lies in curbing young "killers" who want to show off their killing prowess; he prevents the consolidation of a killer identity, as the psychologist would say in the discipline's language. Personally, Majid Khan said, he has never experienced any kind of blood lust even during the worst course of religious violence. This does not mean that he is some kind of a believer in nonviolence when there are riots between the Hindus and the Muslims. He is not a fanatic either way as far as violence is concerned. He has a "healthy" attitude toward the mutual slaughter, an outlook he states as following: "Riots are like one-day cricket matches where the killings are the runs. You have to score at least one more than the opposing team. The whole honor of your nation (*quam*) depends on not scoring less than the opponent."

The other part of his role during a riot consists in liaising with the police and the administration on behalf of the community and in organizing and distributing relief supplies on behalf of his party, the Majlis. Although some accuse him of pilferage ("of the ten bags of rice he keeps seven") and thus of enriching himself on the misery of others, Majid Khan is sincerely eloquent on the great human suffering caused by every riot and about his own modest efforts at its relief. I have the impression that Majid Khan feels much more comfortable talking about human suffering than violence, about the fellowship of misery than the divisions of murderous ethnocentrism. Losing loved ones, seeing one's house and meager belongings go up in flames, the whimpering of children in hunger and fear, is a shared experience of Muslims and Hindus alike and, after all, he is talking to me, a Hindu. Talk of suffering during the riots brings the two of us closer in mutual human sympathy whereas an elaboration on the violence will divide, will keep reminding us of our potential as deadly enemies.

In an earlier meeting with Sahba, who is a Muslim, there had been an absence of constraints imposed by my alien Hindu presence, and Majid Khan had talked freely about his more Muslim sentiments. The Muslims never initiated any attacks; they only defended themselves. They are discriminated against in every field and the police oppression is making the whole community mutinous (*baghi*). One day they will rise up to fight, even against the modern weapons of the police. After all, there are only four fighting communities in India: Sikhs, Marathas, Rajputs, and Muslims. Even badly outnumbered Muslims can hold their own against a far superior Hindu host as long as the police do not turn their guns against them. But this situation too will change. There is nothing like a riot to unite the community and strengthen its collective will for the fight ahead of it.

Testing the Tigers

The Giessen Test (appendix 1) is one of the most widespread test instruments in clinical use in Germany today[1]. Constructed on psychoanalytic and psychosocial considerations, its forty statements are divided into six scales: social response, dominance, self-control, underlying mood, permeability, and social potence. Using it to systematically tap the self-image of the *pehlwans*, the characteristics each ascribed to himself, I found the test to be a particularly useful interview tool which helped me to gain a more comprehensive view of the "warriors" in a relatively short period of time. The *pehlwans* often did not restrict themselves to just marking off an alternative on a statement but would generally elaborate, offering anecdotes from their lives as illustrations. Thus, for instance, in response to a statement, Majid Khan did not simply say, "I am very patient" but went on to add: "I had to learn patience, the hard way," and then narrated an incident from his life where he had suffered because he could not control his temper.

In the first area, social response, which has to do with the person's effect on his environment—whether one is narcissistically gratified or frustrated in social interactions—Majid Khan sees himself as evoking positive responses on the social stage. He finds it easy to attract others and believes people are highly satisfied with his work. He cares greatly about looking nice and feels he has been successful in achieving his aims in life.

In the area of dominance, which on one side has to do with aggressiveness, impulsiveness, stubbornness, and authoritarian tendencies, and on the other with an incapacity for aggression, patience, willingness to conform and the tendency to submit, Majid Khan comes across as particularly dominant and self-willed although he tries hard to control his impatience in public life.

As far as self-control is concerned, Majid Khan is more uncontrolled than compulsive, but not to an extent that would signal delinquency or sociopathic tendencies. It is, however, evident that Majid Khan has a problem in dealing with his aggressive impulses. He has a tendency to let out his anger easily which he struggles to control, lest it break out in episodes of unchecked rage and bouts of violence.

Although Majid lets out his anger and is not at all timid, there are strong indications of an underlying depressive mood. He tends to worry a good deal about personal problems, lets outer changes greatly affect his emotional state, and is often depressed. Coupled with his difficulties with self-control and the fact that he finds it very easy to get into high spirits, I would suspect a disposition where hyperactivity compensates for and sometimes alternates with a dysphoric mood and where there is a marked tendency to blow a fuse in tense situations.

As far as permeability is concerned—the fundamental ways in which the outer world is experienced and how open or closed the person is in inter-action with others—Majid Khan sees himself as very trusting and experi-ences strong feelings in love. Yet he also finds it very hard to come out of his shell, gives away very little of himself, and avoids getting close to another person. The fact that this is true only of personal relations and does not hap-pen in the public sphere, where he can work well with others, would lead one to suspect disturbances in the development of his sense of basic trust and in an openness to his own feelings. It is as if the early contacts with the world were not positive, generating a fear of a hostile environment which led to a defensive closing up and guarding of the core self. I sense in Majid Khan an anxiety about being exploited and abused if he ever opened himself fully to another human being. This way, though he may remain emotionally isolated, he also cannot be destroyed by others. This hypothesis is supported by his responses to other statements in the questionnaire such as that he finds it relatively hard to feel tied to someone for long, that is, he is fearful of per-sonal commitment. He thus comes across as someone who mimics trust and affection without deeply feeling them, something he does quite successfully in his public life since he confesses to being very good at acting and not too particular about truth.

The Violent Poet

Unlike Majid Khan, Akbar is a true *pehlwan*. He has been trained as a wrestler since the age of ten and comes from a family where for the last four genera-tions the men have all been wrestlers. Among the Hindus, he is notorious as a killer, while many Muslims approvingly acknowledge his role in the organi-zation of the community's violence during the riots. Living in a large house with four wrestler brothers and their families, a widowed mother, and three wives, Akbar is a prosperous man who owns a hotel and three *taleemkhanas*, as the wrestling gymnasiums are called in Urdu. Like most other *pehlwans*, the chief source of his income is what the *pehlwans* delicately describe as "land business."

Baldly stated, "land business" is one of the outcomes of India's crumbling legal system. Since landlord and tenant disputes as well as other disputes about land and property can take well over a decade to be sorted out if a redress of grievance is sought through the courts, the *pehlwan* is approached by one of the parties to the dispute to evict or otherwise intimidate the opposing party. The dispute being thus "settled," the *pehlwan* receives a large fee for his services. In the case of well-known *pehlwans* with *taleemkhanas* (or the Hindu *akharas*) and thus a large supply of young toughs as students and all-purpose assistants, land business can be very profitable. Many of the *pehlwans* do not need to use strong-arm methods any longer. The mere fact that a famous *pehlwan* like Akbar has been engaged by one of the parties is enough for the opponent to back down and reach a settlement to the dispute. In some cases, and these are on the increase, if the second party also employs a *pehlwan* to protect its interests, then the two *pehlwans* generally get together and come to a mutually satisfactory solution which, because of the fear they arouse, they can impose on their clients. Built on the threat of physical violence, overt violence is rare in this informal system where a black legality, like a black economy, runs parallel to the state's legal system, and violence occurs only when new *pehlwans* try to muscle into the territories of established "tigers," as the *pehlwans* also like to call themselves, threatening their vital interests and inviting swift reprisals. At least among the Muslim *pehlwans*, Akbar is a tiger's tiger, a well-respected man who is a figure of awe for his prowess as a wrestler, success in the land business, and the high esteem in which he is held by his community. A political career is on the cards. Akbar has been asked to and plans to stand for the state legislature elections on the platform of the Muslim party.

The history sheet of the police, though, is not a respecter of success or sentiment. It goes on to call him a chronic "rowdy" and to list a succession of dates, beginning in the early 1960s, and a few laconic lines in front of the date on the offense committed. Akbar was first convicted of sexual harassment when he was twenty years old—"Eve teasing of a girl,"—as the police history sheet puts it—and was fined ten rupees by the court. A few months later, he came to the attention of the police on a charge of physical assault; the complainant failed to press charges because, the police suspect, Akbar intimidated the victim. He was then suspected of snatching a gold chain, but the first serious crime for which he was sentenced to a couple of years in prison was assaulting a special police party, "causing grievous injury."

There follows a succession of charges of assault, stabbing, kidnapping, and wrongful confinement, most of them in connection with land deals, although he is acquitted every time because either the witnesses or the complainant or both are too scared to give evidence against him in court. A long list of arrests, orders of externment and removal from the city for specified periods, and short jail sentences (many of which he circumvented by getting himself admitted to the prison hospital) follows in monotonous detail.

What is now striking about his record are his increasing confrontations with the police. Abuse of police personnel, threats, and a couple of assaults on police officers are actions which the Hyderabad police, like the police of any other city in the world, view with particular disfavor and on which they come down severely. What is not mentioned in the record is that these confrontations with the police are often in the context of Hindu-Muslim violence where Akbar is seen to be defending Muslim interests in a clear-cut and unambiguous manner by putting his body on the line. This wins him many admirers in the community, especially among the young. And then something strange happens. The rowdy is recruited into the police ranks, undergoes training, and is appointed as a police constable in the armed police, something which can only happen as one of the minor fallouts of a political deal struck by the Majlis with the ruling Congress party at that particular time. Akbar's police career is cut short when he is dismissed for threatening to kill an assistant police commissioner during one of the riots in the seventies. He assaulted a police inspector and landed in jail again, this time for one year of imprisonment. He spent a large part of this sentence in the prison hospital where he continued to be active. Cases of wrongful confinement, assault, and extraction of money are registered as having been organized by Akbar from his hospital bed.

For about a decade now, though, Akbar's history sheet is clean. Akbar is becoming increasingly busy in the political arena and is no longer personally involved in any of the street and *mohalla* violence. He is no more a soldier but is suspected of being a general and one of the chief organizers of Muslim violence during a riot. The police, in their written summary which reveals an aversion to pronouns, concede: "Is very popular. Called *pehlwan* in his locality. Has earned a lot of money in land business. Many local people approach for settlement of domestic problems and civil disputes which he settles amicably. Has car and properties and income from house rents and hotels. Trains many people of locality in wrestling. Of late not involved in any criminal cases. However, close watch is being maintained on his activities."

Akbar questioned Sahba closely when she first met him. He wanted to know the names of the people who had mentioned his name, how she knew his student who had brought her to him, the number of visits she had made to the Karwan area and what the people had said about politics, religion, and violence. He was guarded at first and reluctant to talk, asking why it was necessary to interview him and why should he believe that Sahba was a Muslim except that her dress, face, and ways of carrying herself and talking gave her away as a Muslim. After all his bitter experiences in life, he found it difficult to trust people. If people know about him it was because of the good work he had been doing to uphold the honor (*izzat*) of the Muslim nation. Once his suspicions were lulled, however, Akbar talked to Sahba freely about himself and his view of the Hindu-Muslim relations.

"I am proud to be a Muslim. It is this pride which has carried me through many wrestling competitions I won. My aim in wrestling has not been to achieve fame for myself but to make a name as a Muslim. I always felt thrilled when large numbers of Muslim boys bought tickets because I was fighting in the arena. Each time I defeated a Hindu wrestler, I felt I had not only made a name for myself but for the entire Muslim community, which looked up to me for its honor and fame. I train a lot of Muslim boys in my *taleemkhanas*. I visit the *taleemkhanas* occasionally since I have trained others to do the job. But it is done under my close supervision. Apart from wrestling, the boys are also trained to protect themselves from attack by the enemy. They are trained on the condition that they will never misuse the training to unnecessarily harm someone."

"I also teach my disciples to be good Muslims—to respect their parents, elders, neighbors, and women. A wrestler's life is not easy. He has to observe certain rules very strictly. Besides eating a good diet, he must go to bed early and wake up very early in the morning. Alcohol, cigarettes, and *pan* (betel leaf) are absolutely prohibited. He must not drink tea and loaf around on the streets. I myself have strictly followed these rules and even today I do not drink alcohol or tea, smoke or eat *pan*. To become an example to others, I have undergone a lot of hardship. Today my disciples are very attached to me. If I were to tell them to kill themselves, they will not hesitate for a moment. But they know that their *ustad* will never ask them for their lives. He only works for their welfare. He wants them to be brave."

Akbar was now leaning forward, his voice swelling with pride.

"Your list of *pehlwans* has more Muslim than Hindu names because Muslims are stronger than Hindus. The Muslim has God's strength in him. A Muslim reflects the strength of the nation. Muslims are united and one. The other nation (Hindu) does not have this unity. They are divided. We know our immense strength, given to us by God. A true Muslim is never afraid. The only fear in his heart is of God. The wooden stave of a Muslim or only the cry "Allah-u-Akbar" (God is Great) is more than ten Hindu swords. Whatever is happening today is a test the Muslims have to go through. The Qur'an says very clearly that it is a sin to oppress others but even a greater sin to bear oppression. A good Muslim can never tolerate oppression. Today I am a *pehlwan* because our society, government, and police have forced me to be one. I have faced a lot of *zulm* but have never submitted to it. I have always fought it."

"I was myself a policeman once but I quit the service after I witnessed police brutality. I saw the atrocities they commit on innocent people. One day I openly took on the police in public. I beat up a policeman very badly. Later they ransacked my house and destroyed my hotel. I was charged with assault and jailed for one year. It was solitary confinement. In this one year I changed a lot. My sentiment for God and my love for the nation awakened. I also read the Qur'an and prayed regularly. I decided to dedicate my life to the well-being of my community."

"On my return, I received a hero's welcome. People were so happy to see me back. I did a lot of work for the poor of the community. I am satisfied that I am doing good work—not for myself or for my own good but for others, for my people. A *pehlwan* does not get his strength from the building of his body but from the blessings of the poor and the grace of Allah to whom he prays. To pray to God in the early hours of the morning when others are sleeping is the best. He is not distracted by the prayers of so many others who are still asleep."

There was no trace of banter now, only a deadly seriousness.

"I believe in equality for everyone. There should be no divide between the rich and the poor. I have the communist way of thinking. I am religious and communist at the same time. You might think I am a hypocrite because I own such a big house, a hotel, property. But even in Russia the leaders had everything. I am talking about beliefs and ideas. I hate the rich, their vulgar life style, and the show of wealth. I also hate the whites because they exploit the dark races not only in Africa but all over the world. I also hate the police whose uniform gives them the license to commit such horrible crimes. Today the Muslim's fight is not only against the other nation but also against the police."

"I feel very happy when young Muslim boys are tortured by the police. They should be beaten up even more. My prayer to God is for the police to commit unlimited atrocities on young Muslims. Whenever I hear about Muslim boys being tortured, I feel like dancing with joy. Unless these boys directly experience oppression on their bodies, they will never be able to stand up against it. When they are victims of police brutality they become tigers who join my army. Today, because of God's grace there are hundreds of these young disciples who are spread all over the city." There was no hysteria as he spoke now, just a cold fanatic dedication.

"The impression is false that in every riot more Muslims than Hindus are killed. I can say with complete confidence that at least in Hyderabad this is not true. Here the Muslims are very strong and completely united. More Hindus than Muslims are killed in every riot."

"In another ten to fifteen years the Hindus will be finished as a political force and not only politically. It is important to remember that many Muslim men marry more than once and have large families with many children. Every other Muslim house has at least five to six children. Imagine only two boys in every family growing up to be tigers and it is these tigers who will take them on without fear. Then the Hindus have the caste system in which poor Hindus are exploited. It has happened many times in the past that lower caste Hindus have converted to Islam or Christianity. This is going to happen in a big way now. There won't be many Hindus left."

His expression was again relaxing, a seductive light coming back into his eyes and in the hint of a smile.

"During the riots or at the time of curfew, I often go away from home. Because whenever there is disturbance this is the first place where the police lands up. I get the work I have to do during the riots done but never out of my own house. For the last many years the police have been unable to nab me. I do my land business the same way. I buy and sell land but I am not a land grabber like others. All my land dealings are done at home. No one ever sees me at a site and my signature is never found on any document."

"When you came to meet me, you must have had a certain image of me as a *pehlwan*. But I am sure you will go back thinking differently of Akbar *pehlwan*, I am not like the others."

Sahba's account of her meeting with Akbar had whetted my curiosity. She had been impressed with the dignity with which he carried himself, his elegance and his chaste idiomatic Urdu, liberally sprinkled with couplets from well-known poets. His courtly ways, coupled with the air of menace around him because of his reputation, made him an intriguing figure. Akbar was like the soft paw of a big cat, the talons retracted and almost invisible in the silken fur, a Damascus-steel sword sheathed in a velvet scabbard. I thus went to our meeting with Akbar, which was to take place in his hotel in the late afternoon, with much anticipation.

The rickshaw driver who took us to the meeting place did not need an address more elaborate than our simple instructions to take us to "Akbar *pehlwan's* hotel." The hotel was located near a bus terminal where buses from all over Andhra Pradesh as well as the neighboring states disgorge pilgrims bound for the temple of Tirupati, one of the holiest of Hindu shrines. Families from far-flung villages, often led by wizened women, bent with age yet shuffling along sprightly with faith, stream out of the buses to stretch their legs, use the toilets, and perhaps eat before they take the connecting buses for Tirupati. I found it ironical that Akbar's hotel advertised itself as serving special vegetarian meals for Hindu pilgrims. This time, though, "hotel" was not a misnomer since on one side of the restaurant, there was a flight of stairs leading up to the first floor which had six rooms lined along a narrow corridor. At the end of the corridor, recessed into a wall, there was a sort of, well, reception desk. Behind it, barely visible in the shadows, were three strapping young men. We asked for Akbar and one of the youth, disengaging himself from his companions, told us we were expected. Akbar would be with us in twenty minutes and in the meanwhile to please follow him.

He led us through the corridor to the last room, motioned us inside, and went away. All the other rooms seemed empty and the corridor was silent, with only the subdued late afternoon street noises filtering through its closed windows barred with iron grills. The room was stuffy and dingy, without a single window, the weak whirring of the fan churning the same stale air over and over again. There were two chairs, a twin bed, a television set on a low stool and a red telephone on a table. Otherwise the room was bare without even a poster or a print to mar the uniformity of its ugliness. Above the bed, there was a red bulb sticking out of the wall, baffling as to its purpose. I could feel the stream of perspiration thickening all over my back and my chest as molecules of sweat sought each other to form drops which trickled down to enter the pyjamas at the waist. The fan wheezed slowly, dispensing its miserly breeze only to someone who sat right under it, a space both Sahba and I were too polite to occupy by moving our chairs. The sheets on the bed were washed though they still looked soiled, covered with a profusion of patches, a cheap detergent having changed the color of the original stains to various shades of grey. There were oil stains on the pillows from the heads of guests who believed a daily smearing of coconut oil not only kept the hair thick and healthy but acted as a coolant for the head and tonic for the body. I could not help wondering what the hotel was used for and how many customers rented its rooms for periods shorter than a night's stay.

Half an hour went by but there was no sign of Akbar or, for that matter, anyone else. There was a palpable sense of unease, even fear, as we waited in the room, with the only exit out of the empty hotel leading through a narrow corridor which was blocked at the end by the three young toughs who, like his other disciples, Akbar had told us, were ready even to kill at the merest nod of the master's head. We tried to keep our fearful fantasies at bay through an exchange of light banter, punctuated by loud nervous laughter.

"How much do you think a room in this hotel costs?"

"Oh, you think they rent it by the night?"

"If they try to rape you," I tell Sahba, "keep your protests down to a minimum. I don't want them to get enraged and kill us both. On the other hand, if they do have their way with you, I doubt whether any of us will be left alive to bear witness."

"They throw the bodies under the bridge, remember?" says Sahba.

The red telephone rings. For a few moments we sit rooted to our chairs, staring, before Sahba picks up the receiver. "He will be here in another fifteen minutes," she says.

The minutes pass, very slowly. We have lapsed into silence, alone with our disquieting thoughts. I think of the room as a set from a movie with Ajit, the villain of old Hindi movies whose drawl has spawned a whole industry of Ajit jokes:

"Raabert," says Ajit.

"Yes, *baas*," answers the henchman.

"In the room there is a red bulb."

"Yes, *baas*."

"There is also a red telephone which will ring."

"Yes, *baas*."

"Pick up the phone. I will be at the other end of the line."

"How will I know it is you *baas*?"

Akbar entered the room, leaving my creation of an Ajit joke unfinished. (Frankly, although successful in dealing with my anxiety, I don't think the joke was really going anywhere). A powerfully built man of less than medium height, he wore a white kurta pyjama, the kurta having a faint pink and yellow floral design, so subdued that it was barely noticeable from a distance of ten feet. He was wearing white sandals, the front of the sandals narrowing down to thin strips which curved up like the ends of a proud warrior's mustache. His own mustache was a thin line on an otherwise clean-shaven face. His hair dyed a jet black, it was apparent that Akbar took great care of his grooming and appearance.

After the exchange of obligatory courtesies, Akbar turned his attention to me, his eyes bright and sharp. He asked me about the study, what exactly I wanted to achieve through it, what exactly I did for a living, where I lived in

Delhi and so on. My answers were frequently followed by a witty comment from him which had the intention of mocking my earnestness and exposing my ignorance of the really real life. I complied with the direction in which he wanted to take our meeting, exaggerated my naïveté, pretended to greater stupidity than I feel I am naturally endowed with. My weak laughter at his sallies, a tribute to his easy victories, began to relax him as he often turned to Sahba to receive her appreciative smiles which further sealed his triumph.

He continued in this vein with the Giessen Test. Instead of answering a question, he would toy with me, ask me how I thought he would answer a particular question. With mock humility, he would turn to Sahba, sometimes discoursing on the subject of the question—on patience or strong feelings in love, for instance—with quotes from Urdu poetry, while I waited on the sidelines for an answer I could use for the purpose of the test. There was a coquettishness about him, especially in the way he played with his eyes. He would be looking normally at her while talking and then suddenly the look would become bold, charged with sexual complicity, the boldness further underlined by the briefest flash of a smile before both the look and the smile vanished.

I felt I could sense Akbar's dilemma in relation to me. Clearly, he was far superior in bodily strength, physical courage, and fighting skills. And as for matters of the heart, or soul, was he not a better man here too? After all, he was a poet. Was not a man all about strength and sentiment, both of which he possessed in abundance? Yet he could not dismiss me lightly, this "doctor" from Delhi, who would come to his city for a "study" with a modern Muslim woman as his assistant, a woman who boldly walked in the city's *mohallas* with her face unveiled and talked to men on equal terms. I had better access to the modern world, to its systems of knowledge, and to its new relationships between the generations and the sexes. In terms of his own civilization, Akbar was far above me; yet he could not be easily dismissive of the modern world whose values I understood better and whose symbols I could perhaps manipulate more easily. At that particular moment, it seemed to me, Akbar and I were more than just two men warily circling each other, jousting for advantage; in our individual frames, we also incorporated the collective fates of the Indian Muslim and the Hindu at the end of the twentieth century.

Once I had given up, closed the questionnaire in apparent bafflement and given Akbar the opportunity to remark to Sahba that he had succeeded in making the psychiatrist mentally confused, Akbar became magnanimous in his victory. He was now ready to go through the statements in the Giessen Test with more sincerity.

As I expected, Akbar, unlike Majid Khan, did not give many extreme responses to the statements, further underlining the image of cautiousness which I had formed of him. The only exception was on statements relating to social response scale where Akbar believed that he evoked a very positive response. He felt people were very satisfied with his work. He was easily liked, found it easy to attract others, and was confident that people thought highly of him. Akbar's uncharacteristic emphasis on his social attractiveness made me wonder about his narcissistic vulnerability, whether there was not a strong need for continuous narcissistic gratification which sought to counteract a depressive tendency revealed by his responses to some other statements. Akbar stated that he consistently suppressed his anger and was often depressed. He felt very strongly in love, yet gave away little of himself, found it hard to come out of his shell or to trust others. The cautious and controlled impression he gave also seemed to be an aspect of a tendency toward compulsiveness, manifested in his dealings with money, tidiness, and concentration ability. I wondered whether the control he sought over his inner world and the domination of others exercised in the outer were not aspects of the same defense which guarded against the fragmentation of a self threatened by strong sexual and aggressive impulses; a self in danger of losing its cohesiveness and thus to the outbreak of a full-scale depression.

In brief, Akbar's presentation of the self was of the "strong, silent man" with unsuspected pools of deep feelings which are guarded and bounded by high fences and almost never revealed to a casual emotional visitor or even to those who would like to be close to him. By the time the long interview was over, Akbar was regarding me with a certain distant friendliness. He wanted to give me one of his poems, he said, and I should please write it down.

> Do not trouble to test me
> I am always in the forefront
> when it comes to bearing
> the burden of grief.
>
> When they talked of constancy in her *mehfil*
> I turned out to be the one
> Who was faithless
> In an otherwise constant world.
>
> In these times
> Both of us have achieved fame
> I, in creating her
> She, in destroying me.
>
> A broken mosque
> Can be rebuilt in four days

It takes a lifetime, though,
To knit sundered hearts together.

The wines of yore are there no longer.
The drinkers too are gone
In the wine houses
They drink blood now.

Akbar, guard the mirror
Of your heart with care
It will break
If you show it around every where.

"You will put me in a book," he said resignedly after I had expressed an appreciation of his poetic talent. The final victory will not be his but mine, he meant, for it will be my version of him that will be taken as his reality by the larger world outside Hyderabad. The line in his poem on handling the mirror of the heart with care was also directed at me, a plea which he was too proud to be aware of and would never have dreamt of making openly.

Young Tigers and Pussy Cats

Nissar is one of the soldiers, a twenty-eight-year-old man, a young tiger, who reveres Akbar and other famous Muslim *pehlwans*. He is a handsome young man with broad tapering shoulders, a narrow waist, shoulder-length hair, and a pleasant face with high cheekbones. He wears a thin mustache fashionable among Muslim youth who do not like to sport the beards favored by their elders. Nissar is dressed flamboyantly in a blue shirt of some satiny material, printed with large red flowers and is wearing tight, lemon green trousers. There is a certain reserve in his demeanor, a combination of hauteur and shyness which sometimes cracks when he is youthfully boastful about importing whole bales of cloth from the United States for his shirts or when he coyly asks us to guess the number of people he has killed. It is not eight, the number of murder cases registered against him by the police. Some of them are false, he says, but then with a modest but obvious delight adds that, of course, there are other killings of which the police are unaware. Nissar likes to tell war stories, tales of Muslim throats being cut by the Hindu enemy in underground blood sacrifices to its obscene gods and goddesses, of corpses thrown into the river under the bridges at the dead of night. Akbar and the other *pehlwans* are the protectors of Muslim lives, yes, but also the guardians of a boy's sleep and tranquility in face of such fearful fantasies.

His admiration for the old tigers is proportionate to the number of Hindus they are reputed to have killed. For Nissar they are the fighter pilots whose fame in serving the nation depends on the number of enemy planes each one has shot down. Indeed, it is the military analogy which is most useful in understanding the tigers, young and old. A riot is a battle, an outbreak of hostilities in a long simmering war where the killings do not involve moral qualms or compunctions. On the contrary, to kill under such circumstances is a moral duty higher than the patriotism of a soldier serving a modern nation-state since the killing of Hindus in a riot is in service of the nation of one's faith. Indeed, an outbreak of violence in Hindu-Muslim conflict should no longer be called a riot, with the anarchical connotations of the word. Less planned than a battle yet more organized than a riot, communal violence lies somewhere between the two. The analogies used by Majid Khan, Akbar, Nissar (and, as we shall see later, Mangal Singh) which highlight the warrior aspect of their religious identity should not be surprising. It would be an error to discern in them mere rationalizations for their killings and other acts of violence. As Samuel Klausner has pointed out, riot, assassination, massacre, and terrorism are victim-defined spheres of violence.[2] From the viewpoint of the instigator and the perpetrator, they are defense of faith, crusade, just war, act of purification.

"These are the real people who serve the Muslim nation. All the others are useless, interested in making money and sticking to the chair. The next time a Majlis leader enters this alley he will be thrown out bodily. Our second slogan will be, kill the police. At least two hundred policemen must be eliminated. They have done so much *zulm* on the Muslims. In jail we were so thirsty and hungry, but never received any water or food. After leaving the jail, when I went to the Majlis office, the leader said, "Why are you upset? You are not dead—you are still alive." When Hindus get arrested, a BJP leader immediately arrives and gets them released on bail. We keep rotting in jail. The Majlis is of no use to us. The leaders fight among themselves. They collect money in the name of the poor Muslims like me and then eat it up themselves. They have opened a medical college but the number of Muslim students in the college are only five paise to a rupee (5 perent). Where do they have money for the fees? The college benefits the Hindus more. Actually the biggest school in the world is the mother's lap. The child will grow up to be as capable as the education given by the mother. My mother was a complete illiterate and look at my sorry state!"

Nissar was married, with four children, and sold vegetables from five to eight in the morning. On a good day he could earn as much as a hundred rupees. He also does land business whenever he is called by a senior *pehlwan* to go and negotiate a deal. He is usually paid a commission of 5 percent. He is very proud of his activities as a "soldier" in the service of the Muslim nation. "Our work is to serve the nation [the Muslim *qaum*] and protect our mothers and sisters. We never look at their [Hindu] sisters but their bravery is limited to raping and killing our mothers and sisters. I decided to work for the nation after all I saw during the riots following Rameeza Bi's case. It is always the Hindus who start the trouble. Earlier, we felt very scared. We were often abused when we walked through their alleys. But today I am proud that when I walk through a Hindu lane, the heads bow down. They know me as Nissar *dada.*"

Dada ("elder brother") is not yet a *pehlwan*, but someone who may become one, someone who is high enough in the hierarchy of strong men. As a *dada*, Nissar is not a poverty-stricken vegetable seller, a poor Muslim who needs to defer to the well-off Hindus, but someone who demands and receives respect. Having been trained as a wrestler for many years in different *taleemkhanas*, he stopped the training after he was married since he felt he could not afford the diet of huge quantities of milk, nuts, and meat, required by a wrestler. Now he serves the nation through *chaku-bazi*, wielding of the knife. "If I hear that two of our people have been attacked and killed at the wooden bridge it takes me just five minutes to knive five of them." In Sahba's expression of open interest (obviously, he would not have revealed himself in this way if I, a Hindu, had also been present), Nissar elaborated on his professionalism. "There is a way to kill with the knife. Once I stab with a knife I do not need to turn and look. I am sure the man is dead even as he is falling. Then, on a street, I never make a mistake between a Hindu and a Muslim. We recognize the religion from the face. If I saw you somewhere else, in a different dress, I would know immediately that you are a Muslim. It is clear from your very face."

"Most of the time the police are not able to catch us. We move very fast. All they can do is to suspect. Sometimes we dump the bodies under some bridge which are discovered disfigured after three to four days. Sometimes dogs eat up parts of the body which is then very difficult to identify. We always make sure that if Hindus kill two of our people, we should kill at least four of theirs. This is to scare them away. They must not think we are helpless, frightened or unarmed."

"Personally, I don't take a weapon with me when we go out to kill Hindus during a riot. I only have a wooden stave (*lathi*) but I do have a strategy. I make sure that the first person I confront on the other side is the one with a sword. I disarm him with my *lathi* and then kill him with his own sword. It is easy."

"Scared? What an idea! Once the decision to serve the nation is made where is the room for fear? One has to be brave. Cowards die quietly. Instead of dying inside the house it is better to be martyred outside. Allah is with us. He knows that we are doing good work and He protects us."

"I have told my wife never to worry about me or stop me from my work. I have told her not to wait for me more than three or four days in times of trouble. Where will she look for me? We go everywhere wherever there are disturbances. She should simply break her bangles (the sign of widowhood) and feel proud that I have become a martyr."

Nissar's wife, though, is less worried about his heroics or eventual martyrdom. She complains bitterly about her own situation, about Nissar's attitude toward women that does not allow her to step out of the house. To run their home, she has to depend on her old father to buy groceries, and medicines, and other essentials. He never takes her out since he is embarrassed to be seen with a dark-skinned wife. "If I was fair he would take me out everywhere," the killer's wife sighs in bitter regret. Another man, Aslam, a sullen middle-aged vegetable seller, unemployed for most of the day, who sits across the street wrapped in a mantle of sardonic gloom and has watched our interest in the *dadas* and *pehlwans* gives his own assessment of the young tigers. Pointing to his chapped, dusty feet with grotesque toes and discolored nails, he says: "The police pulled the nails out one by one when they took me to jail during the last riot. I have to keep my feet in water whenever I want to clip the nails. All this tiger business is nonsense, except that they pocket three-fourths of the relief supplies which go through their hands. Otherwise, when the police take them, every tiger turns into a pussy cat."

Spreading the Wind

Mangal Singh is a well-known Hindu *pehlwan*. In many ways he is the Hindu counterpart of Akbar although he does not possess any of Akbar's old-world Muslim graces. He belongs to the Lodha community, economically one of the fastest rising groups in Hyderabad, whose prosperity, observers say, rests on illicit liquor distillation. Brewed in the backyards of houses and stills near the riverbed, the raw liquor is a potent brew which drastically lowers the life expectancy of its hapless customers. Basically distilled from jaggery and the grey oxide powder used to coat the insides of brass utensils with tin (and which can easily dissolve lead), the liquor is expectedly severe on stomach linings. It is believed that anyone who daily consumes half a bottle of the liquor, the *pauwa*, will not survive for more than a year. In the poor neighborhoods of the city where the liquor is mostly consumed, it is not an unfamiliar sight early in the morning to see a corpse or two lying on the street near an *adda* where the liquor is clandestinely sold.

The reputation of the Lodhas is of a mercurial and violent people who are always in the forefront of a riot from the Hindu side. "They will kill as many people in two hours as the rest will in a week," says an old Hyderabad resident who has studied the community closely. They claim to be Rajputs, the traditional martial caste and the sword arm of Hindu society, although this claim is often disputed by others. In spite of their taking a leading part in religious violence, their economic ties with Muslims are close. Muslims are the main customers of their lethal brew, both as retailers and, together with the *dalits*, the poverty-stricken Hindu outcastes, as its consumers. Even socially they have adopted some Muslim customs. Although they regard Muslims as their chief enemy, it does not prevent them, for example, from regularly visiting Muslim shrines, the *dargahs*, in a spirit of devotion.

Mangal Singh's house is in one of the crowded localities of Hyderabad where there is a large concentration of Lodhas. The bazaar running through it has shops stocking somewhat more expensive goods but in essence differs visually from similar other bazaars of the city only in one curious particular. This is the occasional sight of two to three men on bicycles wearing very loose clothes, emerging from one of the alleys and, with a look of determined concentration, furiously pedaling away to turn and disappear into another alley. These are the liquor carriers, wearing bicycle tire tubes full of the illegal stuff tied around their bodies, on their way to various distribution centers in the city.

A young-looking forty, Mangal Singh is a handsome man who laughs easily and has a kind of manic charm about him. He walks with the compact, swaggering gait of a wrestler, with shoulders swinging like a young woman's hips, as he proudly shows us around his house and his *vyamshala*, the gymnasium, both of which are situated in a large compound just off the road and very near the river. The gymnasium, which trains more than a hundred boys and young men, consists of two rectangular halls adjacent to each other. The first hall is used for weight training. There are wooden dumbbells, iron tires to be put around the neck to strengthen the neck muscles, parallel bars, ropes hanging down from iron rings in the ceiling, and many other contraptions for the pulling, pushing, and lifting of weights. The whitewashed walls are lined with colored lithographs and posters. There is the lithograph of the reclining god Vishnu, his faced shaded by the hoods of the hydra-headed snake, Sheshnag. There is a poster of one of Vishnu's incarnations, the god Rama in his heroic pose with a long bow and a quiver of arrows visible above his shoulders. There is the portrait of the goddess Durga in her ferocious form, in the act of killing the buffalo demon, Mahisasura. There are portraits of the Hindu heroes Shivaji and Rana Pratap, who have come to epitomize Hindu resistance to the Mughals; there is also the reproduction of a popular painting of Nehru looking down from the ramparts of Delhi's Red Fort, the Indian national flag flying proudly behind him as he pensively looks down at a large crowd, the faces of the leaders of India's independence movement—Patel, Rajagopalachari, Kripalani, Maulana Azad—clearly recognizable in the forefront.

The other wall, too, is covered with pictures. There are three large portraits of wrestlers, one of them Mangal's own *guru*. The other two are famous wrestlers from the thirties and forties, each in a loincloth and standing with his feet and arms a little apart, in the pose where they are ready for grappling. Pointing to one of the *pehlwans*, who has very close-cropped hair and a thick mustache, Mangal Singh informs me that this man was the prime accused in Hyderabad's first major riot between the Hindus and the Muslims in 1938, when the state was ruled by the Nizam. This *pehlwan*, I forget his name, had killed one of the leading members of the Razakars, the Nizam's unofficial Muslim militia, and then disappeared. He is believed to be still alive in a remote area of Nepal where he now practices the austerities of a holy man.

There are many colored lithographs of scenes from the independence movement—Gandhi leading a long line of volunteers on his march to the sea, the Jalianwala Bagh massacre where British soldiers are shown firing into the trapped crowed, men caught in the pose of falling down, clutching at their chests from which blood is spurting out, open mouthed in silent screams. Then there are lithographs depicting scenes from earlier periods of history: small Hindu children being thrown up and impaled on the spears of the Razakars, Indian soldiers being blown up from the mouths of cannons by the British after the failure of India's first war of independence, the Sepoy Mutiny as British historians called it. Pointing to the Razakar picture, Mangal Singh informs me, "This is what used to happen all the time in those days in Hyderabad. Hindu girls were picked up from the streets or the fields at any time at the will of Muslim nobles and raped. That is why our girls started marrying so early. If a girl had a *mangalsutra* around her neck and *payals* around the ankles (the sign of marriage), she was not kidnapped."

There is a further series of pictures depicting Muslim atrocities from the long period of Islamic rule: Banda Bairagi and his followers being beheaded by Muslim soldiers, the martyrdom of the Sikh Gurus, Mahmud of Ghazni destroying the famous temple of Somnath as shaven-headed Brahmin priests look up with bulging eyes and mouths open in incomprehensible horror. Next we come to a photograph of Subhash Chandra Bose, the stormy rebel of the national movement who sought an alliance with Hitler's Germany and Tojo's Japan during the war to violently overthrow the British empire in India. Next to it is a full-sized wooden statue of Gandhi which is overturned and lies on its side, facing the wall. "There was a high wind a few days ago and Gandhiji toppled over. He has his back to us because he cannot bear to see the present condition of this country," Mangal Singh jokes.

"How is it that you have Gandhiji, the apostle of nonviolence, together with the violent Hindu heroes next to each other?" I venture to ask.

"First, I talk like Gandhiji," he replies with a smile. "Only when talk fails I use force like Shivaji or Bose."

The second hall is dominated by the *akhara* where the actual wrestling takes place. About four feet under the floor level, the *akhara* is a flat smooth rectangle of reddish colored mud mixed with oil and finely threshed stalks of wheat, covering about half the area of the hall. Presiding over it is a Shiva *lingam*; a garland of fresh white jasmine flowers and sticks of burning incense bear witness to its daily morning worship. On the other side of the room, next to the wall, there is a small temple of Hanuman, the ascetic patron god of Hindu wrestlers. The idol is smeared with red paste, flowers are strewn around its feet, and incense sticks burn from between the toes. On the wall itself there are photographs of famous wrestlers—I recognize Guru Hanuman from Delhi among them—as well as photographs clipped from Western bodybuilding magazines and pasted to the walls. The slightly fading photographs show off the oily sheen of bulging biceps, thundering thighs, and sculpted pectorals. One entire side of the hall is without a wall and opens out to the river and a peaceful scene of dark-skinned women with *sarees* tied above their knees, whirling wet clothes above their shoulders and bringing them down with rhythmic thuds on flat stones to clean them of dirt. Mangal Singh draws my attention back to the gym when he points to the corner next to the temple where some loincloths are hanging on a wooden post. "Earlier we used to have spears and swords. Nowadays, of course, they put you in jail if you have even a knife for your self-protection. Many young men prefer to learn karate these days," he continues to enlighten me. "Karate makes the sides of your hands into killing instruments by deadening sensation in that part. They burn the side of the hand and dip elbows in boiling salt water till all sensation is lost. But Indian-style wrestling is still superior where you can kill a man once you grapple with him. Karate is only good for long-distance fighting. Once you get in close to the opponent as in Indian-style wrestling, karate is useless."

The Muslim *taleemkhana* does not differ substantially from the Hindu *akhara*. There will be fewer photographs and, of course, no idol of a Hindu god. It might have an *ayat* from the Qur'an on a wall or a colored print of the *kaaba*, Islam's holiest shrine. Comparatively speaking, with its greater profusion of religious icons, the Hindu gymnasium appears more Hindu than the more neutral *taleemkhana* appears Muslim. The Muslim training regimen is the same as the Hindu one except that the wrestlers will say the prescribed dawn prayers at home before coming to the *taleem*. They too will drink crushed nuts and crystal sugar mixed in water or milk after the training is over for the morning but, in contrast to the Hindu, eat great quantities of mutton.

It had not been easy to meet Mangal Singh. We had to go through friends of friends of friends before the meeting finally took place. Once it happened, though, Mangal Singh talked so freely and without any apparent suspiciousness or guile that I wondered why it had been so difficult in the first place. He did not quite understand what my psychological study of Hindu-Muslim violence was all about (I confess that when I tried to explain the aims of my study to other *pehlwans*, I did not quite understand it myself). He was under the impression that we might eventually want to make a movie on the subject, an impression I did not fully exert myself to correct. In any event, Mangal Singh proved to be most frank about his activities as a scourge of Muslims, perhaps also because he assumed Sahba and I were both Hindus.

The Muslim *pehlwans* had been open with Sahba but understandably guarded when I was also present. With Sahba they could express their bitterness and contempt for Hindus, show their pride in their role in the protection of the community from the Hindu enemy. In my presence, they became less Muslim and more inclined to express universal humanist sentiments. For instance, there was pious talk, not exactly reassuring, that if I were cut my blood would be exactly the same color as theirs. By the end of the interviews, though, all the *pehlwans* were perceptibly warmer. I like to believe that this opening up was because they sensed my genuine interest in them as persons rather than being due to any typical "shrink" "hm-ms," phrases, or inflections. I suspect, though, that their different—although for my purposes, highly complementary—psychic agendas when talking to Sahba and to me were dictated by shifts in their own sense of identity. In other words, with Sahba, a Muslim, their self-representation was more in terms of a shared social identity. With me, a Hindu, once they felt reassured that the situation did not contain any threat, personal identity became more salient, influencing their self-representations accordingly. In any event, when we parted, promises to visit me in Delhi were made, visions of feasting in my house were conjured up, all of which I acknowledged smilingly though not without quaking inwardly at the prospect of the promise being ever kept. There were occasions in meetings with the *pehlwans*—for instance, when waiting for Akbar in his hotel room—where I caught myself thinking that the scholarly work of making a book out of other books was infinitely preferable to being out in the field, anxious and afraid. Besides being perpetually uncomfortable in the heat, dust, bad smells, and biting mosquitoes, I felt envious at visions of friends reading and writing in quiet air-conditioned libraries.

In the meeting with Mangal Singh, the only threat came from his generous but insistent hospitality as he pressed a glass of sugarcane juice on me, delicious but deadly, a prime vehicle for stomach disease and a possible cholera carrier. We were sitting in a room on the first floor of his house where Mangal Singh lives with his two wives. Most of the eleven rooms on this floor are empty. The ground floor has nine rooms, occupied by his widowed mother and his five brothers with their families. The rooms are in the form of a square and open out to a verandah lining a courtyard which has a *tulsi* (basil) plant growing in the middle. "Not *tulsi*, Mother *tulsi*," Mangal Singh had corrected me while demonstrating his Hindu piety at the same time. Besides a scooter and a motorcycle parked in the verandah, there was a refrigerator and a water cooler as well as some toys. Everything looked neat and tidy and freshly scrubbed. Mangal Singh had introduced us to his first wife, a shy, pretty young woman to whom he was openly affectionate. He had married again because she could not have children. "But I actually prefer her," he had said to the young woman's obvious pleasure. "She looks after me well. The other one is also nice but since she is educated she doesn't look after me so well." As with his mother, to whom he had introduced us downstairs, Mangal Singh behaved like a spoilt young boy with his wife, cracking jokes, praising her extravagantly, ordering her about, calling out to her often to reassure himself that she was not far away.

There were three other men in the room when we began the interview, the obligatory *chamcha*s to amplify his statements whenever he paused for breath or effect. They provided emphasis to his statements and strove to increase their truth content by a resounding "That is right!" to his rhetorical "Isn't that so?" Occasionally, when he paused, they sang his praises while he looked on, smiling modestly. "He needs good food to keep up his 'manpower,'" says one. "Manpower" is said in English, the man's rough and ready translation of the Hindi word for strength. "If he lifts his hand, all the hands in the city would rise, such is his 'manpower.'" They showed me the extern-ment order served on Mangal Singh by the police and signed by the commis-sioner *sahib* himself which banished him from the city for six months in "apprehension of inciting violence and breach of peace." "But I'm back after one and a half months. I got a stay from the High Court," Mangal Singh says. The copy of the stay order is also passed on to me by a *chamcha* for my per-usal. A second *chamcha* brings out a sheaf of photographs. The ones shown to me are of police torture. A subdued-looking Mangal Singh, standing in his loincloth, is pointing to his back which is covered with welts. The face is bruised and the eyes puffed. He points to his left eye where the skin under it is noticeably darker. "I have still not completely recovered from that beat-ing," he says with indignation, not at the beating itself but at the surrounding circumstances of which Mangal gives two versions. It seemed a few months ago, at the time of tension over the demolition of the Babri mosque, Mangal received a parcel, very probably from his Muslim enemies. It was kept in the room next to the one where we were sitting. His three-year-old son fell on it and it exploded, killing the boy. In the second version, which is also the statement he made to the police, he had stored firecrackers in the room for the children in the family. His son was playing with them and they exploded, killing the boy. "My son dies and the motherfuckers arrest me and beat me up, claiming I was manufacturing bombs," he says, his indignation quite con-vincing.

There are other occasional contradictions in Mangal's monologue which comes tumbling out at a high velocity. For instance, in talking of the wrestler's ascetic regimen, he had said that he ate exactly at eight every eve-ning and never went out of the house after that. Yet, just before saying good-bye to us, when his wife had come out, he said, "The poor woman makes such nice meals for me but I am so busy I never know when I will be home. I eat at all odd hours. How often she has waited up for me before she could have her own dinner!" Mangal is not exactly a liar in the sense that he wants to deceive his audience. He is an embellisher of facts, some of which may get changed to fit in with what he believes to be true at a certain time. He may also unwit-tingly bend the truth to project a particular image of himself. After a while, the contradictions become a part of his manic charm as I fascinatedly watch the persona he is constructing as much for himself as for us.

The first time Mangal Singh clashed with the Muslims was in 1979. The Muslims had claimed a piece of land on the specious ground that it was an old community graveyard. The man to whom the land belonged had won his case against the encroachment in the court but could not get the land vacated and came to Mangal Singh. His cause was just and Mangal agreed to help him. Mangal would never help someone who wanted illegal possession of land. He only, so to speak, expedited the notoriously lumbering machinery of the law, helped in implementing court orders which would not otherwise be carried out. Mangal settled on a sum of money for his services. Nowadays his minimum fee is a hundred thousand rupees, but he takes it only after the work is done, not like some other *pehlwans* who take the money but refuse to do the work, daring the client to do his utmost. Mangal, on the other hand, is a man of principles.

Mangal went to the site with five of his people. They had a few knives and a couple of swords between them. The Muslims were eight in number, all of them with swords and each an expert at wielding the weapon. But they were old—the oldest being almost sixty—and though thorough professionals, they lacked the staying power of Mangal's much younger men. The Muslims were soon out of breath and Mangal and his men killed six of them. They put four of the corpses in a car and threw them in different parts of the city to confuse the police. He was charged with three murders in that particular incident. He cannot tolerate *zulm*, particularly Muslim *zulm*.

The police report of the incident credits him with only one murder, of which he was acquitted because of lack of evidence. A month later, the history sheet continues, "along with others, he assaulted Imtiaz and his parents with sticks and caused bleeding injuries to them." Two months later, in December 1979, when riots had begun after the Rameeza Bi incident, Mangal Singh is noted to have led an armed group of twenty people who set fire to Muslim shops, attacked Muslims with sticks and knives, and pelted stones at the police. There is a succession of other brief notings over the years: assault, unlawful assembly, rioting. For a few months he was ordered to report to the police every day at eight in the morning and nine at night. But he was never convicted in the court in spite of over forty cases registered against him by the police. Because of the intimidation of witnesses, the police say. Because the people love me and will not let me go to jail, says Mangal. The police record summarizes: "Young and energetic. Very close to the BJP MLA [Member of the legislative Assembly]. Has good contacts with the RSS. Also close to the local Telugu Desam Party MLA. Tries to be close to Congress also. He is a communal element. Very active during communal disturbances and has very good following. Has become very intelligent and never exposes himself personally in crimes but uses his henchmen for creating disturbances. People of the locality very frightened and do not want to complain or become witnesses. Earns a lot of money by settling land disputes."

Mangal Singh freely admits his political links but has a sense of outrage that he was but behind bars in the explosives case. "I was with the Congress party for so many years. I did so much of their work. I also did the personal work of a couple of MLA in getting their houses vacated from tenants. But then I change over to the BJP since that is the only party defending the Hindus. And what happens? The Congress puts me in jail! No gratitude at all!"

During a riot, "strong men" representing different localities, not all of them *pehlwans*, meet almost on a daily basis and decide where "the wind is to be spread" (*hawa phailana*), a euphemism for where the killings have to take place and where they need to be stopped. For instance, it would be decided at the meeting to stop the violence in Dhulpet but start it in the old city. Mangal Singh likes to maintain a tight discipline in his own area. Once, during the riots, a mob collected spontaneously in his locality. He immediately sent a few of his boys who came back in two minutes after doing *satrol* (creating chaos). He then called in the leaders of the mob and told them, "Never do that again without my permission."

Although Mangal Singh enjoys recounting his violent exploits in the land business or in the political field—for instance, when he and his boys did *satrol* to the procession of a newly appointed minister at the behest of his cabinet colleague—what he is really proud of are his clashes with the Muslims in defense of the Hindus. These allow him to identify with and place himself in a long line of heroes such as Shivaji and Rana Pratap, whom he admires greatly for their armed resistance against the Muslim emperors. He tells us of the incident of a Hindu marriage procession when it was stopped in front of a mosque because it was time for the Friday afternoon prayers. An altercation took place and the bridegroom, who belonged to the Lodha community, was pushed off his horse. The incident was reported to Mangal Singh who reached the spot with a few of his men. "Within two minutes," he boasts, "four of their men lay on the ground, two dead even as they fell. The others fled and the marriage procession passed the mosque."

Mangal Singh's psychological profile shows a great resemblance to that of Akbar; the difference is that his responses are much more extreme. He believes he tries to dominate others, is very self-willed and competitive. He, too, is often sad, worries a great deal about personal problems, tends to suppress anger, and always blames himself when things go wrong. Even his choice of favorite songs reflects a preference for the sad and the sentimental. The first is a Mukesh song with the opening lyrics:

> Life's road is full of tears
> Someone should tell her
> I have a long way to travel.

The other is an old hit from a 1950s movie:

> Do not forget these days of childhood
> Today I am laughing
> Do not make me cry tomorrow.

In spite of the dysphoric mood, Mangal feels personally potent and socially gratified. Taking into account the interview and the responses to the statements on the Giessen Test, I would surmise that the outstanding feature of Mangal's personality is a hyperactivity defending against depression, compared to Akbar's more compulsive defenses. And since I am already in the comparison business, let me go further and look at the psychological profiles of all the four *pehlwan*s. Although too small a sample for any definitive statements on the larger universe of "strong men" who carry out the actual acts of violence in a riot, my tentative collective portrait may still be a source of hypotheses for any future psychological studies.

My first observation is that these men are not abnormal in a clinical sense. That is, they are neither psychopaths, highly neurotic, nor delinquent. Their control over their violent impulses is not even greatly impaired. All of them, however, are unusually dominant and of a marked authoritarian bent. There is also a notable depressive tendency in their underlying mood, a threatened depression against which various defenses are employed. Surprisingly, the depressive tendency persists in spite of the *pehlwan*s feeling that they evoke a positive social response; that is, they are narcissistically gratified rather than frustrated by their environment.

Perhaps the need to defend against an emptying and fragmenting self, the inner experience of depression, contributes to the building up of a defensive hyperactivity wherein the cohesiveness of the self is restored and most immediately experienced through an explosion in violent action. The excitement of violence becomes the biggest confirmation that one is psychically still alive, a confirmation of one's very existence.

Psyche and Wrestling

Until now we have looked at the warriors of communal violence, the men who orchestrate the violence and who, in their younger days (and current youthful versions), were directly engaged in it, as moved by specific aspects of their religious and personal identities. Yet in Hyderabad, as well as in many other cities where the *pehlwans* take a leading role in communal violence, we also need to look at their socialization as *pehlwans*. In other words, for a greater understanding of these warriors of religious violence, we need a close look at the culture of Indian wrestling. It may well be the development of the *pehlwans* professional identity which, working in tandem with his personal and religious identities, provides us a more complete picture of the workings of his mind. This is exemplified by an apocryphal story about Sufi Pehlwan, an old *peshawar* ("professional") who retired from the killing business after the 1979 riots. He is reported to have felt that, like everything else in India, riots too were not what they once used to be. Since each one of us interprets the world from the limited view we have of it, Sufi Pehlwan too saw the deterioration of the country through his particular professional lens. The quality of food and thus the toughness of the men's bodies had been steadily degenerating over the years. Bones had become brittle so that when one stabbed a person there was hardly any resistance to the knife blade which sliced through muscle, cartilage, and bone as if they were wet clay. Simply put, there was no longer any professional satisfaction to be obtained from a riot, and Sufi Pehlwan had turned to other, more challenging, if perhaps less exciting pursuits.

The tradition of Indian wrestling, the *malla-yuddha* of the epics, is not equally widespread. Strongest in the north Indian states of Punjab, Haryana, Delhi, Uttar Pradesh, and western Bihar, it is encountered more scatteredly in the rest of the country. Although absent in most of south and central India, wrestling is quite robust in parts of Bengal and Maharashtra as well as in some erstwhile princely states such as Hyderabad where the rulers patronized the art. Wrestling in the Indian context is not just a sport but a whole way of life; it is not only a physical regimen but a moral tradition with changing political coordinates. In the felicitous phrase of the anthropologist Joseph Alter, wrestling is a "meeting of muscles and morals."[3]

As far as the physical regimen is concerned, there is little difference in forms and techniques of wrestling between the various parts of the country or even between Hindu and Muslim wrestlers. Waking up at dawn, the aspiring wrestler runs a few miles to build up his stamina. Ideally, he should then spend some time in contemplation (or in actual prayer in the case of the Muslim) before he makes his way to the *akhara*, *dangal*, or *talim*—the different names given to the wrestling gymnasium. Here he begins with a bath before donning the wrestler's habit, the *langot* or the loincloth. This is followed by the anointing of the body with oil and a collective preparation of the actual *akhara*, the approximately ten-meter square pit. In a Hindu *akhara* there is collective invocation of Hanuman, the celibate god of wrestlers and the symbol of deepest devotion to Rama.

Wrestlers are then paired off by the *guru* (the *ustad* or *khalifa* in case of Muslims) to grapple and practice moves and countermoves under the guru's close supervision and frequent instruction. After two or three hours of this *jor* (literally, "strength"), the wrestler rolls in the earth of the pit to partake of its cooling, reinvigorating, and healing qualities and then finishes with a bath. A large hearty meal consisting of the wrestler's staple foods of clarified butter, liters of milk, and ground almonds (or chickpeas) if Hindu, meat with pistachios and almonds if Muslim (in the days when pistachios and almonds were still affordable) follows. The wrestler then has a short nap and rests for a couple of hours during the afternoon. Then it is back to the *akhara* in the early evening for another two or three hours for individual exercises to build up strength, stamina, and flexibility of joints. Besides various kinds of weight training, the core exercises are hundreds of deep knee bends and jackknifing push-ups. A bath and again a specialized meal later, the wrestler is generally supposed to be asleep by 8 or 9 P.M. so as to get up fresh and energetic at the crack of dawn to repeat the regimen the next day.

The physical regimen is part of a moral and ideological complex, and this is where Indian wrestling is similar to traditional East Asian martial arts, where physicality was inseparable from morality and skills were not independent of ethics. Here, too, traditional wrestling differs from the teaching and learning of judo, karate, or wrestling in the modern context as recreational sports, physical exercises, or fighting skills. The wrestler, though very much a part of society, both looks and experiences himself as a man apart. First, there is the contrast of the bulky but muscled body to the underfed and emaciated bodies of other men in the lower-class neighborhoods from which most wrestlers come. Besides exhibiting the outer signs of apartness, the wrestler adheres strictly to the moral principles of continence, honesty, internal and external cleanliness, simplicity, and contemplation of God which, as Alter points out, he shares with the ascetic—the *sanyasin* or the *sadhu*—who too stresses his liminality to the normal social order.[4] Of course, where the wrestler differs most strikingly from the normal man is in his advocation (like that of the ascetic) of absolute celibacy. Sexuality, and in particular, the loss of semen, are concerns of high anxiety. The image of the wrestler in popular Hindi movies is generally of a strong but simple-minded rustic who goes to absurd lengths to avoid the company of women and thus any occasion for sexual excitement. As Alter tells us, for the wrestler semen is the

locus of all of his strength and character. Milk, clarified butter (*ghee*), and almonds, the primary ingredients of a wrestler's diet, are believed to build up a
store of high-energy semen. Milk and *ghee* are also supposed to lower the
body heat so that the semen is not inadvertently spilt in sleep but can perform its desired function of building bodily strength.[5]

The control of sexuality, and anxiety about sexual concerns, is the cor-
nerstone of all conservative moralities, and the wrestler's ideological universe, with its centrality of celibacy, is very close to the most conservative
parts of the Hindu and Muslim religious traditions. Like the so-called fundamentalist, the wrestler, too, is opposed to the modern entertainment forms of
cinema and television, where sex is so abundantly on display. He disapproves
of modern educational institutions, where boys and girls come into close and
thus dangerous contact. He looks askance at modern fashions in clothes and
bodily care, which he feels are devoted to the excitement of prurient interest.
In general, the wrestler's conservative morality condemns all manifestations
of modernity that arouse the sense instead of calming them, that stoke the
sensual fire instead of dousing its flames.

In the various philosophical and social science discourses on modernity,
there is very often an absence of what many twentieth-century artists,
writers, and film makers—not to speak of psychoanalysts—regard as its central features: the foregrounding of the biographical self and of sexuality (in its
widest sense) in human subjectivity. Psychoanalysis, the study of the sexual
self, is thus a preeminently modern discipline. The protest against the ubiquity, significance, and manifestations of the sexual self is thus inevitably a
basic characteristic of revivalist and fundamentalist rhetoric.

There is one element of the wrestling ideology which at first glance appears to run counter to the conservative label given to it. This is egalitarianism. In the *akhara* there are only bodies, without sectarian, class, and caste
hierarchical distinctions. As a commentator on wrestling remarks, "In every
village everyone from the common labourer to the wealthiest person would
enter the pit together. Everyone on everyone else's back with knees on necks.
There was no stigma, no enmity, anger or threats. The akhara was a pilgrimage point of social equality; a temple of brotherly love."[6] Until the very
recent past, many *akhara*s in Hyderabad were mixed in the sense that they
would have both Hindus and Muslims training under a Hindu or Muslim *pehlwan*. Majid Khan's brother's *khalifa*, for instance, was Chintamani Pehlwan, a
Hindu. In any event, although egalitarianism between men may be missing
from some modern Western conservative ideologies, it can very well be a
part of Hindu conservative traditions and is, of course, available in the ideol-

[margin note:] Why is egalitarianism necessarily not conservative?

ogy of Islam. Egalitarianism, for instance, is a point of emphasis for the deeply conservative ideologies of the RSS, the organizational vanguard in the current revival of militant Hinduism. The litmus test of revivalism and fundamentalism remains the attitude toward sex rather than power.

Morally and ideologically, the wrestler, either Hindu or Muslim, thus welcomes and feels a sense of kinship with forces in his community which would oppose modernity through the revival of traditional values. The changed political coordinates of his position also make it easier for the wrestler to become an active and, given his calling, militant representative of the community. Before the independence of the country in 1947, wrestlers were traditionally patronized by Indian princes who would have court wrestlers just as they had court painters or court musicians. Akbar *pehlwan's* forefathers had been court wrestlers to the Nizam of Hyderabad for four generations. All the physical needs of the wrestler were taken care of by the royal patron. What the wrestler was expected to do was to concentrate on the refinement of his art and the building up of his body. In return for the patronage, the wrestlers would march on ceremonial occasions in royal processions through the streets of the capital, their magnificent physiques testifying to and reflecting on the power of the prince. They would represent the honor of the prince in their competitive bouts with wrestlers from other states—the re-creation of a legendary mode of warfare between kingdoms which has been immortalized in the Persian tale of Rustum and Sohrab.

Although some politicians did try to replace the princes as patrons of wrestling *akharas*, using wrestlers for strong-arm methods to achieve political ends, in general the wrestler had lost the morally elevated view of his calling demanded by tradition and ideology. It is in the polarization of Hindus and Muslims and in the context of religious revivalism that the wrestler is again finding a role as an icon of the community's physical power and martial prowess. Although he may still be used by the politician, employing religious violence for his own purposes, the wrestler can again hold a cherished moral high ground in that he is proud of his new role as "protector of the Muslim (or Hindu) nation."

The traditional wrestling training, although it also graduated religious killers, did have certain advantages in structuring the form of religious violence. Often, the *akharas* and the teachers had mixed Hindu and Muslim students who would never fight each other in or outside the ring and thus had a dampening influence on the battlefield enthusiasm of the two communities. The training also inculcated a strong ideology that bound the fighting and killing by certain rules of combat, where, for instance, the respect for wom-

What?!?

ankind precluded a woman from being a riot victim. In Hyderabad, even now, rape is not used as a vehicle for the contempt, rage, or hatred one community feels for the other, as it is, for example, in Bosnia. As the strength of the *pehlwan's* traditional ideology declines and the role of the *pehlwan* as a channeler of his community's violence gives way to a more brutal free-for-all, religious violence too promises to enter an era of unchecked ferocity. There are, of course, other reasons for the relative absence of rape in a Hindu-Muslim riot, including, as we shall see later, the strong moral disapproval of rape as an instrument of religious violence in both communities. Moreover, unlike in the Bosnian conflict, after a riot the Hindus and Muslims still have to live together and carry out a minimal social and considerable economic interaction in their day-to-day lives. As Mangal Singh remarked: "A few days after the riot is over, whatever the bitterness in our hearts and however cold our voices are initially, Akbar *pehlwan* still has to call me and say, "Mangal *bhai,* what do we do about that disputed land in Begumpet?" And I still have to answer, "Let's get together on that one, Akbar *bhai,* and solve the problem peacefully." Rape makes such interactions impossible and turns Hindu-Muslim animosity into implacable hatred.

As far as the warriors are concerned, their ability to get over the bitterness of the conflict to again work together further attests to their high level of ego functioning. Unlike many other members of their communities who are either unable to hate or cannot stop hating, the *pehlwans* have learned both how to hate and how to get over hating.[7] Killers in the service of their religious communities, they do not fit easy psychological or philosophical categories. There is no evidence, for instance, that they are psychopaths brutally trained to reject human feeling, are sexually insecure, or were abused as children. Endowed with leadership qualities and standing out from their milieu in certain aspects of character, they are not—as in Hannah Arendt's "brutality of evil" hypothesis—perfectly ordinary people with the capacity to behave as monsters.

FOUR

Victims and Others I: The Hindus

O ne of the worst hit areas in the riots was Pardiwada ("settlement of the Pardis") in Shakkergunj. Two miles from Char Minar, the center of the walled city, Pardiwada is an enclave of about fifty Hindu houses surrounded by Muslim settlements. Before the last riot, Pardiwada had a population of about a hundred and fifty families (in a family-centered culture, the population figures, too, are given in number of families rather than individuals) which has now dwindled to fifty.

The narrow lane which branches off the main road to lead into Pardiwada meanders through Muslim *mohallas* where many of the houses show the religious affiliation of the owner by having a window, a door, or a whole wall painted green. The access lane is generally crowded with bicycles, goats, buffalo and fruit vendors pushing their carts through a stream of pedestrians moving in both directions. The pedestrians are both Hindus from Pardiwada and their Muslim neighbors, and the lack of warmth between the two is palpable. A snapshot sticks in my mind: two middle-aged woman, both fat, one a Hindu in a *saree*, the other a Muslim in an ankle-length black *burqa*, though with the face unveiled, walking with the same side-to-side waddle of overweight ducks, pass each other. There is no outward sign of acknowledgment as they squeeze past each other although before the riots, I am told, at least polite greetings would have been exchanged.

The small brick and cement plastered houses of Pardiwada, arranged in uneven rows, were built thirty to forty years ago. Some of them, especially at the periphery of the *basti*, are deserted and show obvious signs of the riot: charred doors and windows, broken electric bulbs and ripped-out wires hanging loose above the chipped and pitted floors. Many have crude "house for seal[sic]" signs lettered in English on their walls, as if the complex of feelings evoked in the seller by such an offer could only be dealt with in an emotionally distancing foreign language rather than in the more intimate mother tongue. They remain unsold. The Pardis believe that the prospective buyers, who are Muslim, are waiting for prices to fall further when the owners will be forced into distress sales.

The street scenes of Pardiwada, though, are cheerful enough. Since the main occupation of the Pardis is the selling of fruits and vegetables, there is a great deal of activity early in the morning when whole families are involved in sorting out and cleaning the fruits and vegetables heaped in front of the houses and loading them onto pushcarts. Many of the women have been up since three in the morning to fetch the fruit from the wholesaler, generally a Muslim, or even from the faraway Muslim-owned orchards at the outskirts of the city. These are traditional business relations which have endured through generations. They are based on trust, where the women take the fruit on credit and make the payment the next day after it has been sold. The riots have disturbed these business—and inevitably, over time, personal—relationships between the Pardis and their Muslim suppliers. The women now feel more apprehensive walking through dark and empty Muslim bazaars or gardens at this time of the morning. In any case, it is a community tradition that the women fetch the goods and the men sell them, a tradition which doubtless persists also because men find it convenient. As one of the women describing the tradition added, "Moreover, my husband does not feel like getting up so early in the morning."

Later in the day, once the men are gone, the teenage boys have been sent on their bicycles to sell onions, garlic, and ginger, and the older children have trooped off to school next to the Hanuman temple, Pardiwada settles down to a more easygoing pace. Free of morning household chores, the women come out to sit in front of the houses, smoking, chatting, and giving baths to babies and young children while old men gather under the shade of trees to gossip or play their interminable games of cards. By one in the afternoon, the working members of the family are back as are the school children. After a lunch of rice and a vegetable curry, this is a time for relaxation and the exchange of the day's news. Children play around on the streets, generally games of marbles, and there is much casual visiting as people wander in and out of each others' houses.

Economically, the Pardis belong to the lower class. Their poverty is reflected in the garbage dump which is clean and uncluttered, with nothing more in it than shards of pottery, small strips of cloth, husks of corn, and a few rotted vegetables. Because the poor use almost everything and throw away very little, their garbage dumps are generally cleaner than those of their richer neighbors. The Pardis may be poor but they are not destitute. They seem to have enough money for simple food, clothes, and even that necessary luxury of the urban poor—a black-and-white television set. The girls and women are dressed in bright colors and wear earrings, bangles, necklaces, and large round *bindis* rather than small demure dots on the forehead, serenely unaware that this particular accoutrement is now a part of the urban chic of upper-class women in Delhi and Bombay. Since their economic life is critically dependent on the prices at which they buy and sell fruits and vegetables, their incomes fluctuate daily, ranging from zero on the day a Pardi does not go out to work to a hundred rupees on an exceptionally good day.

Their housing, too, is decent although overcrowded, not only because of the smallness of the houses but also because of the extended nature of the Pardi family which seems to spread haphazardly in all directions like the roots of a *banyan* tree. In fact, in this extremely close-knit community, there is no clear-cut demarcation of one family from another. Intermarriage has been so rampant that everyone is related to everyone else. The community is divided into four clans, each deriving its name from one of the four goddesses —Chowkat Mata, Shakti Mata, Kali Mata, and Naukod Mata. Theoretically, marriages within a clan are forbidden and the marriage partner cannot be outside the other three clans; it is, however, a rule mostly observed in its violation.

The word *pardi* appears to be a distorted form of *pahadi,* "the hills man," and the group traces its original home to the hills of Chittorgarh in distant Rajasthan in the north, inhabited by the *bhil* hunting tribes. The language they speak within the community is a mixture of Marwadi and Rajasthani, although all are fluent in the Hyderabadi dialect while some also know Telegu. As skilled hunters of birds like quail and partridge and of small animals such as rabbit and barking deer, the Pardis were nomadic hunters who moved southward to Hyderabad two hundred and fifty years ago. According to their lore, the Muslim king who ruled Hyderabad at the time was suffering grievously from a festering sore which did not respond to treatment. One of the king's doctors, a venerable *hakim* of Unani medicine, suggested that the only possible cure was the application of minced meat of a particular kind of quail which was difficult to ensnare. The king had heard of the group of Pardis who had just entered his kingdom and of their proficiency as hunters. A Pardi was summoned to the court and entrusted with the task of snaring some of these quails. The hunter executed the order and brought back several birds whose meat was minced and applied to the royal sore. The worm that was eating into the king's flesh turned its attention to the bird's meat, which was poisonous for it, and it died. The king recovered, and in his grate-fulness decreed that henceforth the Pardis were welcome to take up residence in the kingdom of Hyderabad. In addition, and more materially, he showed his gratefulness by giving them a large tract of land called Jalpalli, which is about ten miles from this particular Pardiwada. Here, the Pardis dug a well for drinking water, built houses, and settled down for the first time in the history of the community in a place they could call their own.

Because of the scarcity of good forests near Jalpalli and the reluctance of the younger generation to learn the arduous skills of hunting, the Pardis began to look for other sources of livelihood. From nomadic hunters they turned into daily wage laborers in the fruit orchards and vegetable farms of Muslim landlords, packing and transporting fruit and vegetables from the farms to sell in the city. Gradually, they moved from Jalpalli into Hyderabad where over the last fifty years they have created various settlements, called Pardiwadas. The whole community still assembles together in the ancestral village of Jalpalli to celebrate certain important festivals like Dusshera and Holi.

Although they are now sellers of vegetables and fruits, the tradition of hunting and the memory of the days when these nomads were considered the scourge of more settled communities are very much alive as a part of Pardi identity and cultural memory. They take a not-so-secret pride in their reputation as a violent and aggressive people. There is little shame in the "recollections" of the men that earlier, in the days of the benefactor king, they were regarded as bandits and thieves and that, whenever a band of Pardis camped near a village for hunting, it had to report daily to the head-man and the police. Generally, though, the "outlaw hunter" is now a dark, occasionally longed-for and rarely fantasized part of the Pardi identity. It comes to the forefront only during the hunting rituals when the community assembles to celebrate its festivals in Jalpalli. In a distorted form, however, I believe it also colors their participation in riots and religious violence, which is experienced in terms of the hunter and the hunted.

The "identity-kit" sketch the Pardis would now have others recognize as their own is of a community that is accepted as a respectable part of settled Hindu society. In their origins myth, the Pardis are intimately related to the Marwadis, India's richest and highly respected business community, which hail from the plains of the same area in Rajasthan where the Pardis roamed the rocky hills. The ancestors of the two communities were brothers; one chose business and the other hunting as his profession. In their further efforts at what the sociologist M. N. Srinivas has called the process of Sanskritization, the Pardis strive to emulate and adopt the manners and mores of high-caste Hindu communities in an effort to raise their ritual status.[1] The erstwhile subsistence hunters now have very strict prohibitions on the eating of beef. Drinking of liquor, too, is frowned upon, although in an earlier generation even women were regular drinkers as some of the older women still continue to be. Marriages used to be simple affairs, with the families of the bride and the groom sitting down together with some elders of the community under a tree to decide on the arrangements and the sharing of expenses. The head of the community then conducted a simple ceremony. Today, marriages follow the more elaborate pattern of other Hindu castes. The groom's family demands and receives a dowry from the girl's side. Brahmin ritual specialists are involved in the matching of horoscopes, in determining the auspicious days, and in presiding over the elaborate wedding ceremonies.

The Pardis' Sanskritizing effort to raise their ritual status in Hindu society is paradoxically accompanied by what can only be called attempts at de-Sanskritization in the socioeconomic sphere. This is because of the reservation policy of the Indian state which seeks to benefit the historically backward and deprived sections of society through preferential quotas in school admissions and government jobs. The Pardis, who were once classified as a "scheduled tribe" and were thus on the lowest rung of the socioeconomic totem pole (thereby having first claims on the state quotas in education and employment), have been recently reclassified as a mere "backward caste." The elevation has brought with it the loss of many economic benefits, and the Pardis are currently engaged in a battle with the bureaucracy to prove that their backwardness is greater than that of a backward caste and thus to recover their earlier, lower status.

With very few exceptions, anthropologists have generally not described the many reasons why a community reveals itself to an outsider. Perhaps this reserve is because many anthropologists believe that the information they receive is primarily due to their personal qualities, such as a special gift for establishing rapport with strangers, fluency in the community's spoken language, evident sympathy with its ways, or other markers of an irresistible personal attractiveness which it would be immodest to talk about in public. The community's expectations of the researcher, which both encourage and skew a community's self-revelations in a particular direction, are rarely discussed. These expectations may be frankly material, as in case of Napoleon Chagnon's Yanomono Indians of Venezuela who expected a constant stream of presents in exchange for their cooperation in furthering the anthropologist's academic career.[2] There, the community operated according to the principle of the goose who laid golden eggs: "If you want more eggs, be nice to the goose." In other communities, expectations may be linked to more nonmaterial benefits: the prestige of associating with a white *sahib* if the anthropologist is European or North American, or (in a more literate community) help with admission and scholarships for a relative to the *sahib's* university. As far as the Pardis were concerned, it was evident that their initial ambivalence toward me, the motivation both to hold back and to talk, was colored by their preoccupation with getting themselves reclassified as a scheduled tribe. Their suspicion was of strangers who might be agents of the government, gathering data which would harm their cause, like the researcher who had come twenty years ago and on whose report the government had acted: "For his own career, he ground a whole community into dust." The hope, which finally triumphed over the doubt, was of my being a potential helper in their dealings with the state, given my obvious high status. The motivation of the Muslims in talking to me—or, rather of their leaders in sanctioning our conversations—was of a different kind which can be expressed in words thus: "You want to write about us and we would like to be written about in a way which suits our political purpose of appearing as victims." In contrast to the Pardi leaders' faintly whining, complaining tone, the leaders of the Karawan Muslim community were firmly courteous, barely betraying their slight contempt of a Hindu liberal and do-gooder whose guilt about the Muslim minority they hoped to manipulate. I was thus aware that the accounts I heard were not only self-representations of individuals and the community but were also designed to accomplish particular pragmatic actions. Thus their conversational context needed to be kept constantly in mind.

A Pardi Family

The two-storied house of Badli Pershad, of the Naukod Mata clan, is smack in the heart of Pardiwada. On top of the doorway which opens into a courtyard are two painted baked clay idols, each about a foot high. The monkey god Hanuman, with a golden mace resting on his powerful shoulder, stands on the left side, guarding with his legendary strength the inhabitants of the house from the evil forces that surround human beings. The idol of god Rama stands on the right side, with a smaller Hanuman kneeling in front of the god in his equally legendary devotion. Badli Pershad, who is about seventy years old and blind for the last five years, is usually to be found in the room to the right of the courtyard. Except for a cot, the room is empty and scrupulously clean. Its floor, made of grey paving stone, is swept and washed every morning.

Badli Pershad has four grown children, two sons and two daughters, of which his youngest son Rajesh and his family live with him. The others live separately in different parts of the city. Both his sons are college graduates who reluctantly took up the traditional family occupation of vending fruit from pushcarts because they could not find other jobs. Their feelings of bitterness and humiliation are very close to the surface. Besides his son, daughter-in-law, and two grandchildren, Badli Pershad's ninety-year-old mother also lives with him. His sister, Laloo Bai, stays in a separate part of the house, occupying most of the second story, with her eldest son and his family. The kitchens are separate but on many evenings, especially in the summer when it gets very hot, the sister and her family come down to the courtyard with the food they have cooked, and both the families eat together.

.This is a snapshot of the family at one particular instant in the winter of 1991, since a major feature of a Pardiwada family is its fluidity. Family members come and go and stay for varying lengths of time depending upon the impact of external events on their lives and the ebb and flow of internal family life and relationships. Badli Pershad's eldest son, Satish, lived in the same house with his family till a few months ago and moved out to a safer area after the December riot of last year. If his economic situation worsens, he may soon be back again. In this kind of shifting family, expanding and contracting like a giant membrane with an irregular rhythm, the only constant presence for young children is their parents (and, to some extent, their grandparents), especially the mother. Although it is both exciting and reassuring to have many caretakers who can compensate for parental shortcomings and mitigate the strong emotions aroused in a small, nuclear family, the frequent comings and goings of other adults in an extended family can also make children clutch to their own parents, especially the mother, with a marked intensity as they seek to establish an intimate, enduring, and trusting relationship in their inner, representational worlds—to establish "object constancy," in psychoanalytic language. In one of my earlier writings, I had attributed the intense bond between mother and son in Hindu India solely to the vicissitudes of a woman's identity—to become a mother of a son is to finally become a woman in the eyes of the patriarchy—with all the radical improvement in her status in the family that such a transition implies.[3] I increasingly realize that the son, with his need for at least one figure to stand out clearly from a labyrinthine flux of relationships, actively furthers the mutual emotional investment of mother and son.

The experience of fluidity is not only from within the family, which constantly constitutes and reconstitutes itself, but also in relation to the wider community which, in fact, is an extended family. Badli Pershad's eldest son is married to his sister's daughter and his youngest daughter is married to one of his sister's sons. There are so many such interconnections by marriage in the Pardi community that Badli Pershad would not be surprised to discover that he was the nephew of his daughter! One of the consequences of their being such a closely knit community is the great similarity in their views and opinions on different issues and in the way they think and follow a shared logic. This can be helpful in the sense that one can be reasonably sure that even a small sample would be accurately representative of the larger community. On the other hand, it can get boring to listen to very similar responses and a shared, common discourse unenlivened by individual quirkiness.

Badli Pershad's wife, one of the economic mainstays of the family, who earned fifty to sixty rupees a day selling fruit died in 1988. He misses her terribly. "Her absence is unbearable at times. She used to look after all my needs. Since I cannot see, she brought me my food and medicine, took me to the bathroom. I have been a diabetic for thirty-five years and can only eat a restricted diet of wheat *rotis* and vegetables. I am not allowed to eat rice. She understood that these restrictions upset me and sometimes added meat gravy to my food."

"Although my children and grandchildren are quite obedient, I feel they get tired of taking care of me to such an extent. Sometimes I think I am a major burden on them because of my lack of sight. If only I could have this [cataract] surgery, I would be more independent. My mother here, who is probably ninety years old, is still fit and healthy, and people say she is my daughter and not my mother in the way she looks after me. She brings me my food, takes me to the bathroom, bathes me, and sees to all my comforts. Even at this age, she is active and alert. When my daughter-in-law goes off to her mother's house, she does all the cooking by herself."

"I had more say in family matters when I had my eyes. My children were also younger. I was strong, worked hard, and people looked up to me for making all the major household decisions. Now I feel dependent, a burden on the family. They still respect me and are concerned about my needs and wishes. I, too, feel it is their life now and they should be allowed to do what they want to. Therefore unless someone asks my opinion I try not to force my views on others."

The deference paid to Badli Pershad is not only perfunctory but extends to issues vital for the family's welfare. His sister and his sons want him to sell the house and move out of Pardiwada since their sense of security has diminished precipitately after the last riot. In the past, Badli Pershad has resisted the demand although he is now resigned to the move: "This house carries memories of my youth, my wife, my children, and the good times that we spent together. Given a choice, I would not like to leave this house till I die. But under the circumstances, where we cannot hope for security or peace, I am forced to think of selling. The reason I have not done so is because the buyers are mainly Muslim who are offering very low prices for such a good house."

Pardis and the Modern World

Badli Pershad's younger son, the forty-year-old Rajesh, is bitter that he could not find the job he feels his college education entitled him to. It is with a sense of aggrieved humiliation that he drives an auto-rickshaw to earn a living, in addition to helping out with the family's vegetable and fruit business. He has a baffled feeling of betrayal, of unkept promises, although he would be unable to say what the promises were or who made them. He blames the changing times, as do many of his friends, for this feeling of nagging dissatisfaction. Rajesh mourns the passing of an earlier era when the world was a simpler and kinder place and the bonds between the Pardis much stronger than they are today. "In Hyderabad, our *jaat* (a word denoting both a caste and a community) was once the best in the mango and grape business. No other *jaat* could even touch us. Now we compete against each other. We have become the best in the infighting business. Everyone is running after wealth, looking out only for himself. We were happier when we were together."

"In olden days after you earned twenty thousand rupees, you relaxed. There was enough to eat for six months and after that we'll see. We went back to the village, lazed about, talked day and night. Now no one's desires are ever satisfied. Everyone wants more—bigger house, better food, more this, more that. It is good that a persons thinks, "I must progress, I must raise myself." But this raising is done by pushing someone else down. We were happier when we earned less but lived in friendship and love.

"Even the nature of our business has changed. Nowadays, it is all just calculation. Earlier, we would go into an orchard and estimate the yield of trees and come to an agreement with the owner. Most of the time the fruit would be more than the estimate and one made a little extra money. Then came these packing boxes. We do not buy the fruit on the trees anymore but get it in exactly weighed boxes. You have to deal with agents, contractors, truck owners, each one measuring, weighing, calculating. There is no more

walking around in orchards in fresh air, looking up at the trees, and estimating the yield."

Of course, a part of Rajesh's mourning for the "good old days" may well
be the normal expression of what Christopher Bollas calls a "generational
consciousness" as it yields place to the consciousness of a new generation.[4]
Rajesh's nostalgic ruminations are thus also occasioned by the waning of a
youthful vitality which made the world come alive at a particular time of his
life. The inner feeling of the dimming of life for a whole generation then gets
expressed in a sense of loss which is attributed to changes in the modernizing
outside world. Many of us pass down this consciousness of loss to our young,
although it is not strictly their own, and which most of them thankfully succeed in renouncing sooner or later. On the other hand, the raising of a generation's consciousness occurs precisely because of severe dislocations such as
the process of modernization. Without a crisis of this historical magnitude,
the demarcation between the consciousness of a preceding and a succeeding
generation is not so marked; the change is not big enough to become a subject of reflection.

Rajesh's elder brother, the forty-five-year-old Satish, although sharing
some of his brother's feelings of bitterness and disappointment—he too
could not get a job in spite of his education—would confront the dislocations of modernity more actively. He is a passionate advocate of change in
the community's attitudes and values. A small, intense man, whose sense of
his own dignity is in constant conflict with an anxious desire to please, Satish
would make the next generation a vehicle for his hopes rather than weigh it
down with despair.

"You know our business is such that we cannot earn a lot of money to buy
property or have savings. It is a hand-to-mouth existence. Our most valuable
property is our children. So we are very careful about how we bring them up
and what they will make of their lives. That is why we not only want to feed
and clothe them properly but also give them the best education we can. We
do not want our children to get into bad habits. Therefore I have bought a
black-and-white television so that if they want to watch a film they can do it
at home. Otherwise once the children are in their teens it is easy for them to
fall into bad company and spoil their lives. But I know that not everyone in
our community feels like this. They think that children are there for the financial support of the parents in their old age, and this is why they want to
make them study and find a good job. Not for the children's sake but their
own. We [indicates his wife] are not selfish like that. It is our duty to bring up
the children as good people and if they feel like taking care of us in our old
age then it is our good luck."

"Our people have certain fixed festivals like Bonal, Holi, and Dusshera which we have celebrated since the time of our ancestors. But now, seeing other Hindus celebrate so many festivals, our people also want to celebrate them. Festivals like Ganesh, Diwali, Ugadi, are nothing but occasions for wasteful expenditure. In the name of the festival it becomes compulsory to buy new clothes, prepare good food, spend money on useless things like crackers and decorations. It is the spirit of sacredness and not the show that is important. Unfortunately, these days show and the amount of noise one can make seem to have become a sign of one's importance. And sometimes although the menfolk may not be interested in celebrating all the rituals of a festival, they may have to do so because of their wives. I am lucky that my wife shares my ideas. Many of my friends complain that they are unable to meet these expenses but have to undertake them to please their wives. These women have no thoughts of their own. They want to do everything other women do. I am very particular that blind customs and useless rituals are discarded."

"Another custom I would like to change is the burial of dead bodies. I feel it is better to cremate than bury the dead. This is because space is becoming a major problem these days. Our ancestral village of Jalpalli is now only full of graves. The sad part is that these graves do not get respectful treatment from those who are alive. After a few years, the land is dug up and used for construction. Therefore I feel it is better to finish off once and for all so that there is neither a problem of space nor disrespect to the dead. Moreover, many times some of my Hindu friends have questioned me about this practice. They ask why despite being Hindus we bury the dead like Muslims. I feel very embarrassed. Now it is a mixed situation. Some families have started cremating their dead and some continue to bury them. This kind of behavior makes you the laughingstock of others, especially these Muslims. They are always on the lookout for our customs that are odd. This is the main difference between their religion and ours. They have fixed rules which no one can flout."

"The other thing I would like to change is our custom of marriage between members of one family. Earlier, people followed it because it ensured that all family members lived in one place. Now there is no need for such a custom because there is so much overcrowding. I feel that one must send our daughters to different families and get girls from new families because it will help us establish new relationships."

Satish's main strategy in dealing with the dislocations caused by rapid change seems to be aimed at reducing the isolation—of the family by integrating it into a network of other families, and of the community by bringing

it closer to the customs and usage of a Hindu "mainstream." He exemplifies
the spirit of agency among the Pardis, both individual and collective. In their
vigorous pursuit of community self-interest which manipulates all the levers
that can influence decision making in a modern democratic state—from preparing detailed, petitioning briefs for the bureaucracy to persistent lobbying
of their elected representatives—the Pardis are by no means mere passive
victims of the modernizing process.

The Night of Long Knives

The thirty-five-year-old, plump and cheerful Lalita, Badli Pershad's eldest
daughter-in-law, remembers that particular Saturday evening well. It must
have been 7:30 and they were all gathered around the television set listening
to the local news which comes on during the intermission of the Saturday
movie. (It was *Swami Ayappa*, a religious-mythological in the classification of
Indian movies.) The riots had started in another part of the walled city that
morning and a curfew had been in force since five in the evening. The news
announcer informed them that the curfew would be lifted for one hour the
next morning so that people could go out and buy essentials such as milk and
medicines. Suddenly, they heard a crowd's deep growl of "Allah-u-Akbar!"
"Kill! Kill!" and panicky answering shouts of "The Mussulmans have come!"
Lalita knew what to do. It was the third time since her marriage that Pardiwada had been attacked in a Hindu-Muslim riot. It always happened at
night. The women and older children went downstairs and started collecting
stones for the men to throw at the Muslim mob. Children's school bags were
emptied to serve as pouches for the stony ammunition, *saree*s and bed sheets
were taken out and tied around the men's foreheads to prevent serious head
injuries. The women could not see much whenever they looked out into the
alley. There were "hundreds" of Muslims with swords and spears, their faces
covered with pieces of cloth so that only their eyes were visible. Prema, the
thirty-three-year-old daughter-in-law of Laloo Bai, Badli Pershad's sister, is
certain that the attacking Muslims were not outsiders. They knew which
houses belonged to the Hindus and in fact would call out the owner's names.
Perhaps there were a few *goonda*s from outside but "the whole thing was
planned by our Mussulmans here." Prema's mother's brother was killed that
evening as was her sister-in-law Kalavati, who had run out in panic to get
back her four-year-old son who had slipped out of the house to investigate all
the excitement happening outside. Both the mother and son were chopped
down by sword blows before they could get back.

Kamla Bai, Badli Pershad's "cousin" (I have given up the effort to chart more precise relationships), who lives some houses away at the outskirts of Pardiwada, had a narrow escape. Her family had just eaten and was rearranging itself before the television set when the Muslims broke into the house. She ran out with her children, pleading with the men to spare their lives. One Hindu was killed in front of her but Kamla Bai was allowed to pass through unharmed. She hid in a neighbor's house. The ration shop and the vegetable shop next to her house were looted and set on fire. "One of my neighbors has four children who are not normal in the head. They killed her with a sword. Her head was literally in two pieces. One of the woman's relatives came out to help. They caught hold of her and asked her where her husband was. When she refused to tell, they cut off her arms and legs. She died. They broke into Ratnaram's house and killed him. His young daughter Krishnavati hid herself behind an almirah to save herself. They dragged her outside and killed her. They did not even spare old women."

The attack on Pardiwada, which left twenty-four people dead, ended around eleven at night when the police arrived. The Pardis were not sure whether it was the police or a new Muslim mob disguised in police uniforms. "Pelt them with stones," was the general consensus on the action to be taken. "The police would not be scared but the Muslims would run away." More men and women now started to come out, and the alleys of Pardiwada, eerily lighted by magenta-tinged smouldering fires, began to fill with the sounds of women's wailing and weeping as corpses of close relatives were discovered and mourned.

Rajesh, Badli Pershad's youngest son, was standing under a tree next to the Hanuman temple. Because of the curfew he had been playing cards with his friends, Nambre and Anto, the whole afternoon. He had just come out for a pee when he saw a group of Muslims running toward the temple with swords and tins of kerosene. Rajesh hid behind the tree, glad that he was shirtless and only wearing underwear and was thus less easy to spot in the dark. As he watched the Muslims throw lighted kerosene rags into the temple as they ran by to attack the house that he had just left, his only thought was that he would have died like his friends if he had not come out to ease his bladder.

For Rajesh, the Muslim attack on Pardiwada was not entirely unexpected. His Muslim friends, a couple of whom he had known since childhood, had been warning him of just such an eventuality. "We are very worried about you," they would say as they drank tea in a hotel. "You are staying there, your wife and children are there. You should leave." One day before the attack, the Muslim friend told Rajesh to go away for a few days. "Why are you after my life?" Rajesh replied in some irritation. "Whatever happens, will happen." Rajesh had reported the Muslim warnings to the community elders such as Dalyan Singh, the unofficial leader of the Shakkergunj Pardis. The police have made all arrangements for their safety, Rajesh was told, and Dalyan Singh pointed to the three policemen who had been assigned to Pardiwada and with whom he was playing cards.

Running back from the temple, Rajesh met a distraught Dalyan Singh on the way. "The Muslims have attacked from all sides," Dalyan Singh said. "I am trying to find the policemen." Many Pardi men had come out. They tried to stop the attackers from entering the heart of Pardiwada by directing a barrage of stones at whichever corner a Muslim breakthrough seemed imminent. "The men of our community are brave. We were unarmed and still did not run away from their swords and spears." Later at night, as soon as Muslims began withdrawing from the heart of Pardiwada, Rajesh rushed to his sister's house located at the outskirts. The door was closed from inside. Rajesh banged on the door, shouted and screamed, but there was no response. "'It is all over,' I thought. 'They are all dead. Everyone has been killed.' I went up to the police inspector. They were picking up a corpse. 'My sister and her family are dead,' I said. Then I saw them coming out of a neighbor's house who is a Muslim. 'We are here,' they said. The Muslim family had given them shelter, saved their lives."

When the police finally arrived, Rajesh was active in helping them identify the dead bodies and gather together the injured for further transport to the hospital. This was when he saw two men bring in a seriously wounded Dalyan Singh. He had been stabbed by Jafar, the men said. Jafar was the leader of the area's Muslims and a friend of Dalyan Singh. The two had worked closely in the past, liaising with the city administration in keeping the relations between the Hindus and Muslims peaceful whenever there was communal tension in the city. (Later, it was discovered that the assassin was not Jafar but another man accompanying him.) At this time someone informed Rajesh that his "uncle" had been killed and the body taken to Osmania hospital.

The police jeep took a long time in coming, and Rajesh offered to take some of the seriously wounded to the hospital in his auto-rickshaw. He could then also claim his uncle's body and bring it back. As he drove out of Pardiwada around one in the morning, his adrenaline-fueled courage evaporated. He had to pass through Muslim areas where groups of men roamed the dark streets in shadowy, menacing packs. "I will surely die tonight," Rajesh thought, or rather felt, in his terror. But as the headlight of the rickshaw bore down on the men, they scattered into the bylanes. They had taken it to be a police motorcycle, and Rajesh, soon cottoning on, heightened the impression by driving at full throttle while roaring threats and abuse like a real police inspector.

Osmania hospital, named after the last Nizam of Hyderabad, famed for both his wealth and his reluctance to spend it, was in total chaos. The harried doctors and staff were unable to cope with the stream of injured and dead descending on them from all over the city. Rajesh unloaded his grisly cargo on the floor of the admissions hall and hurried from one corridor to another searching for his uncle's body in the pile of corpses that were haphazardly stacked outside the wards. He did not find his uncle's body but became instrumental in saving the life of his niece, Pushpa. In one of the mounds of corpses, he saw a hand moving. As he tugged at the hand and pulled out the body, he saw it was Pushpa, who was still alive although unconscious with a severe head injury. A passing doctor was successfully importuned and cajoled into arranging for surgery, and Pushpa was saved.

Rajesh returned to Pardiwada to find the Pardis preparing to move out of their homes. "I was against such a step and vehemently protested. To evacuate is to run away. It was a question of our self-respect. It would always stand as a shameful black mark against our community. But rumors were going around. 'The Muslims have attacked here; they have attacked there.' People were getting very frightened. Then Jaggu and Suraj *pehlwans* appeared on the scene. 'We have brought trucks,' they said. 'The *basti* must be vacated immediately.' I was still unhappy but followed their instructions. My brother refused to leave. I was very angry. If everyone else was leaving what was the need for him to stay? I asked the police to help and they forced him to come with us. The trucks brought us to Gandhi Bhawan."

It was my strong impression that the mental processing of the events of the riot is different in women than in men. It is not only that women's memories of the riot tend to be circumscribed by what happened inside the house rather than outside and that their anxieties are centered around the danger to their children. With women, anger at Muslims is not the baffled rage I encountered among men. Women also find it easier to think and plan of moving away from their endangered homes, to leave it all behind, and get on with their lives. Men seem to find it more difficult to free themselves from the impact of recent violent events. They agonize over leaving Pardiwada and the implications such a move may have for their own self-respect and the community's sense of honor. The men brood over the events of the riot more.

They take the betrayal by their Muslim neighbors, who they believe helped the violent mob by identifying the Hindu houses (if they themselves were not a part of the mob), much more personally. Their sense of betrayal and perfidy is perhaps due to the fact that the men's relationships with their Muslim neighbors were more personal; some were even friends. Women's friendships were (and are) firmly within the Hindu community. With their Muslim women neighbors, the relationship was limited to the exchange of polite greetings. Women do not have to deal with the trauma of the neighbor suddenly being revealed as a deadly enemy to quite the same extent as do the men.

Although the riots have had an impact on the friendships between Hindus and Muslims, not all of these friendships, especially those that go back to childhood, have snapped completely because of the heightened conflict and violence between the communities. As an outsider, it is difficult to judge the depth of a friendship, and it may be, as studies across the borders of other antagonistic groups such as the Protestants and Catholics in Northern Ireland and the French and the English in Quebec have suggested, that such friendships are more illusory than real or are qualitatively different from one's friendships within one's own in-group.[5] This particular social-psychological theory predicts that such friendships can be maintained when individuals dwell upon their similarities rather than differences, avoid the divisive issue of religious affiliation, and shape their interactions so that the salience of their group membership—of one friend being a Hindu and the other a Muslim—is lowered. It appears from my observations, however, that the salience of one's religious group membership is not lowered by avoiding the issue, at least as far as deep friendship is concerned. Such an avoidance may smooth the course of fleeting Hindu-Muslim encounters that are temporary from the very outset. The maintenance of lasting Hindu-Muslim friendships, on the other hand, seems to demand (and never more so than after a riot) that the fact of friends belonging to antagonistic groups be squarely confronted before being negated as of little consequence. Rajesh, for instance, in the days following the riot, openly berated his Muslim friends for what their co-religionists had done to the Pardis. In more normal circumstances, friends seek to periodically dissipate the tension which arises from antagonistic religious affiliations by jokingly addressing each other deliberately in negative stereotypical terms such as "Come here, O you Hindu idolator," "O you Muslim violator of four wives," and so on. Such a joking relationship between friends strives to reduce the antagonism which has its source in the conflict of their religious groups by acknowledging the difference while at the same time downplaying it.

Many Pardi families, including that of Satish, Badli Pershad's eldest son, moved out of Pardiwada to safer areas after the riot. Some of them have come back for reasons of both economics and sentiments. It goes without saying that they missed the homes they had grown up in. They missed the nutrients for the soul provided by the closely knit community life they had left behind to settle among strangers. They have also been unable to sell their Pardiwada houses at reasonable prices. The only interested buyers are Muslims and, though Pardis would reluctantly reconcile themselves to the idea of selling an ancestral home to a Muslim, the prices quoted are very low—the Muslim buyers content to wait till the Pardis' fear of staying on becomes greater than the wish.

The disruption in their lives caused by the riot has been considerable. "When we all sit together to talk, certain things bring back the memories of that day, especially the sight of broken and empty houses," says Satish. "Even after so many months, we are very scared that it may happen again. Before we plan to celebrate any of our religious festivals on a community-wide basis, we think ten times about the likely consequences. The experience was terrifying! These days we feel a little more confident about staying here because a police picket has been permanently posted in Pardiwada. But you know the police are not very reliable. Where were they that evening? They arrived three hours after all the damage was done."

"Our business has been badly hurt. We also used to sell our stuff in Muslim areas and most of the time we went in alone. Now we are afraid to go there even in small groups. I keep on thinking about going back to the place we moved out to after the riot. But our business runs on various personal contacts which I developed over the years. To start such a business in a new locality where you neither know the people nor the place becomes difficult."

Badli Pershad, who is resisting the family pressure to move out of the home he built forty years ago, is naturally more sanguine about the future. "The next riot," he feels, "will not occur for another five to ten years because the last riot was very severe. Both the Hindus and Muslims suffered great losses and are fully involved in repairing and trying to restart their lives. Therefore they will neither have the time nor the inclination to trouble the other community." His children wish they could share his optimism in the force of human rationality.

For the women, the riot has had the consequence of drastically reducing their freedom of movement. "We used to come out at night and play in small groups," says Lalita. "Now we can't even sit out. The policemen shoo us back." The number of women who go out to buy fruits and vegetables from the Muslim wholesalers early in the morning has also declined. The women

do not let the children venture far from their homes and have become especially watchful of the movements of young girls. "What if Muslim boys harass one of our daughters and another riot starts?" asks Prema.

"The relations with the Muslims of our own *basti* have become more formal. The older ones still address us as "daughters" and claim they did not
recognize our attackers in the dark. We cannot believe them. Earlier, the
Muslims used to come when we invited them for any of our community cele-
brations and we went whenever they invited us for theirs. When Jafar's
daughter got married in Secunderabad, all of us went and helped in making
the wedding arrangements. Now there are no more invitations, either from
us or them." The riots have hastened the process of Pardi differentiation and
separation from their Muslim neighbors. They have given another push toward making the Pardis more Hindu, contributed to a sharper etching of
Hindu and Muslim identities.

Pardis and Muslims: The Past

The Pardis recollect their shared past with Muslims with a measure of ambivalence. They are aware that their ancestors served the Muslims as farm laborers during the latter's long rule and that they have been influenced in
many ways by their erstwhile masters. The influence is evident in the way
they dispose of their dead, in the many Urdu words which have crept into
their dialect, for example, *valid* for father, *mazhab* for religious faith; and, till
recently, in the not too seldom use of Muslim names for their children. Rajesh's wife Sakila, for instance, has a Muslim name, a fact of which he is
deeply ashamed and for which he blames his illiterate in-laws who had no
idea of the meaning and importance of names.

In the more recent past, Satish recalls playing football, cricket, and *ka-
baddi* as a child with Muslim boys of the neighborhood. He visited their
homes freely, as they did his, and was even friendly with their womenfolk
who did not observe any *purdah* from him. Accompanying his mother on her
rounds through the Muslim areas, he would carry the fruits and vegetables
right inside the houses and was never made to feel unwelcome. The understanding that existed between Hindus and Muslims of the previous generation, Satish says, has disappeared in the younger one which is a hot-blooded
lot. Whereas the older Muslims were tolerant, the young ones are aggressive
and are provoked to violence at the slightest of pretexts. Kamala Bai agrees
with the assessment, as do others, that it was easy to live together with the
older generation of Muslims but it is impossible to do so with the younger
who are all turning into *goondas*.

The easier coexistence in an earlier era does not mean that the Pardis ever *liked* the Muslims or did not feel resentful toward them. The Pardi version of the history of Hindu-Muslim conflict, articulated by Badli Pershad as an elder of the community, goes thus: "The clashes between Hindus and Muslims started long ago in the period of the Nizam and his *razakar*s (a marauding, unofficial army) who were very cruel to the Hindus. They used to harass our girls, rape them. This happened not only in villages but even in Hyderabad. We feared the Muslims. The rule was theirs, the king was theirs, the police were theirs, so it was hard for the Hindus to resist. We were also poor and no one supports the poor. Some *Marwadi*s may have been well off but the majority of Hindus was poor. The Muslims were close to the king. They were moneylenders, charging high rates of interest. Thus they were rich and the Hindus poor and though we lived together Muslims dominated the Hindus."

"We never used to mingle closely with them. Hindus feared Muslims a lot. They were very aggressive. They eat *bada gosht* (beef) which kept Hindus away from them. They used to prepare *kheer* (rice pudding) on their festival days but they cooked it in the same vessels. So we never ate even the vegetarian food they sent to our houses. People only drank tea together."

"Anyway when the oppression of the Hindus came to the notice of our leaders in Delhi, they wanted to do something about it as the British were not going to help. After independence all the leaders wanted Hyderabad to become a part of Hindustan but Gandhi was hesitant. So Nehru, Patel, and Rajendra Prasad felt Gandhi needed to be eliminated and had Gandhi killed. Then they could free the Hindus in Hyderabad from Muslim rule."

Badli Pershad's account of Hindu-Muslim relations in the pre-independence era, except for his version of the murder of the Mahatma which not every one agreed with, represents a popular consensus among the Pardis. As the historian David Lowenthal has observed, it is only academic versions of the past which are variable, contested, and subject to different interpretations; popular history, on the other hand, is a timeless mirror which gives accurate reflections of historical events, beyond questioning or doubt.[6]

Image of the Muslim

The two chief components of the contemporary Pardi image of Muslims are of the powerful and the animal-like Muslim. Shared alike by men and women, the image of the Muslim's power seems to be more pronounced in men. The image of the antagonist's powerfulness is certainly influenced by the Pardis' direct experience of being an embattled enclave in the walled city, surrounded by a numerically greater Muslim host. It also contains their historical memory of being serfs on the farms and estates of Muslim landlords. This image of Muslim power is in relation to the Hindus' lack of it. What is repeatedly stressed is the weak Hindus—weak because divided—rapidly losing ground against a united and purposeful nation. "Anything happens in a Muslim community, they all become one. We don't because of our different castes. Every caste has its own customs and lifestyle."

"We are not united. Each one is engrossed in himself. The rich try to exploit the poor. This does not happen with the Muslims. Though they have rich and poor at least at the time of prayer they are one and they all do it together at the same time. It develops unity among them. Our system is not like that. Each one goes to the temple to perform *puja* at his own time and in his own way and then leaves. There is no communication between us. If we could also show togetherness in our prayers, we can definitely become united and stronger than the Muslims."

"The problem with Hindus is that because of the number of castes they are not united. Reddys fight with Kapus, Pardis fight with Komtis, Yadavs fight with Naidus. If only they could unite like the Muslims! Muslims may be small in number but their do's and don'ts with regard to religion are very strict and they are forced to gather together at least for the Friday prayer. Their leaders use these occasions to forge religious unity. I don't speak Arabic but I am told many fiery speeches are made in mosques every Friday afternoon where they talk of driving the Hindus away from Hyderabad and making their own independent Pakistan here."

The Muslim is powerful because he is united, armed, favored by the state in India and supported, perhaps even armed, by a state outside, Pakistan. "Muslims have a constant supply of weapons coming from Pakistan or may be they are locally made. They are always well stocked. Even the poorest Muslim house will at least have a butcher's knife because they all eat meat. Hindus are not so well equipped. If the government continues to please the Muslims and makes rules against the Hindu majority, these riots will continue forever. If processions are to be banned, both Ganesh and Muharram processions should be banned. Why is only the Ganesh procession banned? It is like blessing and protecting only one community (*sir per hath rakhna*) and behaving like a stepmother toward the other."

"They want to dominate us. Just see how they are planning to make the old city into a Pakistan. In Hyderabad, the mosques always had four minarets. But now they have started building mosques with a single minaret, just like in Pakistan. Hindus are willing to adjust but Muslims are stubborn. Our government also supports them. On Shivratri day, the markets will be closed but during Muharram they will remain open day and night. Why?"

It was strikingly apparent that the Pardis' self-identification as Hindus occurs only when they talk of *the* Muslim; otherwise the conversation is of Pardis, Lodhas, Brahmins, Marwadis, and other castes. It seems a Hindu is born only when the Muslim enters. Hindus cannot think of themselves as such without a simultaneous awareness of the Muslim's presence. This is not so for the Muslim, who does not need the Hindu for self-awareness. The presence of the Hindu may increase the Muslim sense of identity but does not constitute it. Little wonder that Hindutva needs "the Muslim question" for the creation of a united Hindu community and the expansion of its political base and, in fact, will find it difficult to exist without it.

In the bitter complaints directed at the government, the *mai-baap* ("mother-father") of an earlier era, the psychoanalyst cannot help but hear echoes of a collective sibling rivalry, of the group-child's envy and anger at the favoring of an ambivalently regarded sibling by the parent. This does not mean that there is no factual basis to these accusations, but only that, like many other such perceptions in the emotionally charged era of Hindu-Muslim relations, they are neither merely real nor merely psychological.

The image of Muslim animality is composed of the perceived ferocity, rampant sexuality, and demand for instant gratification of the male, and a dirtiness which is less a matter of bodily cleanliness and more of an inner pollution as a consequence of the consumption of forbidden, tabooed foods. This image is an old one, also found in S. C. Dube's thirty-year-old anthropological account of a village outside Hyderabad: "The Muslims are good only in two things—they eat and copulate like beasts. Who else except a Muslim would even think of going to bed with his uncle's daughter, who is next only to his real sister?"[7]

Badli Pershad contrasts Hindu and Muslim sexual natures explicitly: "Muslims always had an eye for our women. This habit persists. Good thoughts and thoughts of God come into their minds only when they shout "Allah-u-Akbar!" Rest of the time they simply forget morality and go on sexually harassing our women. We never took a single woman of theirs. They used to take ours all the time. They were rich and the rulers and did what they wanted. We are moral (*dharmic*) and would never do such things even if rich. We treat all women as mothers and sisters. They force themselves on women; they are obsessed by women and sex. Look at all the children they produce, dozens, while we are content with two or three."

Most Pardi women concur with these views and in fact go further in linking the outbreak of violence to the "fact" of the Muslim's lewd sexual nature. Kamla Bai remarks, "Muslim boys are especially prone to harass our girls. Unlike Muslim girls, we leave our women free to walk around and go out of the *basti* if they wish to. Many times the girls are victims of very vulgar behavior on part of Muslim boys. If it was only kept to the verbal level, it is O.K. But the Muslims often use physical harassment. This makes our boys very angry. Sometimes these fights take on a communal coloring and in the past they have been main triggers for the outbreak of riots."

The Muslim animality also lies in a heedless pursuit of pleasure without regard for the concerns and obligations which make one human. "Their children are completely spoilt. They drink a lot. They are used to a carefree, uninhibited life. The young ones are only interested in enjoyment. Everything they do is for enjoyment. Hindus are cowards because they are worried about cultivating the land, education for their children, and so many other things. Muslims don't worry at all."

The Pardi image of the Muslim and the arguments employed for its construction are strikingly similar to the ones used by the *sangh parivar* to attract Hindus to its cultural and political fold. (Whether this convergence of perceptions is due to the *sangh parivar's* articulation of a widespread Hindu sentiment or whether it is the *parivar's* creation through a manipulation of Hindu symbols is a question I shall discuss later.) In any event, an understanding of this component of the Hindu image of the Muslim gives us an insight into how people belonging to a vastly superior demographic majority can still psychologically experience themselves as an endangered minority.

Viewing an antagonistic group as dirty, and thus subhuman, whereas one's own cleanliness is not only humanely civilized but next to godliness, is commonplace in ethnic conflict. "Dirty nigger" and "dirty Jew" are well-known epithets in the United States. The Chinese regard Tibetans as the great unwashed, perpetually stinking of yak butter, while Jewish children in Israel are brought up to regard Arabs as dirty. In the Rwandan radio broadcasts inciting the Hutus to massacre the Tutsis, the latter were consistently called rats and cockroaches, creatures associated with dirt and underground sewers, vermin needing to be exterminated. Serbs and the Bosnian Muslims, the Turks and Kurds, and so many other groups in conflict are outraged by each other's dirtiness. Again, there may be a grain of reality in some of the accusations because of a particular group's poverty, food habits, or the climatic conditions of its habitat. If the attribution of dirtiness falters against too great a discrepancy in factual reality, it will no longer be attributed to the opponent's body but to the soul. In some ways, the dirtiness is now even worse; it is a moral dirtiness which is more than skin deep, a blackness of the heart.

As a poverty-stricken community, the Pardis are not in a position to call Muslims physically dirty, an accusation which is more the province of the higher Hindu castes. One of the jokes I remember from my childhood is of the Muslim saying to the Hindu, "You Hindus are so dirty. You have a bath today and then (now speaking in an exaggeratedly slow drawl) you will baathe agaain tomoorrow. But we Muslims, we have a bath (in a rapid fire delivery) Friday-to-Friday, Friday-to-Friday!" "The Muslims who work are dirty, others are not. We work hard to survive. So where is the time for us to appear neat and clean?" asks Badli Pershad plaintively. Muslims, however, are dirty in a more fundamental way; they eat beef.

Beef eating is the most heinous of sins among the Pardis (as it is among most Hindus), a more serious violation of the moral code than marriage to a Muslim or conversion to Islam. "*Bada gosht* [beef] is their favorite dish. If any of us even touches it he must have a bath. All Muslims eat *bada gosht*. That is why we keep ourselves away from them. We do not even drink water in their homes," says Lalita. "We pray to the cow because it is our [mother-goddess] Lakshmi. Hindus revere even cow dung, use it for cooking, decorating the house, and for many other things. *They* eat the cow!" says Badli Pershad, his disgust palpable. The Muslim eating and the Hindu abomination of beef creates an effective barrier between the two; it is difficult to be close to someone with whom one cannot share a meal and whose eating habits one finds disgusting.

Gandhi, Psychoanalysts, and Cows

The Muslim eating of beef and thus the killing of cows has perhaps historically been the most important source of Hindu bitterness toward the Muslim. In Tipu Sultan's dominions, Abbé Dubois tells us, though Hindus witness the slaughter of cows without uttering loud complaint, they are far from insensible to the insult, contenting themselves with complaining in secret and storing up in their hearts all the indignation they feel about this sacrilege.[8] Pious Lingayats come up to the Abbé with tears in their eyes, imploring him to use his influence as a priest with the local Europeans to stop them from eating beef. Hindus who had been forcibly converted to Islam could not reconvert even if they had eaten beef only under duress. From the nineteenth century onward, Hindu revivalism has been closely associated with movements against cow slaughter.

The ferocity of Hindu emotions, chiefly disgust at the eating of beef and rage at the slaughter of cows, would automatically draw attention from psychoanalysts for whom the presence of strong emotions in a relationship implies the operation of unconscious factors. In 1924, the British army psychiatrist Owen Berkeley-Hill wrote a paper on the theme of Hindu-Muslim conflict, a paper which served as a topic for discussion at the meeting of the Indian Psychoanalytic Society in Calcutta to which Gandhi was also invited.[9] In this essay, Berkeley-Hill identifies two main hurdles in the way of Hindu-Muslim unity. The first is the Hindu's "motherland complex" wherein the ancient cults of mother-goddesses have become associated with the ideas of women, virgin, mother, and motherland—Bharat Mata—which the Muslims violated through their conquest of India. (The colonel does not explain why there is no such Hindu bitterness against the British for a similar "violation".) The second obstacle is the Muslim slaughter of cows which, Berkeley-Hill tries to establish, were once a totem animal for the Hindus (as it still continues to be for certain tribes in central and south India) and thus an object of the ambivalent feelings of cherishing and destruction which are directed against all totems. Following Freud's ideas in *Totem and Taboo*, Berkeley-Hill argues that one who violates a taboo, becomes a taboo and thus an object of detestation—more especially in the case of the Muslim because the violation of the taboo, the cow slaughter, often took place to ratify Muslim victories or show contempt for Hindu susceptibilities. The violators of a taboo are contagious and must be avoided for they arouse both envy (why should they be allowed to do what is prohibited to others?) and the forbidden desire to emulate the act. Christians and Jews, who also kill cows, do not provoke the same hostility because they do not kill cows ceremonially as do the Muslims or with a clear intention of offering insult to the Hindu. Berkeley-Hill's solution, "in line with the fundamental ideas which underlie totemism," is that "any reconciliation between Hindus and Muslims would demand as a cardinal feature some form of ceremonial in which cows would be killed and eaten, either actually or symbolically, by Hindus and Muslims in concave. It is quite conceivable that this killing and eating of cows could be so arranged as to fulfil every demand from a psychological standpoint without involving the death of a single animal, although in view of the great issues at stake, namely the formation of a real and permanent pact between Hindus and Muslims, the actual sacrifice of every cow in India would hardly be too big a price to pay."[10] We do not know what Mahatma Gandhi, a strict vegetarian who shared the Vaishnava veneration of the cow, thought of this suggestion.

Even at a distance of seventy years, Berkeley-Hill's paper remains intriguing, although Freud's ideas on totemism has fallen into oblivion. I am surprised that, given the wealth of evidence and the ubiquity of Hindu worship and references to the cow as mother, Berkeley-Hill did not simply include the cow in the Hindu's "motherland complex" but sought a separate explanation in terms of totem and taboo. Any unconscious Hindu ambivalence toward the eating of beef, which he might have observed underlying a conscious abhorrence, could then be traced back to the infant's ambivalence toward the maternal body and the breast it cherishes and would keep alive, but also tears at and would destroy. But, of course, Melanie Klein had not yet formulated her theories of infant love and violence, guilt and reparation, and Berkeley-Hill, who was in charge of the Ranchi psychiatric hospital, used the theories he had available to explain his observations, though they now seem forced.

Muslim "animality," as expressed in dirtiness and the male's perceived aggressivity and sexual licentiousness, are of course a part of human "instinctuality" which a civilized, moral self must renounce. The animality not only belongs to an individual past—to infancy and early childhood—which needs to be transcended by the institution of a constantly endangered adult moral self, but also to the Pardis' collective past which is still a part of their folk memory. Visions from the past of themselves as aggressive hunters, killing and eating whatever animals are available (perhaps also the cow?), drink- ing and lazing around in the village without a thought for the future, are too dangerous to the cultural identity the Pardis are now trying to construct for themselves and others. The Muslim must be kept at a distance because that animality is too near, even within, the Pardi self.

Here, the Pardis are not different from Hindus in many other parts of India. Some years ago, while studying the phenomenon of possession by spirits in rural north India, I was struck by the fact that in a very large number of cases, fifteen out of twenty-eight, the malignant spirit possessing Hindu men and women turned out to be a Muslim.[11] When, during the healing ritual, the patient went into a trance and the spirit started expressing its wishes, these wishes—for forbidden sexuality and prohibited foods—invariably turned out to be those which would have been horrifying to the patient's conscious self. Possession by a Muslim spirit, then, seemed to reflect afflicted persons' desperate efforts to convince themselves and others that their imagined transgressions and sins of the heart belonged to the Muslim destroyer of taboos and were farthest away from their "good" Hindu selves. In that Muslim spirits were universally considered to be the strongest, vilest, the most malignant and the most stubborn of the evil spirits, the Muslim seemed to symbolize *the* alien in the more unconscious parts of the Hindu mind.

The reasons why Muslims are *the* hated out-group for the Hindus (and vice versa)—rather than the Sikhs, Parsis, or Christians in India, or the "modern West" outside the country—have not only to do with the sheer size of the Muslim minority which can thus withstand the absorptive and disintegrative pressure of the Hindu majority. They lie also in certain social-psychological axioms on scapegoating and displacement of aggression which have been systematically listed by Robert LeVine and Donald Campbell and that seem to fit the case of Hindus and Muslims to a tee:[12]

—An out-group is a target for hostility if it is a source of frustration in its own right, as Hindus have perceived Muslims to be over centuries.

—An out-group with the most disparaging images of the in-group, as Muslims have of the Hindus, and whose ethnocentrism the in-group is in a position to "overhear," will be the most hated.

—The out-group which is seen as the most ethnocentric, in terms of unwarranted self-esteem—the Hindu view of Muslims—will be the most hated.

—The most hated out-group will be the one which is used most as a bad example in child training. In other words, groups indoctrinate their young as to against which targets to vent their hostility.

The existence of the image of the Muslim I have described above, with all its unconscious reverberations, does not mean that a coexistence of the communities, at least in the public arena, is impossible. The hope for such a coexistence comes from many directions. First, there are many instances of Muslims and Hindus protecting each other during a riot. Badli Pershad's own daughter and her family escaped certain death by taking shelter with their Muslim neighbor who, at some risk to his safety, did not betray their presence to the marauding mob. Second, often enough there are acknowledgments of their common ancestry and the recognition that the two communities have to share the same physical space. "We love our *jaat*," says Badli Pershad, using *jaat* more in the sense of a way of life than a physical group. "They love theirs. We should live together because we have the same blood."

The Pardis would be willing to go even further in seeking this coexistence by accepting intermarriage with the Muslims, but they believe that here they come up against a Muslim inflexibility about matters of faith, even bigotry. Badli Pershad elaborates: "Actually I feel marriage between Hindus and Muslims would be one method of building communal harmony. But in my opinion Hindus should never make the mistake of marrying Muslims because the Hindu is not allowed to retain his or her religion at any cost. So many of our women have got married to Muslims, either because they were in love or by force because these women were working as servants in Muslim households. None of them has been allowed to remain a Hindu or practice Hindu religion. All of them have been converted whereas the same cannot be said of the Hindus. They are more tolerant and allow the other person to follow whatever religion he or she wants."

"We used to have a young Muslim girl coming to our house a few years ago. She was my daughter's friend. She used to spend long hours in our house. Although her family did not like her visiting us she continued to do so. She would discuss many things about Islam and the Hindu *dharma* with me, and one day she stated that if she marries at all she will marry a Hindu only and not a Muslim, because Hindu religion is more humanitarian and tolerant and not as violent as Islam. She married one of our men and to this day she practices both Islam and Hinduism. She not only observes *rozas* (a month of ritual fasting), Muharram, celebrates Bakr-Id but also installs Ganesha idols in her house, celebrates Diwali and Dusshera and participates in Holi festival along with all of us. Her children have both Hindu and Muslim names. They were living happily as a family when the mother of the girl started telling her Hindu son-in-law that he should convert to Islam. When the boy did not agree, they started threatening him. This is the problem with Muslims. They are so particular about their religion. Even the suggestion of conversion or practicing the Hindu religion can spark off another riot."

"Unfortunately, it is more frequent for Hindu girls to marry Muslim boys. This is partly because Hindu girls are not kept in *purdah* like the Muslim girls and therefore come into contact with Muslim boys. We do not get even a chance to see a Muslim girl once she attains puberty. And love is such a thing that once bitten by it, our girls seem to forget everything about their community or religion or family. They are willing to do whatever their husbands want. They get converted, their children carry Muslim names, go to *madarsa*s, learn the Qur'an but nothing about any other religion. The tragedy is that some of the women who married Muslims twenty-five, thirty years ago are now old and deserted by their husbands. This woman sitting here was married to a Muslim and had four children. The husband has left her and refuses to pay a minimum maintenance. She used to earn something when she was healthier and younger. Now she is ill and goes from house to house begging for her daily food. She has no home, sleeps wherever she can, and no one treats her well. Our people don't accept her because they think it was wrong for her to marry a Muslim. That is why I think it is important to hold on to the religion of our ancestors under all circumstances. Otherwise, you not only lose the respect of your community but the other community also looks down upon you."

It is difficult to say to what extent the Pardi attitudes toward Muslims are shared by other Hindus in Hyderabad or are generalizable to Hindus in the rest of the country. On the one hand, as victims of recent riots one may expect the Pardis to be especially bitter. On the other, they are a lower, "scheduled" caste, and we know from other studies that higher-caste Hindus evaluate Muslims much more unfavorably than the lower castes.[13]

Children's Tales

To get some impressions of the way children view and experience Hindu-Muslim conflict, I adapted the "toy construction" method used by Erik Erikson in his research on the identity development of Californian boys and girls in the 1940s.[14] Using toys such as a family, some uniformed figures, wild and domestic animals, furniture, automobiles, and wooden blocks, Erikson asked the ten- to twelve-year-olds to imagine that the table was a movie studio; the toys, actors and props; and they themselves, movie directors. They were to arrange on the table an exciting scene from an imaginary movie. My own toys consisted of two families of dolls, each with a set of grandparents, parents, and four young children divided equally between the sexes. The dolls were identifiable as Hindu or Muslim from their dress or other markers of religious group identity: long black *burqas* for Muslim women, *sarees* and *bindis* for the Hindus; pyjamas, *sherwanis*, round caps and beards for Muslim men, *dhotis*, *kurtas*, and turbans for the Hindus. In addition to the Hindu and Muslim dolls, there were dolls of a man in a uniform with a gun slung over one shoulder, of two sinister-looking, masked men in undershirts and jeans, and of a few domestic animals such as a cow, a sheep, and a dog. The dolls were placed on a stool next to a large wooden table which was used as the stage. The instructions to the child were to imagine himself or herself as a film director—the children are avid fans of popular Hindi cinema—and to construct an exciting scene for the shooting of a film, using as many or a few dolls as desired. The child was then asked to identify the dolls and after the mise-en-scène was over, the young director was asked to describe what was happening in the scene and why. The test, conducted in the one-room school next to the temple, aroused great excitement, and it was not easy to keep hordes of enthusiastic volunteers of all ages from pushing and shoving their way into the room to get into the action, or to stop them from shouting comments through the window which had to be kept open because of the heat. Hyderabad not being San Francisco and Pardiwada not being Berkeley, it was impossible to conduct the proceedings as a "standardized test under controlled conditions," and therefore I will dispense with reporting my results in the proper scientific format in favor of more informal observations.

The sample consisted of fifteen boys and fifteen girls, ranging in age from ten to fifteen, with a median age of thirteen for both boys and girls. The lower age limit of ten was determined by trial and error since we found that the task was not comprehensible to a child below that age—not that I have much confidence in the reported ages.

Both boys (twelve out of fifteen) and girls (eleven out of fifteen) made an immediate identification of the dolls as Hindu or Muslim. The three boys and two of the four girls who first identified the dolls in term of age or gender and had to be prodded to make the religious identification, were younger children of eleven or less, confirming the findings of other studies that awareness of one's own religious affiliation and the prejudice against religious outgroups increases with age.[15] Boys typically used a large part or the whole of the stage and were generally more confident in the construction of the exciting scene than girls, who tended to start from a corner of the table and then gingerly spread out to use a bigger part of the stage, though rarely as much as the boys. The different approaches by boys and girls to the task and the use of stage space is intriguing, and some speculations accounting for gender difference are certainly in order. One could hypothesize that the different use of a public, even an exhibitionistic space, simply reflects the relative positions of boys and girls in a Pardi family where, in spite of the women's relative social freedom and economic importance, the boy is still at the center of the stage while the girl hugs the corner. I could also speculate that the imaginative activity required by the task has an object of identification (film director) and a content (exciting theater) that are closer to a boy's than a girl's imagination in this particular social group. Another line of argument, complementary to the other two, would hold that these particular uses of space are expressions of a broader male-female difference in patriarchal societies. The work of Luce Irigaray on women's language, especially with regard to syntax, suggests that women do not put themselves in the center of space they open by their utterance.[16] Their subject is hesitant, open to interaction, asking questions rather than asserting. The male subject, on the other hand, is easily dominant, at the center of the stage, operating in terms of an expanded "we."

In the construction of the exciting scene, boys generally arranged Muslim and Hindu dolls in separate groups engaged in some kind of violent confrontation. The fighting between Hindus and Muslims (presented by ten of the fifteen boys) is relatively absent in girls' constructions, where only three of the fifteen girls staged such scenes of conflict. Girls use dolls to construct peaceful scenes from family life, even when they identify the families as Hindu and Muslim. Their stories emphasize relationships between the characters, couples watching animals, and, especially, parents watching children play. Hindu and Muslim dolls are often mixed together. The excitement occurs at the periphery of the scene: a fight between the policeman and a robber, animals being chased by a *goonda*, a man running away from a soldier. A typical scene constructed by a fifteen-year-old boy has a Hindu wedding taking place at the center of the stage, the Hindus watching the dancers. They are surrounded by four Muslims, one in each corner, two of whom are identified as *goonda*s. The Hindu dolls move closer together for protection, wondering how to save themselves. The police dolls run away. Rather than be killed by the Muslims, the Hindus commit suicide.

A scene by a girl, a thirteen-year-old in this case, has Hindu and Muslim families in semicircles next to each other, along with the animals who are an integral part of the tableau. The Hindu family is having coffee and bread. The Muslim family is saying its prayers. Small children are playing. The excitement of the scene is in a corner where a *goonda* is being chased by the policeman after a robbery.

The Muslim children, nine boys and nine girls from Karwan, the other location of this study, ranged in age from ten to fifteen with a median age of thirteen years. They did not differ from the Hindu children as far as immediate identification of the dolls as Hindu or Muslim was concerned, the younger children having more difficulty than older ones in identifying the dolls according to their religious rather than gender affiliation or according to age. Like the Hindus, the Muslim girls were shyer than the boys in their approach to the task and used less of the stage space for their constructions. As with the Hindus, less than half the Muslim children constructed scenes of violent confrontation between the communities although the distribution of the scenes between girls and boys was different from the Hindu sample. Whereas somewhat more Muslim than Hindu girls (40 percent versus 20 percent) constructed scenes of conflict, Muslim boys showed significantly less interest than Hindu boys in communal violence (20 percent versus 70 percent). It is not that violence as the source of excitement was absent from the scenes of Muslim boys. The violence in their story lines was, so to say, more traditional—between policemen and robbers or the hero and the villain, the *goonda*. The fantasy of Muslim boys is thus more of the Hindi film variety wherein a hero skilled in one of the martial arts such as karate rescues a damsel in distress from the unwelcome attentions of the *goonda*. Though the *pehlwan* as a hero occurs in one of the stories, I am afraid that in children's fantasy traditional wrestling is being consigned to oblivion and is being replaced with the more modern import of karate. The fantasy of Muslim boys has not yet been overlaid by the real-life events of the riots to the same extent as in the case of the Pardi boys. I can only account for this difference by the children's actual experience of the riots. The experience of the Muslim boys from Karwan has never been as traumatic as that of the Pardi boys who have seen their homes burned and their close relatives killed by an attacking Muslim mob.

On the other hand, the dolls of the army soldier and the policeman play a greater role in the constructions of the Muslim children, either as hostile figures ("The soldier has been helping the Hindus and not Muslims") or a benign presence ("The army is telling the Hindus and Muslims not to fight"). This reflects the actual experience of the children in Karwan where police and paramilitary forces have often been employed to patrol the area during a riot or to conduct house-to-house searches for hidden arms. Reflecting their experiences of the riots, the Muslim children are also much less informed than the Hindu boys about the "causes" of Hindu-Muslim confrontation; the Hindu boys often ascribe the outbreak of communal violence to the Muslims' throwing of *bada gosht* into a temple.

Two examples will give a flavor of the children's stories:

A twelve-year-old boy, studying in the sixth class, immediately identifies the dolls as Hindu or Muslim. He uses all the toys and the full stage for the construction of his scene where the Hindus and Muslims are not in any kind of confrontational posture, although the Hindu dolls are clustered together on one side. He explains the scene thus: "The animals are saying to each other, 'Don't fight among yourselves. It gives other animals a chance to come in your area.' The army man is telling the Hindus that they should think of their country and not trouble the Muslims. The Muslims are saying their Id prayers. The older Muslim woman is telling other women (including the Hindu women) that a good woman always wears a veil (*burqa*) and they should all do so."

A thirteen-year-old girl, who studied till the third class and is now a school dropout, also identifies the dolls immediately and uses all the toys for the construction of her scene which takes up half the stage. She explains: "Hindus and Muslims are fighting. [She doesn't know why.] First, the children fight then the adults. The soldier is saying don't fight. The Hindus brought in a *goonda* to attack the Muslims. The Muslims brought in a karate expert who put the *goonda* to flight."

To summarize: In spite of the endemic Hindu-Muslim violence in the old city of Hyderabad, less than half the children constructed scenes of this violence in their play constructions. This number may be seen as too large or too small, depending on one's own inclination to view the glass of Hindu-Muslim relations as half empty or half full. In any event, a communal orientation is present in a significant number of children between the ages of ten and fifteen. This orientation, however, varies with age—older children being more communal in their imagination than younger ones—and with gender—girls, especially Hindu girls, prefer to construct scenes from family life rather than from communal conflict. Scenes of Hindu-Muslim violence, when they are created, seem to express the child's unresolved anxiety in relation to his or her personal experience of the riot—for instance, the fear of imminent death at the hands of an attacking Muslim mob in the case of the Pardi boys. Unsurprisingly, the direct, personal experience of a riot as a victim is the strongest impetus to the development of religious hatred and communal imagination in a child.

In conclusion, let me note that both Hindus and Muslims do not perceive their conflict in terms of local issues but as one involving the "essential" nature of a Hindu or Muslim which does not change over history. Such an essentialization, found in many other ethnic conflicts (such as the one between Jews and Blacks in New York, where local issues get linked to the perceived global nature of the "Jew" or the "Negro"), will always make a conflict more intractable.

FIVE

Victims and Others II: The Muslims

K arwan or, to give it back its original name, Karwane-Sahu ("caravan of merchants") was planned as a camp for traders when Hyderabad was being built. In the seventeenth and eighteenth centuries, it was a thriving commercial area with many inns, mosques, and storehouses for the convenience of merchants from all over India and abroad who camped here on their trading visits to Hyderabad. During the Qutub Shahi period most of the Gujarati and Marwadi merchants lived here. Today, Karwan is one of the most economically backward sections of the city.

Dotted with mosques, graveyards, and *dargahs*, the Muslim character of Karwan is unmistakable. The shops in the cobbled streets sell cheap goods requiring low financial investment: spices, bangles, metal scrap, a small assortment of Indian sweets and savories. There are the inevitable general stores which stock most of the items needed by a poor neighborhood, from pencils for children to hair oil, packets of inferior brands of tea, and cheap detergents for the household. Some of the streets have Hindu women vegetable sellers squatting at the edges along with their young daughters. With their oiled black hair rolled into buns and their mouths strained a brick red from chewing tobacco or betel nut, the women sit behind heaps of fresh vegetables which are kept moistly glistening by frequent sprinklings of water. Cars—except for old, beat-up Ambassadors—are rare, yet the streets still manage to be clogged with pedestrians, auto- and cycle-rickshaws, bicycles, and the rattling buses of Hyderabad's road transport system.

Occasionally employed in road construction, as grave diggers, or as kitchen helpers in large weddings, many men have only intermittent work. Others are vegetable sellers and rickshaw drivers while a few lucky ones work in the factories of the new city or at low-paid jobs in government offices. The few signs of affluence are manifested in newly built houses—"Gulf   119 money," one is invariably told—and in restaurants on street corners owned by Muslims in city politics or in "land business" (Majid Khan's restaurant is on one of these street corners). These eateries and the pan shops which stay open late into the night are places where the men like to congregate to talk and catch up with news and friends.

Rashid's family lives in one of the lanes of Kulsumpura which forms the southern part of Karwan. Rashid's house in on a lane at the edge of the Muslim quarter, the street at the back of the house separating it from the Hindu majority area. Each lane in Kulsumpura has twenty-five to thirty-five houses on either side, with a meandering ribbon of open space of varying width between them which at its narrowest permits only one bicycle to pass through at a time. The houses are generally one room tenements with thatched or tiled roofs. They are kept scrupulously clean. The mud floor, given a fresh mud coating at least once a month, is covered with faded cotton durries or, among the poorest, with pieces of jute sacking stitched together. The access to the inside of the houses is guarded by flimsy wooden doors, barely supported at the hinges. Worn-out curtains hang at the entrance, their varying heights often permitting glimpses of the dark shapes of women and children moving inside the room. Although nominally in *purdah*, there are times during the day, especially at mid-morning, when one sees groups of women sitting in the doorways, chatting, chopping betel nuts into small pieces or shaving them into mottled brown slivers while they keep a watchful eye on the children playing outside. Twice a day, in early morning and late afternoon, at the public water tap provided by the municipal corporation, the women come to fetch buckets of water for daily use. Unlike women in Hindu areas, the Muslim women in Kulsumpura are not seen bathing their children or washing clothes at the tap, the community norms dictating that they be out in the open for as little time as possible. Yet even as they wait their turns with the bucket, the water tap becomes the women's counterpart of the restaurant or the pan-stall of men—a meeting place to exchange views, information, and gossip, mostly of a familial kind rather than the more political exchanges favored by the men.

Rashid's Family

With eight years of schooling, the fifty-five-year-old Rashid is the most educated person in his family. Nominally headed by his mother who is in her eighties, the family consists of a sixty-five-year-old brother, a forty-eight-year-old younger brother, a widowed sister in her late sixties, and another thirty-eight-year-old sister, all of whom live with their own families in separate households next to each other. With five to six children in each household, the extended family consists of about thirty persons.

Rashid's occupation is that of an occasional vegetable seller. Both his brothers are unemployed. The elder brother earns a little money by helping out as a cook at weddings. The younger brother runs errands for one of the "big men" of Kulsumpura who owns a restaurant and is active in local politics. The brother-in-law drives a cycle-rickshaw and one of his nephews sells vegetables. Two others, in their early twenties, are unemployed. Unlike the Pardi women, the Muslim women only work from their homes. Rashid's younger sister sews blouses and petticoats for the neighbors, but most other women chop betel nuts to earn three to four rupees a day, a welcome addition to the family's perpetually tight budget. Except for Rashid's younger brother and a nephew, both of whom have had three years of school, all other adults in the family are illiterate.

This situation is changing in the younger generation, at least as far as boys are concerned. The girls are still not sent to school, much to the regret of the fourteen-year-old Shakira, Rashid's niece. Even Shakira, however, gets some kind of education at one of the neighborhood institutions for young girls, opened all over the city with state support. Here, Shakira learns sewing, embroidery, Urdu, basic English, and is also taught some fundamentals of her faith. After she returns home in the afternoon, Shakira's day passes in cleaning the cooking utensils, preparing the evening meal, and looking after her younger brother. Shakira's only other outing is going to the *dargah* with other women every Thursday. Like a grown-up woman, Shakira wears the veil when she goes out, a garment that needs some practice to get used to. She is an avid fan of Hindi movies but must satisfy her desire for films through television since going to the cinema with friends is strictly forbidden by the family. The other women, including Shakira's mother, chafe at the restrictions to their freedom yet accept their necessity. The women's *izzat*—their honor, so inextricably intertwined with the honor of the family and the community— is much less safe out on the street after the riots. Yet even at the best of times, women had freedom of movement only after marriage and that too before the arrival of children. Although Rashid's younger sister-in-law grew up in Hyderabad, she had never seen the city's architectural glories such as the Char Minar or its main bazaars till she was married. Now, of course, the riots have further curtailed women's freedom. Some years ago at the public water tap, Shakira's mother inadvertently broke the pitcher of a Hindu woman. She was beaten by her husband for this mishap which could have raised the tensions between Hindus and Muslims to a dangerous level. After that she was forbidden to fetch the water from the tap, the errand being delegated to another woman in the family.

Early marriages, repeated pregnancies, and unremitting economic hardship have not broken the women's spirit nor exhausted their zest for life which, I suspect, is continuously renewed by a vibrant community life, especially with other women of the family. There are the many weddings and festive occasions such as the circumcision of a boy or the piercing of the nose and ears of a girl. There are the religious festivals, especially Id, which are celebrated without regard for expense. If there is no money, it will be borrowed to buy new clothes and the goat for the festive meal. This is an extravagance needed by the poor to transcend limits imposed by the outer reality of their lives and thus regain the vitally important feeling of agency and freedom, something which those influenced solely by notions of economic rationality deplore but rarely understand. The women often offer their *namaz* together and after finishing the household chores sometimes chat and sing together till late into the night.

Another source of the women's strength lies in their religious faith. They freely admit their ignorance of Islamic tenets and traditions. None of them knows what is exactly contained in the Qur'an, although a few younger ones have been taught to recite from it in Arabic without understanding the import of the words they are repeating. Their faith consists of following a simple moral code which makes them feel pious: cleanliness of body and purity of mind, respect for the aged, remembering Allah often, saying your *namaz* when the call comes from the mosque, keeping the ritual fast of the *rozas*. From a modern individualist viewpoint which stresses the woman's rights as a person rather than the duties and obligations prescribed by faith, her religious belief may contribute to the woman's feelings of integration with the community and to a personal well-being which comes from an approving conscience, and yet keep the woman imprisoned in a "false consciousness." The faith makes women accept their inferior status in relation to men who are deemed to be physically, mentally, and spiritually superior. It makes them only tenants rather than owners of their minds and bodies which have a more transpersonal than individual cast. For instance, when asked whether after giving birth to six children why she had not got her tubes tied, Rashid's younger sister replies: "If you undergo such an operation your *namaz* is no longer legitimate. It is said in the Qur'an that Allah does not forgive you for this sin even on Judgment Day. On that day you will find your face having turned black in color. Allah does not accept your *namaz*, even the one on Id, if you have prevented the birth of a child. My sister-in-law who had her tubes tied has stopped offering her *namaz* and is becoming unhappier by the day. All I can do is pray to Allah that He stop giving me children and bless someone else."

Days and Nights of the Riot

To continue in the woman's voice, here of Kubra Begum, Rashid's wife: "It was Friday. I was buying vegetables around ten in the morning when the children came running and told me that a fight had started between Hindus and Muslims. Why? I asked. They said a Muslim woman was buying vegetables when the *bhoi* (a Hindu vegetable seller) pulled at her arm and her veil and shouted at her. Perhaps she had not paid the right amount. Twenty to twenty-five of their men and a similar number from our side rushed to the site of the quarrel. When I saw that the men were armed with sticks and swords I hurried home and told everyone to get ready for trouble. Things were already bad with that quarrel about Babri masjid (mosque) where many people died and which made Hindus so angry. Then there was the attack on Majid *bhai* (brother). One knows a riot is about to start when one sees the Hindus sending away their women and their belongings."

"We did not even have the *lathis* in their house. The women started collecting stones and stacking them in piles near the men who took up positions at the two ends of our alley. First, the Hindus started throwing stones from their side of the road. The men retaliated from our side. The police arrived. They tried to disperse the Hindus but could do so only after firing tear gas shells. At night there was again a barrage of stones from the Hindu side. We did not go out. Then there were shouts of "Allah-u-Akbar" and screams of "Help! Help!" None of the men went out because we all know this trick. A truckload of young Hindus dressed all in black comes to a Muslim area, gives the Muslim rallying cry and there are screams for help. Anyone who ventures out to investigate is killed and the truck drives off into the darkness of the night."

"Everything was quiet the next morning. The men went about their work. On Sunday night there was again heavy stone throwing by the Hindus. Two of my nephews received serious head injuries. I started crying, "Allah, how long must the Muslims bear this oppression!" The curfew was in force but when it was relaxed for a couple of hours more people were killed. An old woman and her grandson went out to buy vegetables. The *bhois* stabbed the boy. His name was Amjad. A rickshaw driver was killed in front of my eyes. They pulled him out of the rickshaw and knifed him repeatedly. The dust on which his body lay turned into mud from his blood."

"The curfew is the worst. If a man earns twenty-five rupees a day and has to feed six children, then what will the children eat if he cannot work for four days? And a curfew can go on for weeks! Last time I had enough flour for four days and we ate *rotis* with chillies. After that, boiled rice was all we could get for days. In the beginning people try to share but later it is every family for itself—a man is no longer a brother, nor a woman a sister."

For women who have lost a family member in the riot, their faith and its tradition of mourning give both succor and structure to their grief. The journalist Anees Jung gives us a sensitive description of one such woman, Mehdi Begum, whose daughter was sick for ten days while the curfew was on. Mehdi Begum could not get medicines or milk for the daughter because the husband was unable to go to work. She blames no one for her daughter's death and attributes it to the will of Allah. "As my child was dying I was chanting the elegy my grandfather wrote about the death of the young daughter of Imam Husain, Sakeena, who after her father's death was dragged to a prison and left alone to languish and die. My daughter's death pales in comparison." "Azadari, mourning in the memory martyred imams," Jung comments, "for generations has provided women like Mehdi Begum a release and lent their grief a focus."[1] Indeed, I generally have found that women, both Hindu and Muslim, with their better-established traditions and rituals of mourning, are less bitter and more reconciled to the violent deaths of their loved ones; those who weep and mourn their losses are no longer filled with warlike anger.

The men's accounts differ from the women's in that the riot is placed in a more historical perspective and conveys less immediacy. Although so far the worst in terms of the number of lost lives and damage to property, this riot is described as part of a series—sixteen in the last twenty years. When the city's wholesale vegetable market was located here, Karwan was especially riot-prone as Muslims and Hindus jostled for a larger share of the business. Many Hyderabad riots began here before spreading to other parts of the city. The market has since been shifted and Karwan no longer takes the lead in communal rioting but is content to go along with the general ebb and flow of violence in the rest of the city.

The men's reports emphasize tales of masculine heroics and martial prowess in contrast to the women's anxiety about the safety of their families. With men, we hear much talk about how a small group of Muslims triumphed over a vastly superior force of attacking Hindus. Their riot stories resonate with echoes of Badr, the first battle of Islamic history, where heavily outnumbered Muslims trusting Allah and armed only with their faith succeeded against a vastly superior foe.

Another characteristic of the men's narratives is the space given to the encounters with the police. After the start of a riot, the police may descend on Kulsumpura at any time of day or night in search for hidden weapons or to recover goods reported to have been looted from their homes by the Hindus. Men of all ages, from fifteen to fifty, are routinely taken away for questioning so that many of them do not sleep at home at night while the curfew is on. When the police arrive, there are tense confrontations, say between a young Hindu policeman intent on entering and searching a house and a Muslim youth defending what he believes is the honor of his family. Indeed, in many towns and cities of north India, such as Meerut, the confrontation between the police and the Muslims have led to violent explosions.

Psychologically, what occurs between Hindu policemen and young Muslims is marked by the same dynamics as the encounter between white cops and black kids in the United States described by the psychoanalyst Rollo May.[2] As they come face to face, the young policeman and the Muslim youth are very much alike in their pride and their fear, in their need to prove themselves and their demand for respect. For the Hindu policeman, who additionally incorporates the state's authority and power, which he identifies with his own masculinity and self-esteem, it is essential he insist that the Muslim respect this authority. Laying hands on the other man's body, violating its intactness by rough handling without retaliation or protest, is one way of having the power over the other person acknowledged. Another way is to enter his home without invitation or permission. The Muslim youth, on the other hand, equally impelled to protect his own masculinity and honor, must resist any violation of both his body and home. It becomes imperative that, even when he must bow to the policeman's superior might and tolerate the incursion into his most private space, he remain defiant. His submission should not be perceived as voluntary and under no circumstances be reflected in his eyes. This, of course, is the only kind of submission which will satisfy the Hindu policeman as the young men proceed to become prisoners of an escalating conflict.

Babar's Children

Both men and women agree that Hindu-Muslim relations have greatly deteriorated over the last two decades, especially after the Rameeza Bi incident in 1975. The earlier participation of Hindus and Muslims in each other's festivals has all but disappeared, and ties of friendship reaching across the communities have snapped. Old Hindu friends are now only acquaintances, to be politely greeted when one passes them on the street, but one no longer stops to exchange further courtesies. The women, who meet at the public tap, are not yet as distant from each other as the men, perhaps also because they were never especially close earlier. Ghousia (Rashid's younger sister) reports Hindu women telling her: "If you are cut the same amount of blood will come out as when we are cut. All religions are not the same but all human beings are. We wear the same clothes and it is difficult to make out who is a Hindu or Muslim if we did not wear a *bindi*." The killers often ask the name of their victim before they strike because they need this additional information to make sure of the victim's religious affiliation. When there is no chance of making a certain identification by asking the man to strip and show his penis (Muslim if circumcised, Hindu if not), the marauding mobs have found other, bizarre ways of making sure of the victim's identity. A man may be first hit on the head with a *lathi*. If while falling he takes the name of a Hindu god or goddess, he is then stabbed if the attackers are Muslim; if the involuntary cry is "Ya Allah!" he is spared.

The Muslims are concerned about the children who, unlike their own generation, do not even have memories of good relations with the Hindus. Whereas their own parents used to forbid them to talk in terms of "He is a Hindu; he is a Muslim," and instead stressed their shared humanity, today's children are acutely aware of being either one or the other from an early age.

My general impression is that Hindus are disliked and looked down upon but not passionately hated, even after so many riots. In contrast to the self-image of the Muslim who is compassionate, the Hindu is seen as cruel and without a trace of pity. "If a Hindu woman or child walks through a Muslim street, the Muslim will let them go, thinking the fight is between men and should not involve women, children, and the aged. A Hindu does not think like that. It is enough for him to see the other person is a Muslim before he strikes without regard for age or gender."

"Hindus are also cowards who can fight only when they are in a large group. Muslims are not afraid even if they are few and unarmed and their opponents have swords. Allah gives them courage and they know if they die the death will not be in vain but a martyrdom which Allah will reward in paradise."

"Hindus also have no control over their impulses and behavior. There are no fixed times or formats to their prayers nor do their books give them instructions on how to lead a good life like the Qur'an does. They go to the temple any time of the day or night, ring the temple bell, and give their God instructions: "Do this for me, do that for me!" And, of course, having been slaves for thousands of years, they have no experience of governance like the Muslims. They may be more educated by they are illiterate as far as governing is concerned."

Most of all, the Muslims feel baffled and hurt at the thought of being unwanted in the country of their birth. They seem to be struggling against a growing conviction that, irrespective of its formal constitution, India is a Hindu country and they may be living here on Hindu sufferance. Ghousia says: "We hear they are saying all over the country, 'Go to Pakistan. Pakistan is your country, Hindustan is ours. Not a single Muslim should be seen here.' They think if they harass us enough, we will leave for Pakistan. They have trains ready for our departure. We feel if we have to die, we will die here; if we have to live, we will live here."

"Babar ki santan, jao Pakistan" ("Children of Babar, go to Pakistan") is today one of the most popular slogans of Hindu mobs during a riot or in the preceding period of rising tension between the two communities. The crudity of the slogan should not blind us to its significance in the shaping of contemporary Hindu-Muslim relations. It reflects the Hindu nationalist's deep-seated distrust of Muslim loyalty to the Indian state and a doubt regarding Muslim patriotism if the community is faced with a choice between the country of its birth and that of its coreligionists. The slogan contains the accusation that Muslims may prove potential traitors in any conflict between their loyalty to the state and their loyalty to Islam.

Though repressed in elite political discourse, this accusation is perceived to have enough substance to arouse a sense of unease among many other Hindus who are not sympathizers of Hindu nationalism and yet subscribe to the notion of the nation-state as a definer of their political identity. The importance of this accusation as a prime irritant in Hindu-Muslim relations is also recognized by a large section of Muslims, and, as we shall later see, it evokes an emotionally charged response from the community's religious-political leadership.

Currently fueled by events in Kashmir where a large section of the Muslim population is demanding independence or accession to Pakistan, the suspicion of Muslim loyalty to the Indian state has two main sources. First, there has been a historical tendency among upper-class Muslims (or those aspiring to higher status in the community) to stress or invent Persian, Arab, or Turkish ancestry rather than rest content with their more humble Indian origins. The tendency, more pronounced among Muslim fundamentalists, is to see themselves as superior beings from outside India who share Indian history only as the country's erstwhile rulers.

Second, as we shall again see in the next chapter, the specific Muslim history the community's conservative spokesmen would like to construct and exalt is the one shared with Muslims of the Middle East, especially the sacred history of early Islam and of the Dar al-Islam between the seventh and fifteenth centuries, when Islamic civilization was at its zenith and Muslims had conquered half the world. Hindu nationalists believe that only a minority of Muslims accept the Indian nation-state as a definer of their political identity and container of their loyalty. They are inclined to believe that Bernard Lewis's thesis on Muslims of the Middle East is equally applicable to the Indian context, namely that "there is a recurring tendency in times of crisis, in times of emergency, when the deeper loyalties take over, for Muslims to find their basic identity in the religious community; that is to say, in an entity defined by Islam rather than by ethnic origin, language, or country of habitation."[3] The nature of the vicious circle is immediately apparent: the anchoring of Muslim identity in Islam spurs Hindu suspicion of Muslim loyalty to the nation, which makes the Muslims draw closer in the religious community for security, which further fuels Hindu distrust of Muslim patriotism, and so on.

Empirically, there is some evidence in a twenty-five-year-old study that a situation of actual conflict between India and Pakistan is a stressful affair for Indian Muslims which makes them emotionally close ranks. Yet, in spite of increased Hindu hostility toward Muslims during the actual period of warfare, Indian Muslims do not feel any closer to their Pakistani coreligionists but in fact feel more distant toward them than in the period preceding the outbreak of hostilities.[4]

The Victim Response

Among the poorer Muslims, I was acutely aware of a weary resignation in their dislike of the Hindus. Their diatribes were often mechanical, lacking energy and that fire in the belly which leaves some hope for the transformation of various states of withdrawal into an active advocacy on one's own behalf. I wondered if there was not a repression of anger, even hate, operating here—the maintenance of repression imposing a drain on energy and depleting the aggression available for assertive action. The psychological portrait I repeatedly drew when the talk shifted from the private to the public, from the familial to collective realms with respect to the current situation

[margin note: The repression of hate drains the energy to act aggressively?!?]

of Indian Muslims, was of the Muslim as a helpless victim of changed historical circumstances and the demands of the modern world. One of the main
refrains was that since the *hukumat*—used in the sense of rule, political authority, regime—was now of the Hindus, discrimination against the Muslims
was to be expected. However galling to the individual and collective sensibility of the Muslims, this was a fact of life with which one had to come to
terms. A few women even took a melancholy (and I thought, masochistic)
satisfaction from this turn of the historical wheel which had reversed the position of subjects and rulers and of the accustomed directions of inequality
and injustice. Most, though, bemoaned the discrimination against Muslims
without expressing much hope for a foreseeable change in the situation.

"The Hindu likes the Hindu and not the Musulman," says one woman.
"The *hukumat* is Hindu. They can now oppress us, take revenge for the thousand years of our *hukumat*."

"They are doing *hukumat* since forty years and will try their best to make
the Musulman weak and insignificant," says another woman.

"Jinnah was right," says a man who works part time for the Majlis, "Living
in a Muslim nation is the only protection from oppression by the Hindus."

Another woman, echoing the old *mai-baap* ("mother-father") attitude toward the state, is more plaintive: "The *hukumat* should treat both Hindus and
Muslims equally. When a mother has borne more than one child she looks at
each child with equal favor."

Rashid tries to make the abstraction of "discrimination" more concrete
by describing his own experiences. "For fifteen years I worked in the vegetable market. Then I applied for a job in the Road Transport Corporation.
When I went in with my application, the clerk said, 'Don't even bother to
register your name. Muslims can't get a job here.' I applied to at least ten
other government departments but the moment they heard my name they
told me to go away. I finally got a job in the railways by hiding my identity
and changing my name to Babu Rao. After two years when the time for promotion came they found out Babu Rao was not my real name and that I was a
Muslim. I gave up after that and started working with the Majlis. I said to
myself, 'How can you work with the Hindus when even your name is unacceptable to them!'"

"It is difficult for the Muslims to be self-employed. The Hindus control
most businesses. If we ask for credit, they will refuse us and extend it only to
members of their community. If I buy goods from them I will have to pay ten
rupees, but a Hindu will pay only eight. Because of our poverty we cannot
send our children to school. If there is only one man who earns twenty-five to

thirty rupees a day and has eight mouths to feed, where is the money for the extra expense of school to come from?" Rashid, however, does not completely blame the modern external world for the Muslim's plight. "Hindus are better off not only because they are favored by the *hukumat* but also because their mothers, sisters, daughters, all work. We do not educate our women or make them work because of *purdah*," he says, not in a spirit of criticism of the tenets of his faith but as a pure statement of fact. Indeed, it is the loss of faith which he holds ultimately responsible for what has happened to the Indian Muslim: "If we had unshakable faith, then our *hukumat* would not have gone. When faith went, everything went."

He ties his faith (its strength) to power/control.

This, then, is the striking difference between the Hindu and Muslim poor: the former feel less as victims and have a greater sense of agency and mastery over the circumstances of their lives than the latter. In the victim response of the Muslims, the loss of collective self-idealization which sharply reduces self-esteem is perceived as a result of overwhelming outside forces of which they are hapless victims. The Muslim poor convey an impression of following a purposeless course, buffeted by the impact of others in a kind of social Brownian motion.[5] There seems to be a kind of institutionalized fatalism at work which makes them act as ready victims of circumstances and leaves them little ability to defend themselves against exploitation. This is not to maintain that the victim response of the Muslims is only "in the head," without a basis in reality. Like the notion of the "enemy," discrimination too is neither merely real nor merely psychological but a blend of the two.

Whereas the loss of collective self-idealization due to changed historical and socioeconomic circumstances evokes a depressive response among the Muslim poor, for many sensitive members of the community—including some of its writers, scholars, and artists—this loss of Muslim power and glory is explicitly mourned. The despair at the moral decay and political decline of Muslim societies, the historian Mushirul Hasan tells us, is a recurrent theme in Urdu poetry, literature, and journalism.[6] Ideally, such a mourning should clear the decks for the birth of new ideals and a more confident encounter with the future. For many, though, the mourning is never completed; its stock of narratives of loss and their elegiac mood become a part of the family heritage that is passed from one generation to the other. For these men and women, the poet Iqbal's line, "Lightning only strikes the hapless Muslims" (*Barq girti hai to bechare Musulmanon par*) has acquired a personal significance which has been incorporated into the social aspect of their identity. In other words, whenever a person feels, thinks, and acts as a Muslim rather than as an individual, there is a perceptible undertone of grief, a miasma of mourning in what has been called "the Andalus syndrome."[7] The syndrome, of course, refers to the great Muslim civilization on the Iberian peninsula that ended abruptly in the fifteenth century, plunging the Islamic world into gloom and leaving a yearning for its lost glory in Muslim societies on the rim of the Mediterranean. In the Indian situation, the Andalus response, I believe, is more the province of the upper and middle classes rather than of the vast number of Muslim poor. Of course, in Hyderabad, with its history bearing a striking similarity to the fate of Andalusia, especially in the abrupt ending of Muslim rule, the heartbreak is more widespread than in most other parts of the country.

Gilani Bano, a novelist from Hyderabad, is one of the more eminent Urdu writers who has tried to capture the elusive spirit of the Andalus response in her fiction. In her novel *Aiwan-e-ghazal*, she takes as her subject a slice of Muslim life just before and after 1948, the year in which Hyderabad abruptly ceased being an independent state with its own administration, ruler, and ethos, and became part of India—a country which was geographically contiguous with Hyderabad but was emotionally distant for many of its inhabitants. The title of the novel is from the name of the family mansion of an old aristocratic (*nawabi*) family. Literally, it also means "the palace of the *ghazal*," the *ghazal* more often than not being an elegy of unhappy love where the lover bemoans the loss, the inaccessibility, or the turning away of the beloved.

One of the main characters in the novel through whose eyes the events of those years are viewed is Nawab Wahid Hussain, a man in his early fifties, steeped in the ethos of a vanishing world, who is fearful and contemptuous of the change that is poised to destroy the old civilization. Wahid Hussain looks down at what he considers the crass commercialism of the modern era and deems the writing of poetry and the play of love with a favored mistress—normally an accomplished courtesan—as the only worthwhile occupations of a civilized man. He admires his grandfather whose dead body was discovered one morning surrounded by sheets of paper covered with Urdu calligraphy while the flame in his bedroom lamp burnt low. The family had thought that the papers pertained to the affairs of the family home which the British Resident, acting on complaints of debauchery and the kidnapping of girls, had demanded for his inquiry. The papers, however, turned out to be the final drafts of fifteen *ghazals* which the old *nawab* had composed throughout the night in a burst of feverish activity. With the threat of the inquiry and eventual disgrace looming over him, they were yet some of the best *ghazals* his grandfather had ever written. Wahid Hussain ruminates on Hyderabad's fate: "[He] opened his eyes and saw the portrait of Quli Qutub Shah on the wall opposite the portrait of the last ruler, Osman Ali. Wahid Hussain saw Quli Qutub Shah's eyes brimming with contentment as if he was searching for a *ghazal* or, standing on the ramparts of Golconda, lost in the dream of a beautiful city springing up on the forested land around the fort. The city he founded for Bhagmati to live in was like a garden, its magnificent buildings like lotus flowers lit with the lamps of civility and culture. He looks as if he is saying to one of his lovers, 'Prepare the festivities. The tender shoots of Urdu are coming out but we do not have much time left. Behind the hills of a few centuries, the caravans of time are moving in our direction. Soon the plunderers will fall upon us. Under the rubble of Golconda people will search for our stories. The dust particles of our fallen glory will become a diamond glittering in the crown of a queen in a distant land.'"[8] The diamond, of course, was the Kohinoor; the queen, Victoria of Great Britain.

Morality of Violence

Although they live in separate *bastis*, the inevitably close contact between Hindus and Muslims in the crowded inner city leads to interactions between the two which span the full emotional range from friendship to deadly hatred during the time of a riot. The exchanges with members of the other community which are considered to be transgressions of the group's code governing such transactions were of particular interest and invited a more systematic exploration.

In this exploration, my focus was not on questions close to the hearts of moral philosophers such as whether it was reason, reason dependent upon individual desire, religious prescription, role obligation, or a convention that was being violated by a particular action. Nor was I concerned with the religious foundations of the morality governing Hindu-Muslim relations; with what, for instance, the Qur'an has to say on a Muslim's various interactions with those who are outside the faith. My aim was more to understand the way people experienced these interactions and the psychological processes underlying the experiences.

It was evident from the preliminary interviews that these interactions had to be divided into two parts: those which pertain to normal, peace-time life and others which take place during a riot. In both Hindus and Muslims, riot-time interactions deviated substantially from the code that governs their actions during normal times. There are, however, as we shall see later, still a few acts that invite universal moral condemnation from both sides, independent of their temporal context—normalcy versus riot. These obligations are considered universally binding. Even within context-dependent obligations, there are interactions which are perceived as binding on one's own group and not on others; they are viewed as distinctive expressions of the community's moral qualities, uniqueness, and traditions. These obligations are perceived as objective and moral and yet not universally binding. Their violation is usually remarked upon by the phrase, "A good Muslim (or Hindu) does not do that," implying that the bad Other may indeed do so.

Using the method developed by the anthropologist Richard Shweder, who in a series of studies has explored the moral ideas of children and adults in India and the United States, I have attempted to examine adult Muslim and Hindu interpretations of nineteen behavioral cases of Hindu-Muslim interaction in the "Morality Interview" (appendix 2).[9] The first twelve cases represent different kinds of interactions in normal times while the last seven *and* cases are descriptive of certain interactions during a riot. Examples of normal interactions are: "A Muslim rents his house to a Hindu"; "'A Muslim girl marries a Hindu boy." Examples of riot-time interactions are: "Some Muslims rape a Hindu girl"; "'Some Muslims loot Hindu shops." Further interview questions seek to elicit the respondent's view of the seriousness of the violation and the kind of sanctions it should invite.

Before discussing the results of the interviews, I need to sound a note of caution. The interactions between Hindus and Muslims had also come up during the more freewheeling conversations with some of the same respondents. I had the impression that people became "more moral" in the situation of a structured interview using a questionnaire than they were in *an* the unstructured setting where they were more uninhibited in the expression of violent sentiments. The "questionnaire morality" is perhaps inclined to be more conservative than the actually lived one.

It seems, and this may be of methodological importance in collection of psychological data, that the expression of an individual's views on subjects close to one's heart becomes more and more controlled as the setting changes from an informal conversation, to a formal interview, to the filling in of a questionnaire, to writing for wider dissemination, and, finally, to the most controlled expression of all, the enactment of one's views in the public arena. *interesante ...* Differently but tentatively stated, it is perhaps less the nature of the medium in which self-disclosure is made than the imagined intimacy with the presumed recipients of our views which is important. Our openness and honesty in revealing ourselves decreases in tandem with the degree of intimacy we believe we share with our ultimate listeners (although on rare occasions, such as an encounter on a train, we may for a time imagine sharing great intimacy with a total stranger). Writing a book for an impersonal audience is less intimate than talking to long-standing disciples; filling a questionnaire is less intimate than a friendly conversation which, in turn, is less intimate than responding to someone even closer than a friend.

The Muslim sample from Karwan consisted of ten men and ten women. The women ranged in age from eighteen to fifty and all except the youngest were illiterate. The ages of the men were between nineteen and seventy-five. A couple of the men had a few years of schooling but none had finished high school. A third of them were unemployed while others worked in low-paid jobs as casual laborers, vegetable sellers, and auto-rickshaw drivers.

Before I discuss the morality judgments of the Muslims, there are two general remarks that need to be made. First, the idea of convention, the idea that the disapproved interactions with the Hindus could be based on a consensus within the community and are relative and alterable, is almost totally absent. Once a behavior is seen as a violation it generally tends to be viewed starkly as a sin and it does not matter if it is done secretly or openly or whether it is permitted in other places. These interactions, except in the area of religious faith, tend to be viewed as part of a moral order, categorical, imperative, and binding on all Muslims. Second, the moral code, to follow Dworkin's distinction, is duty- rather than right- or goal-based.[10] In other words, a duty like "obedience to Allah's will as expressed in the Qur'an," is taken as fundamental and given priority over a right such as the "individual's right to freedom of choice" or a goal like "improving the welfare of the community." The morality is traditional or customary, deeply connected to the ancestry and narrated history of the group. The transgressions of moral ways of acting are accompanied by anxieties relating to the unexpected and the fear of narcissistic injuries such as being excluded from the group or the loss of a fantasized union with others of the community.

The statements on which there was a consensus—a consensus referring to judgments of right and wrong shared by at least 75 percent of the sample—are the following:

PERMITTED INTERACTIONS

In Normal Times
To have Hindu friends.
To eat with Hindus.
To work with Hindus in a factory.
To learn the Gita from a pandit.
To beat up a Hindu boy for whistling at a Muslim girl.
To beat up a Hindu who is making fun of Allah.

In Riot Time
To give shelter to a Hindu.

WRONG INTERACTIONS

In Normal Times
A Muslim girl to go to the cinema with a Hindu boy.
A Muslim girl to elope with a Hindu boy.
To throw a dead cow in a temple.

In Riot Time
To rape a Hindu girl.
To kill a Hindu woman.

Let us begin by looking at the interactions which are consensually considered wrong. In normal times, the strongest reaction is evoked by the idea of a Muslim girl going to the cinema with a Hindu boy. This is not only a serious violation of the moral code but unequivocally a sin. "The other day we beat up one such pair," says a nineteen-year-old man, "We watched them for three days and followed them to the cinema. I slapped that girl and informed the girl's brother. He was ready to poison himself and die as he could not bear the dishonor that his sister was caught with one of their [Hindu] boys." Almost a third of the respondents would have the girl killed, expecting the parents to quietly poison her, bury her alive, or themselves commit suicide. Here, of course, our "law" that "expression is contingent upon its medium" also works in the reverse direction. The outrage which is being expressed in such violent words will generally be more controlled if and when it comes to concrete action. Then we can expect a beating rather than murder, wounding words, yes, but rarely the sharp stabs of a knife.

The younger Muslim women, whom I would expect to identify more with the girl, are at one with their menfolk in considering the action a grave sin. They are, however, much less harsh in the punishment they envisage as adequate. Most would be content if the girl got a good thrashing, and a couple recommended marrying the girl off against her will. In fact, the only two voices which do not consider the behavior a sin, though it remains a serious offense, are women.

What is the culture-specific aspect of the moral code which invites such wrath on the head of a Muslim girl who goes to a movie with a Hindu boy? Preeminent here is a notion of the family which is not an association of individuals but a structure with differentiated roles and obligations. The structure itself is a part of and in service of a larger whole, the Muslim community. The movie-going of a Muslim girl is not an individual affair but the establishment of a particular kind of relationship with the other *qaum* which is a deadly insult to the Muslim community. Yet the ferocity of the imagined punishments arouses the suspicion that there are also some unconscious fantasies involved in this act which, for instance, are absent in the case of a Muslim girl eloping with a Hindu boy. To an outside observer, with a different moral code, the latter would seem to be a far more serious affair. Although considered a sin, the punishments for elopement are not so severe. The girl should not be readmitted to the home and should be considered dead by the community, is the general tenor of opinion in dealing with this particular "sin." My hunch is that going to the cinema gives rise to images of hot, hurried gropings in the darkness of its foyer, fantasies of forbidden sexuality between the pair, whereas the elopement makes sexual congress between the couple more acceptable in that it is legitimized by marriage. The girl who has married a Hindu is outside the bounds of the community, dead as far as the Muslim *qaum* is concerned. The girl who went to the cinema is still a part of the community, a boil which must be lanced.

Throwing a dead cow in a temple is the only violation which is not considered a sin but a minor transgression. It is wrong because it hurts the religious sentiments of the Hindus and, more rationally, can lead to outbreak of a riot. Some will content themselves with pointing out to the offender the error of his ways while others will consider handing him over to the police.

During riot time, the two consensually forbidden acts of violence relate both to Hindu women, namely, their rape and murder. In contrast, there is no consensus on the moral status of the killing of men, looting, and arson. Although both rape and killing of women are regarded as sinful, there is a hesitation, almost reluctance when it comes to punishment of the guilty. What comes to the fore here is the conflict between the perceived interests of the community and its moral codes. "The men who have raped and killed are our own. Who will protect us if they are severely punished or handed over to the police?" expresses the nature of the dilemma. The recommended punishments range from educating the culprit, leaving it to Allah, letting the law take its course, to handing over the men to the police.

In the case of rape, there is no difference of opinion between men and women in either perception of the act or punishment of the wrongdoers. Of the two in the sample who favor the severest sanctions—castration and killing of the man—one is a man and the other a woman. During a riot, a time of danger to individual and collective survival, identification with the community outweighs all other identifications, including the identification with one's gender.

Killing and rape of Hindu women are sins because they are forbidden by Islam. This is elaborated through the idea of Islamic chivalry where a riot between Hindus and Muslims is a battle exclusively between men in defense of the honor of their *qaums*. The women are noncombatants. Weak and vulnerable, they are entitled to protection, even by men of the enemy host.

Rape of a Hindu woman, though, has some surprising twists to the nature of its sinfulness. The seventy-five-year-old man regards rape as a sin because a Hindu woman is *haram*, forbidden to the Muslim like the eating of pork or meat of an animal not slaughtered in the ritually correct manner. Rape of a Muslim woman, on the other hand, is not a sin because she is *halal*. This view is echoed by another, much younger man, who reacts with horror to the idea of raping a Hindu woman and thereby entering the polluted and contaminating inner regions of an infidel body. In these two cases rape is not a violation of the moral code that forbids the causing of harm to another individual but the breaking of a code that decrees the preservation of one's own sanctity.

Turning to permitted interactions in normal times, there is no difficulty in Muslims having Hindus as friends. There are three sceptics, all women, who believe such friendships are no longer possible after the riots of the last decade. They mistrust the Hindus; '"Hindus are sweet outside but have poison in their hearts."

It is also alright to eat with the Hindus. The only reservation is that since the Hindus eat *haram* foods, a Muslim might inadvertently eat something which is forbidden.

Working with Hindus in a factory does not pose any problem. It is a matter of work, of survival, and beyond the personal control of any single individual or even a community.

Learning Hindu scriptures from a Hindu priest is also not wrong. The Gita, too, is the voice of God in their language so it is not wrong to listen to it, opines one respondent. To do so is to gain knowledge which is pleasing to Allah, says another. It does not matter if one does so, says a third, after all a Muslim will remain a Muslim. The few dissenting voices express the fear that an exposure to unbelief (*kufar*) may corrode a Muslim's own faith.

I must confess to a mild surprise at this evidence of tolerance in matters of faith, reminding me once again not to underestimate the impact of the Hindu images from my childhood of the Muslim as a religious fanatic. This becomes especially true if we look at the dissensus on the question of a Muslim who converts and becomes a Hindu, an action I would have expected to be overwhelmingly rejected as wrong and sinful. Even the ones who condemn the conversion are reluctant to punish the offender. Others see such a conversion as a matter of personal choice. Of course, such an action is not a matter of indifference. It is an affront to the Muslim community yet does not call for its interference. Ironically, "religious fanaticism" is the least in the religious domain, in interactions at the level of faith, less than in any other area of social exchange with the Hindus. The otherwise duty-based moral code is suspended here as the individual's right to freedom of choice takes precedence over duties.

Beating up Hindu boys for whistling at a Muslim girl or for making fun of Allah are retaliations for straightforward insults to the collective honor and earn consensual approval. The qualifications are minor. In the first case, try to explain and then beat, says one man; another man will let the whistling go unpunished if the girl was out without a veil because then she has invited this unwelcome male attention. In the second case, a couple of respondents recommend forbearance in face of this stupidity. Mostly, though, violent reprisals are fully in order, as in the case of Salman Rushdie, whose example was specifically cited by two respondents.

But during a riot, giving shelter to a Hindu is the only consensually approved action. This is viewed as a religious duty owed to Allah. It is a duty independent of one's personal feelings about Hindus in general and the individual seeking shelter in particular. It is the expression of the compassion and mercy in the heart of a good Muslim and is enjoined by Islam.

On several significant actions, the sample of twenty Muslims did not establish a consensus. The question of renting a house to a Hindu in normal times produced several reactions. The dissenter's argument is based on the pollution of the Muslims by a Hindu living among them. Hindus plaster the floors and walls with cow dung, eat pork, will perform *puja* where *ibadat* has been done. A few feel more strongly: "My mother said if you give alms to a Hindu your hand will burn on Judgment day." It is not a sin but certainly an error to be avoided. The assenters argue that not all Hindus are bad, and there is nothing wrong with renting your house to a good Hindu.

Dissensus existed on a number of actions if taken in riot time. Those who see setting fire to a Hindu house as a wrong act do not consider it a major violation. It is a minor offense during a riot, and the offenders should be properly counseled. Others who approve look at it as something inevitable during a riot.

Looting of Hindu shops is an action that produced pro and con arguments that are the same as in the case of arson.

The respondents, both men and women, are almost evenly divided on the action of killing a Hindu man during a riot. Those who consider it a sin will still not sanction any punishment by the community. Some will allow it only in retaliation. Others who consider nothing wrong with killing a Hindu in a riot liken the situation to a time of war when killing and being killed is the normal order of things.

Morality and the Hindus

The Hindu sample from Pardiwada consisted of ten men and ten women. The men ranged in age from twenty-two to forty-five with a median age of thirty years, while the age range of women was between twenty and fifty-nine, with a median of thirty-five years. The Hindu women, like their Muslim counterparts, had had no schooling, whereas the Hindu men were better educated than the Muslim sample, with an average of seven years of schooling. Economically, too, the Pardis, though poor, were visibly better off than the Muslims from Karwan. Most of the men were fruit vendors while two drove auto-rickshaws for a living.

Before I discuss the Hindu responses to each of the behavioral cases, there is one general observation that needs to be made. As compared to the Muslims, the Hindu respondents were much more relativistic and contextual in judging a behavior as a transgression and more easygoing in proposing punishments for actions judged as wrong. Irrespective of age and gender, "It all depends" was an almost reflexive response, and the individual had to be persuaded to engage further with the standard interview.

In responding to cases of interaction with the Muslims, both during normal and riot times, which were not clearly labeled as unobjectionable at the outset, the answers were almost always framed in terms of a context, temporal or spatial. The linking of the morality of an interactions with time would be typically expressed thus: "It was wrong when times were different but it is not wrong now." By "different times," the person is alluding to a past golden era of individual and collective morality as compared to the degenerate Kali-yuga of today. The individual can thus convincingly state that an action is wrong in right times but right in wrong times. Similarly, demographic space seemed to be intimately involved in moral judgments, and I was often told that actions such as the beating up of a Muslim or arson and looting of Muslim shops were wrong if you lived in a Muslim majority *mohalla* but alright if you were living in a Hindu majority area. This appears to have less to do with morality than with prudence and expediency unless, of course, one is willing to consider the case for an expedience-based morality. As a consequence of this contextual stance, it is understandable that the envisaged punishments by the community for wrong actions were nonexistent or weak and evoked far less emotion and righteousness than the corresponding sanctions among the Muslims against the violators of their community's moral codes.

This striking difference between Hindus and Muslims can be accounted for in religious terms. The difference in the approaches to morality may be seen as a consequence of the difference between humanist and authoritarian religions (Fromm) or between precept-based and prophetic religions (Obeyesekere).[11] In more culturalist terms, as I have discussed elsewhere, in Hindu philosophical and ethical tradition, the rightness or wrongness of a proposed action depends on the individual's *desa*, the culture in which one is born; on *kala*, the historical era in which one lives; on *srama*, the efforts required of one at different stages of life; and on *gunas*, the innate psychobiological traits which are the heritage of a person's previous lives.[12] "Right" and "wrong" are relative; they can emerge as clear distinctions only out of the total configuration of the four coordinates of action.

The Hindu approach to the making of moral judgments may well be a part of a basic Hindu way of thinking which the poet-scholar A. K. Ramanujan has called "context-sensitive."[13] Hindus, Ramanujan believes, idealize context-sensitive rather than context-free rules. Whether it is in medical matters, where the context is vital in diagnosis, prescription, and preparation of herbal medicines, or in music, where the ragas have their prescribed and appropriate times, the context sensitivity extends even to space and time, the universal contexts, the Kantian imperatives, which in India are not uniform and neutral. Every moral rule thus has a number of exceptions, each of these additions a subtraction from any universal law so that one falls back on the universal only if one fits no context or condition (which is rare). Yet before wholly embracing the religious-culturalist explanations, as I am tempted to do, we must remember that the Pardis are not completely context-bound in their moral judgments. The rape and killing of a Muslim woman are unequivocally condemned as sins, unalterable by any contextual considerations. To me, even more significant than the differences between the Hindu and Muslim approaches to morality is their similarity in the condemnation of the rape and killing of the other community's women; both groups regard these acts unalterably as sins. At an emotionally more neutral level they also share a common disapproval of acts which hurt the religious sentiments of the other community. What is most encouraging is the fact that this disapproval is often couched in terms of empathy: "Their feelings are the same as ours and we would not like it if it were done to us." The existence of this empathy—even if it is in a restricted sphere—demonstrates that the history of violence be-

[handwritten margin note:] Empathy for the "other" reveals that a dehumanization has not taken place between Hindus + Muslims.

[handwritten bottom note:] (What would he say about the atrocities that are committed? — i.e. were they possible because of a dehumanization?)

tween the communities (which can fairly be said to have made enemies of Hindus and Muslims, at least in the poor underbelly of the city) has not yet dehumanized the enemy. There is still empathy on both sides which does not let a Muslim consider a Hindu—and vice versa—less than human and therefore a deserving prey for every imaginable brutality. Empathy with members of the other group, even when considered the enemy, defends the Other from the untrammeled aggression which can so easily be let loose against all those considered subhuman.[14]

The Hindus, I have noted above, are far more easygoing than the Muslims in their moral judgments of interactions with members of the other community. In normal times, although a Hindu girl's elopement with a Muslim boy is consensually disapproved of, it is not considered a sin. Having Muslim friends, eating and working with Muslims, renting your house to a Muslim, learning the Qur'an from a Muslim priest—are all consensually permitted though some may express reservations about this conduct. The dissensus is on a Hindu's conversion to Islam, a Hindu girl marrying a Muslim boy or going out with him to the cinema. The latter action, so violently disapproved of in the Muslim sample, elicits divided opinions. Its opponents would discourage such a practice because it may lead to an interfaith marriage, with all its attendant problems. Those who see nothing objectionable in the girl's action, most of them women, look at it as something which happens all the time in today's world and is not something over which one should get unduly exercised. Whether the greater Hindu permissiveness with regard to interactions with the other community is a function of the Pardis' low status in the caste hierarchy, and whether high-caste Hindus wall themselves off much more from the Muslims, as anecdotal evidence seems to suggest, is a question which can only be answered by future empirical work.

As with the Muslims, rape and killing of women of the other community during a riot, especially the former, elicited consensual condemnation as sins—the only actions the Hindus were prepared to label as such. Similarly, giving shelter to members of the other community during a riot is not considered wrong. There is dissensus on the morality of other riot-time actions such as arson, looting, and the killing of men. The riot-time morality of the Hindus is thus strikingly similar to that of the Muslims in its contents, though not in the emotional intensity with which this morality is invested. The two communities share in common the commandments "Thou shalt not kill . . . a woman" and "Thou shalt not rape," but the outrage associated with the transgression of these commandments is stronger among Muslims than among Hindus. Indeed, as I noted earlier, the emotional reaction of Muslims to any violation of the community's moral code of conduct is intense and especially violent in cases involving a Muslim woman's sexualized interaction with a Hindu man. In such situations, I believe, the self-representation of the community becomes identified with the woman's sexual stance in its more servile aspect, with images of being "fucked"—not in a joyful but in a contemptuous sense—by the Hindu. To penetrate the Other, whether a woman or another group, is to be superior, powerful, and masculine; to be penetrated is to be inferior, weak, and feminine. It is a blending of the images of power and sexuality in a phallocentric vision which makes many men all over the world, for example in parts of the Middle East and Latin America, regard only the man who is penetrated by another man as a despised homosexual while the active inserter on the "top" is considered as a "normal", even macho male.

Violence between religious-ethnic groups is, then, also a struggle over the assignment of gender, a way of locating the desired male and denigrated female communities. As a Hindu patient, echoing the sentiments of a few others, remarked in a session during the 1984 anti-Sikh riots in Delhi: "It serves them right! Every one of these cunts (chutiye) behaves as if his prick is at full mast!"

SIX

A New Hindu Identity

Great disorders lead to great devotions.
                    —Emile Zola

Some fifteen years ago, when what is today called the Nehruvian project of a modernized secular India was still vigorous and fundamentalism was a distant gleam in the eye of an occasional *imam* or *mahant*, I tried to peer into the crystal ball of the future. In my conclusion to *The Inner World*, I wrote that *modernisation=* as modernization picks up pace, individuals will increasingly seek member- *individualism* ship in groups with absolute value systems and with little tolerance for devia- *fundamentalism=* tion from their norms. To quote: "Whereas initially the appeal of these *collectivism* groups may be limited to sections of society who are most susceptible to the pressures of social change—for, example, youth and urbanized classes—we can expect an ever-widening circle of participation as more and more people are sucked into the wake of modernisation. . . . In short, we can expect an increasing destruction of the nascent, western-style individualism as more and more individuals seek to merge into collectivities that promise a shelter *) These are* for the hurt, the conflicted and the ship wrecked."[1] *} the by-products of modernisation*

If I again take up the theme of those large social formations through *?* which many individuals in India seek a sense of their cultural identity (a term which I prefer to the more sociological "ethnicity"), then it is not to derive a melancholy satisfaction from any perceived prescience but to offer some psychological observations on an issue which is normally seen as the domain of political scientists and social commentators. First, to get definitional mat- *There's nothing* ters out of the way, by "cultural identity" I mean a group's basic way of orga- *basic about it.* nizing experience through its myths, memories, symbols, rituals, and ideals.[2] Socially produced and thus subject to historical change, cultural identity is not a static affair even while it makes a decisive contribution to the en- hancement of an individual's sense of self-sameness and continuity in time and space. This definition is particularly apt for the Hindutva movement— characterized by some as Hindu fundamentalism—through which a large

143

number of Hindus today seem to be seeking a sense of their cultural identity. Let us again remember that "fundamental" does not mean "traditional." As in other parts of the non-Western world, revivalism or fundamentalism in India, Hindu, or Muslim, is an attempt to reformulate the project of modernity. Like its counterparts elsewhere, the leadership of Hindutva, for instance, has never been traditional but decidedly modern, consisting of individuals who turned their backs on their own Western education.[3] Keshav Baliram Hedgewar, the founder of the Rashtriya Swayam Sevak Sangh (RSS), the core institution and the driving force of Hindu revivalism, had his schooling in English and went on to study medicine in Calcutta. In his youth, he is reported to have felt that orthodox Hindu ritual was rather silly. His successor, Golwalkar, was the son of a civil servant, did his master's degree in biology at Benares University, and was a lecturer in zoology at the same institution before he joined the RSS.[4]

Shadows of Mourning

Haunting images of loss and helplessness among large groups of people underlie many literary and scholarly accounts of transnational historical changes. These images constitute the somber mood with which scholars have often reflected upon the periods and processes of significant transformations in human history. When Max Weber paints the portrait of Western man in the wake of enlightenment, we see a face aglow with the promised triumph of rationality in human affairs, yet also etched with deep shadows of mourning. From Weber's canvas, we see modern man peering out with hopeful though disenchanted eyes at a future which offers vastly greater control over nature, society, and man's own destiny. Yet the portrait also conveys a palpable grief for the lost spontaneity and immediacy which the social forms and symbols of the Judeo-Christian religious tradition had built up and guaranteed.

Nearer to our own times, as we study the anthropological, psychological, and above all, fictional accounts of another transcultural historical process, the process of modernization in the non-Western world, we again encounter the ghost of depression seated at a banquet table laid out for eagerly awaited dishes of economic development and the fruits of industrialization. Let me, then, first outline the social-psychological processes which are a consequence of modernization and which I believe are the foundation on which the edifices of the new Hindu and Muslim as well as other cultural identities in India are being constructed. These processes are, of course, not particular to India but common to most of the non-Western world.

[margin handwritten note: Why just the non-Western world?]

First, population movements which take place during the modernizing process involve the separation of families and the loss of familiar neighborhoods and ecological niches. Psychologists report and novelists describe the feelings of bereavement and states of withdrawal among those mourning for old attachments and suspicious of creating new ones. These tendencies are not only harmful for individuals but also hinder the birth of new social structures and forms while they rob community life of much of its vitality and therefore its capacity for counteracting the sense of helplessness.[5]

With increasing globalization, migrations are no longer confined by national boundaries. Globalization, too, encroaches upon traditional group solidarities and the established relationships between different groups, whether in Cochin or Moradabad. The shifting demands of global markets for particular kinds of goods and labor make for rapid and bewildering changes in the relative status of many groups in a particular society. Whereas some groups dramatically increase their earning power (and thus claims to a higher social status) through their access to international markets in goods, services, and labor, others are as dramatically impoverished, with many forced to migrate from their traditional geographical and cultural niches.

The vast internal migrations also give rise to overcrowded living conditions in urban conglomerations, especially in the sprawling shanty towns and slums with their permanent air of transience. On the one hand, it is undeniable that urban slums, however awful they seem to middle-class sensibilities, represent to the poor a hope of escaping from deadening economic deprivation and the relatively rigid, caste-based discrimination and inequities of rural society. On the other, there is the lack of cultural norms in dealing with relative strangers whose behavioral clues cannot be easily deciphered, so different from the ritualized predictability of interactions in the communities left behind in villages or small towns, which compel the person to be constantly on guard. One is in a state of permanent psychic mobilization and heightened nervous arousal.

In addition, the rapid obsolescence of traditional roles and skills as modernization picks up pace seriously dents the self-esteem—when it does not shatter it completely—of those who are confronted with simultaneous loss of earning power, social status, and identity as particular kinds of workers. For the affected and their families, especially children, there is a collapse of confidence in the stability of the established order and of the world. What looms instead is the specter of a future which is not only opaque but represents an overwhelming threat to any sense of purpose.

The feelings of loss are not limited to the migration from geographical regions and cultural homes or to the disappearance of traditional work identities. They also extend to the loss of ancestral ideals and values. For instance, compared to what many believe was a traditionally healthy eroticism, modernity, with its popular cinema, television, fashions, the commingling of sexes in schools, colleges, and at work, is sexually decadent. "People have lost their brahmacharya (celibacy), their character is destroyed and everyone has become an addict of bad habits. If you cannot control your libido, you cannot be pure."[6] Once the enlightenment values of universal equality, liberty, and fraternity, of the preeminence of reason and moral autonomy of the individual were formulated through the political revolutions in the non-Western world, they became a universal heritage, inevitably triumphant when in conflict with the norms and values of the local culture. In spite of the disillusionment of some postmodern Western intellectuals with the enlightenment mentality, its values continue to constitute what has been generally regarded as the most dynamic and transformative ideology in human history.[7] Yet the enlightenment has a dark side, too. The modernization project is riddled with its own inequities, repressions, and unfraternal conflicts. There is thus bound to be a palpable grief for the values of a lost—and retrospectively idealized—world, when in the brave new one progress often turns out to be glaring inequality, rationality becomes selfishness and the pursuit of self-interest, and individualism comes to mean unbridled greed.

Secret Wounds

Whereas loss and helplessness constitute one stream of feelings accompanying the modernization process, another stream consists of feelings of humiliation and radically lowered self-worth. One source of humiliation lies in the homogenizing and hegemonizing impact of modernization and globalization, both of which are no respecters of cultural pluralities and diversities. The imperatives of economic development, which see many local cultural values and attitudes as outmoded or just plain irrelevant, are a source of humiliation to all those who have not embraced or identified with the modernization project in its totality.

For the masses, there are other occasions for blows to self-esteem such as the increase in the complexity and incidence of bureaucratic structures, with their attendant dehumanization, which has been a corollary of development. The cumulative effect of daily blows to an individual's feelings of self-worth, received in a succession of bureaucratic and other impersonal encounters, cannot be underestimated.

For the elites of the non-Western world, there is an additional humiliation in their greater consciousness of the defeat of their civilizations in the colonial encounter with the West. This defeat is not merely an abstraction or a historical memory but one which is confirmed by the peripheral role of their countries in the international economic and political order of the post-colonial world. Their consciousness of being second-class citizens in the global order is reinforced by their many encounters with the more self-confident Western colleagues in the various international forums. An example of the role played by loss and sensed humiliation is seen in case of those Indians, economically an elite group, who have migrated to the United States and are frequently exposed to indifference or condescension toward their cultural tradition. When they have not abjured their cultural identity altogether in what I would consider an "identification with the aggressor," they have turned back to embrace their cultural identity as Hindus, Muslims, or Sikhs with a revivalist fervor which is far in excess of their counterparts in the home country. Of course, migration itself plays a significant role in the revival of cultural identity. Global migrations, tourism, and communications confront people in a society with a foreignness of others which is unprecedented in their experience. All over the world our encounters with strangers are on a larger scale, over longer periods of time, with the strangers possessing a higher degree of strangeness than has ever been the case before. Observations such as "They think like that," "They believe this," "Their customs are like that," inevitably lead to questions which may not have been self-consciously addressed before; "'What do *we* [however that "we" is defined] think?" "What do *we* believe?" "What are *our* customs?" In bringing together people in closer proximity, the processes of globalization paradoxically increase the self-consciousness which separates and differentiates.

The portraits of loss and helplessness may sometimes seem to be overdrawn. Human beings have a remarkable capacity for adaptation, for creating new communities when old ones must be abandoned, for planting new gardens of love around them where old ones have withered. Yet before fresh psychological and social structures can emerge, there is a period—permanent for some—of apathy, chronic discontent, or rebellious rage at those who are held responsible for the loss of old social forms and ideals. Historical and social changes, working through the psychological mechanisms of loss and humiliation thus lead to the widespread feeling of being a victim rather than an active agent of events which are buffeting the individual and his or her group. Millions of people become patients in a broad sense, even if temporarily, patienthood being essentially a condition of inactivation. After all, *patiens*, as Erik Erikson has pointed out, denotes a state of being

[handwritten margin note: His explanation for {fundamentl's} "7."]

exposed to superior forces from within and without which cannot be overcome without energetic and redeeming help.[8]

Cultural Identity and Cure

The required energy and redemption to restore *agens*, that inner state of being which sanctions initiative and encourages purposeful activity in the outer world, is most often sought through increasing, restoring, or constructing a sense of cultural identity. Cultural groups are not only a shelter for those mourning lost attachments but also vehicles for redressing narcissistic injuries, for righting what are perceived as contemporary or historical wrongs. The question of why such "primordial" group identities as "Hindus" and "Muslims" are generally preferred rather than identities based on class, profession, or other criteria cannot be discussed here. Perhaps the latter lack an encompassing worldview, are impoverished in their symbolic riches and devoid of that essential corpus of myths in which people have traditionally sought meaning, especially at a time when their world appears to have become meaningless.

Is this change from meaning to meaningless

A core attraction and vital therapeutic action of self-consciously belonging to an cultural community lies in its claim to the possession of a future which, in a state of *patiens*, is felt to be irretrievably lost. To outsiders, this future may appear to be a simplistic perspective on the world such as a promise of restoration of the perfect civil society of the ancestors, what the Hindus, for instance, call *Ram Rajya*. It may be the reproduction on earth of a paradise envisaged only in sacred texts. It may be the hedonistic enjoyment of more and more goods and services in a heaven presided over by a benign, supply-side God. The promise is of a future, not seen, but which "works."

a fair/accurate representation?

The cultural group, which brings the "primordiality" related to shared myths, memories, values, and symbols to the fore, thus assumes a vital healing function. One of its most important aspects is to replace feelings of loss with those of love. This insight into the way groups work psychologically goes back to Freud, who postulated eros at the vital cohesive force in a group.[9] He believed that ties of love among members of a group come into existence through their emotional bond with the leader. In more technical terms, members of a group put the same object, the leader, in place of their ego ideal and consequently identify with each other. This shared idealization gives rise to the love ties which are experienced in the feelings of loyalty, esprit de corps and, in the more intense moments of group life, in feelings of fusion and merger. Experientially, it is a reordering and opening up of the

There's something to this...

inner world of the individual to include members of the group who, in turn, open up to include the individual in their psychological space, a mutual affirmation which lies at the heart of love. In cultural groups, the shared ego ideal may not be the figure of a single leader but many historical and mythical figures from the group's tradition, its ideals and values, and even its social and intellectual traditions.

We are all aware of the profound effect the group can have on the consolidation of a person's "sense of identity" and in increasing the cohesiveness of the self. Even in individual psychotherapy, we often see that it is not unusual for patients in a state of self-fragmentation to achieve a firmer and more cohesive sense of self upon joining an organized group. The Nazis are not the only group who turned quasi-derelict individuals into efficiently functioning ones by providing them the framework of a convincing world image and the use of new cultural symbols and group emblems such as shiny brown uniforms. As Ernest Wolf perceptively observes, "It seems a social identity can support a crumbling self the way a scaffolding can support a crumbling building."[10]

Psychology versus Politics?

Before I look at the construction of the new Hindu identity, I would like to address the objections to a psychological approach to the subject. There are many social scientists and political analysts who would locate the enhancements of ethnicity (cultural identity in my terms) in a particular group not in social-psychological processes but in the competition between elites for political power and economic resources. In fact, this has been the dominant explanation for the occurrence of Hindu-Muslim riots and is best exemplified in the work of Asghar Ali Engineer.[11] This "instrumentalist," as contrasted to the "primordialist" view I advocate here, has been succinctly formulated by Paul Brass: "In the process of transforming cultural forms, values and practices into political symbols, elites in competition with each other for control over the allegiance or territory of the ethnic group in question strive to enhance or break the solidarity of the group. Elites seeking to mobilize the ethnic group against its rivals or against the state strive to promote a congruence of a multiplicity of the group's symbols, to argue that members of the group are different not in one respect only but in many and that all its cultural elements are reinforcing."[12]

Cultural identity according to this view is not a fixed or given dimension of communities but a variable one which takes form in the process of political

mobilization by the elite, a mobilization which arises from the broader political and economic environment. Brass questions the import of the primary
dimensions of ethnicity in the subjective lives of individuals. Most people, he
says, never think about their language at all. Millions, both in traditional and
modern societies, have migrated to other countries out of choice (or necessity). And though many may have an emotional attachment to their place of
birth or ancestral religion, many others have chosen to assimilate to their
new societies and have lost all connection to their origins.

Brass's case for the relative insignificance of primordiality appears to be
overstated. Cultural identity, like its individual counterpart, is an unconscious human acquirement which becomes consciously salient only when
there is a perceived threat to its integrity. Identity, both individual and cultural, lives itself for the most part, unfettered and unworried by obsessive and
excessive scrutiny. Everyday living incorporates a zone of indifference with
regard to one's culture, including one's language, ethnic origin, or religion.
It is only when this zone of indifference is breached that the dimensions
of ethnicity stand out in sharp relief and the individual becomes painfully
or exhilaratingly aware of certain aspects of one's cultural identity. The
breaches in the zone of indifference, like the ones which took place in the
aftermath of the demolition of the Babri mosque, are not only made by momentous external events such as actual or threatened persecution, war, riots,
and so on. Inner psychological changes at certain stages of the life cycle may
also cause these fateful incursions. Thus, for instance, youth is regarded as a
period of life when issues of personal identity become crucial, when the conscious and unconscious preoccupation with the question "Who am I?"
reaches its peak. Many migrants, who have willingly chosen to thoroughly
assimilate themselves into their new societies and appear to have lost all
traces of their ethnic origins, are surprised to find that the issues of cultural
identity have not disappeared. They have only skipped a generation as their
sons and daughters, on the verge of adulthood, become preoccupied with
their cultural roots as part of their quest for a personal identity.

I do not mean to imply that the instrumentalist approach is without substance. It is also not a monopoly of professional social scientists but is shared
by many people in other walks of life. In Indian towns and cities where there
have been riots between Hindus and Muslims, I have normally found that
"men of goodwill" from both communities invariably attribute the riots to the
machinations and manipulations of politicians pursuing political power or
economic advantage rather than to any increase in primordial sentiments, a
perspective which is also shared by people who are far removed from the

[margin note: All of which makes it easier for charismatic leaders to be manipulative.]

conflict. The instrumentalist theory of ethnic mobilization thus becomes an "instigator" theory of violent conflict among religious groups. In concentrating on the instigators, it underplays or downright denies that there are "instigatees," too, whose participation is essential to transform animosity between religious groups into violence. The picture it holds up of evil politicians and innocent masses is certainly attractive since it permits us a disavowal of our own impulses toward violence and vicious ethnocentrism. We all have different zones of indifference beyond which our own ethnocentrism, in some form or the other, will become a salient part of our identity.

The appeal of the instrumentalist or instigator theory, however, is not only that it allows us a projection of the unacceptable parts of ourselves onto "bad" politicians. Its allure is also due to a particular historical legacy of the literary elite in all major civilizations. This legacy devalues nonrational processes—what psychoanalysts call "fantasy"—which form the basis of the primordial approach. As has been pointed out by others in a different context, the culture of fantasy lacks all meaningful status in the realm of serious public discourse which is comprised of the discussion of ideas, not of shared fantasies.[13] Fantasy is regarded as primitive, primordial, before reason; it is unconscious as compared to conscious, mythic as compared to scientific, marked by the pleasures of connotation rather than the rigors of denotation. A sensitive, introspective discussion of socially shared fantasies (rather than ideas) as the moving force behind the ideals and ambitions of large groups and communities is generally not possible. Steeped in a long tradition of respect for the culture of ideas and their own professional role in its production and propagation, the scholarly elite of a society are not easily receptive to the culture of fantasy.

I do not mean to imply that the political and psychological, the instrumental and the primordial, approaches should be viewed in either/or terms. Both the approaches are complementary to each other. Whether it be the history of Hindu-Muslim relations, or the analysis of the causes of the riots between the two communities (economic-political versus social-psychological), or the explanation for the basis of emerging religious group identities (instrumental interests versus primordial attachments), the arguments are invariably couched in a dualistic either/or mode. This, of course, is a testimony to the strong hold of the Aristotelian and Cartesian ways of thinking on modern minds. Like most shared habits, we do not recognize this kind of thinking as mere habit but take it for granted as an unquestioned verity, as the way things "naturally" are. Complementary thinking does not mean that "anything goes," in a vulgar postmodernist sense. It has its own definitional constraints and boundaries; for instance, the more incompatible (not outlandish) the explanations for a phenomenon, the more complementary they will be. Complementarity is the belonging-together of various possibilities of experiencing the same object differently. The wave and particle theories of light in physics, the primary and secondary processes in psychoanalysis, *mythos* and *logos* as modes of knowledge, are a few of the many examples of complementarity. Forms of complementary knowledge belong together in so far as they pertain to the same object; they exclude each other in that they cannot occur simultaneously. Complementarity is the acceptance of different possibilities and not their splitting and the exclusion of some. To describe a phenomenon complementarily is to reveal its wholeness, to understand its different aspects.[14] None of these aspects is more true than others; each is irreplaceable. In brief, the logic underlying complementary thought is not of an either/or kind but of an "as well as" variety. Thus, without the psychological perspective to complement the political-economic one, we will have only a partial and thus dangerously inadequate understanding of the reasons for the success of political formations based on religious mobilization.

Search for Hindu-ness

The instrumentalist approach to cultural identity, however, makes an important contribution by pointing out that these identities are not fixed and immutable but more or less variable. The self-consciousness of being a Hindu today is not of the same order as at other times in India's history. What is today called "Hinduism" has emerged through many encounters between dissenting sects professing diverse beliefs and with other, more self-conscious religions, such as Islam and Christianity.

Today, there is a new Hindu identity under construction in many parts of India, especially the northern and central states. It is a process which is undoubtedly propelled by the fact that this identity is also the basis of political mobilization by the main opposition party, the Bharatiya Janata Party (BJP). Created out of a preexisting though ill-defined and amorphous "Hinduism," the new identity bears only a faint family resemblance to its progenitors. Indeed, as we saw in the first chapter, some scholars argue that the sharply differentiated cultural identities of Hindus and Muslims which we encounter today, with their heightened self-consciousness, the kind of commitment they command, and the intensity with which these identities are pursued politically, are a creation of the British colonial period. They are not only a product of the colonial "divide and rule" policies which led to the emergence of "identity politics" but are also a consequence of the imposition of alien modes of thought on native Indian categories. The political scientist Don Miller remarks: "By their education, legislation, administration, judicial codes and procedures and even by that apparently simple operation of 'objective' classification, the census, the British unwittingly imposed dualistic 'either-or' oppositions as the 'natural' normative order of thought. In a multitude of ways, Indians learned that one is either this or that; that one cannot be both or neither or indifferent. The significance of identity thus became a new, paramount concern . . . an orthodoxy of being was gradually replacing a heterodoxy of beings."[15]

Leaving the issue of pinpointing the time and place of birth of the new Hindu identity in the late twentieth century to historians—an identity which its critics have decried as Hindu nationalism, Hindu militancy, or Hindu fundamentalism—we can only observe that this identity selects many of its symbols, myths, and images from a traditional stock. The cultural values and forms it endorses have a recognizable ancestry. In its strong links with the past, this Hindu identity is neither wholly new nor completely old. It is constructed, yet also revived; it is a combination of the made and the given. The social and political forces which are self-consciously active in its constructed revival, the *sangh parivar,* have some truth on their side when they maintain that the elements of this new Hindu identity were always there; it is just that people did not see them before. The question of whether those propagating the new Hindu identity are embarked on its construction or merely on its articulation for others does not have a simple answer. The answer depends upon whether the vantage point is of an outside observer or of the insider directly engaged in the process. In any event, the political countering of this Hindu identity will involve the offer of a different Hindutva with other images, symbols, and myths of the Hindu ethos rather than any abstract concept of secularism, which for most Hindus is empty of all psychological meaning.

The Virtuous Virago

To look more closely at the constructed revival of Hindu identity, I have chosen as my text a speech by *sadhavi* Rithambra, one of the star speakers for the *sangh parivar,* the prefix *sadhavi* being the female counterpart of *sadhu,* a man who has renounced the world in search of personal salvation and universal welfare within the Hindu religious worldview. It is reported that Rithambra was a sixteen-year-old schoolgirl in Khanna, a village in the Punjab, when she had a strong spiritual experience while listening to a discourse by Swami Parmananda, one of the many "saints" in the forefront of Hindu revivalism.[16]

Rithambra abandoned her studies and home and joined Parmananda's *ashram*. Soon she began traveling with her guru to religious meetings in the Hindu heartland and after a while addressed a few herself. Her oratorical talents were noticed by the political leadership of the *sangh parivar* and, after being given some training in voice modulation, she was well on her way to become the leading firebrand in the Hindu cause.

The speech I have chosen was given at Hyderabad in April 1991, a few weeks after the general elections for the national parliament and many state assemblies were announced. The speech is a standard one which Rithambra has given all over India to the enthusiastic response of hundreds of thousands of people. The political context of the speech is the bid by the BJP, the political arm of the *sangh* family, to capture power in some north Indian states in the coming elections and to emerge as the single largest party in the national parliament. In the preceding months, the BJP had determined the country's political agenda by its mobilization of Hindus on the issue of constructing a temple to the god Ram at Ayodhya, his reputed birthplace. The construction of this temple had become an explosive and divisive issue since the designated site was already occupied by Babri *masjid*, a mosque built by Babar, the Muslim invader from Central Asia who was the founder of the Mughal dynasty that ruled over large parts of India for over four hundred years. There had been much bloodshed five months earlier as many Hindus, the *kar-sevaks*, lost their lives in police firing when they attempted to defy legal orders and begin the temple construction, a step which required demolition or at least relocation of the existing mosque. The killings of unarmed Ram *bhaktas*— devotees of Ram—in Ayodhya, led to a spate of riots between Hindus and Muslims in other parts of the country, including Hyderabad, a city with an almost equal proportion of the two communities and where the tension between them over the years had regularly erupted in communal violence.

The political context of the speech, the theme of temple versus mosque, the abundance of imagery and allusions in its text to the narratives of the epics Ramayana and the Mahabharata, and the person of the speaker herself are all replete with symbolic resonances, evocations, and associations. They virtually reek with a surfeit of meaning that burrows deep in the psychic recesses of the audience, going well beyond the words used as its carriers. Listening to her speak, the earlier question is once again raised: Is she an elite manipulator of Hindu cultural symbols (instrumental theory) or is she an articulator of what many Hindus feel but cannot express (primordialist viewpoint)? The answer is again not in terms of either/or but of the simultaneity of both processes. Rithambra appeals to a group identity while creating it.

She both mirrors her listeners' sentiments and gives them birth. My impression is that the images, metaphors, and mythological allusions of her speech have a resonance for the audience because they also have a resonance for her. This does not imply that the speech is a spontaneous pouring out of her heart. Like an actor she has honed this particular speech through successive deliveries and knows what "works." It is not raw feeling but carefully crafted emotion; an epic poem rather than a scream or a shout. Rithambra's power lies less in her persuasiveness on an intellectual, cognitive plane than on the *poetic* (Greek *poiesis*—a making, shaping) that permeates her speech. It is this poetic which gives a first form to what are for her audience only vaguely or partially ordered feelings and perceptions, makes a shared sense out of already shared circumstances.[17]

As a renouncer of worldly life, a *sanyasin*, Rithambra conjures up the image of selflessness. Associatively, she is not a politician stirred by narrow electoral considerations or identified with partisan interest groups but someone who is moved by the plight of the whole country, even concerned with the welfare of all mankind. As an ascetic who has renounced all sexual activity, she evokes the image of the virgin goddess, powerful because virgin, a power which is of another, "purer" world. There is also a subtle sexual challenge to the men in her audience to prove their virility (vis-à-vis the Muslim) in order to deserve her.

The key passages in the text of her speech are delivered as rhyming verses, in the tradition of bardic narration of stories from the Hindu epics. Perhaps people tend to believe verse more than prose, especially in Hindu India where the transmission of sacred knowledge has traditionally been oral and through the medium of rhymed verse. In any event, implicit in her speech is the claim to be less tainted with the corruption of language, a corruption which is widely laid at the door of the politician and which has led people to lose faith in what they hear from public platforms. If Rithambra is a politician, hers is the politics of magic that summons forces from the deep, engaging through coded ideas and ideals the deeper fears and wishes of her Hindu audiences whom she and the *sangh parivar* are determined to make "more" Hindu. As I listened to her I was once again reminded of Milan Kundera's statement that "political movements rest not so much on rational attitudes as on fantasies, images, words and archetypes that come together to make up this or that political kitsch."

Hail Mother Sita! Hail brave Hanuman! Hail Mother India! Hail the birth place of Ram! Hail Lord Vishwanath [Shiva] of Kashi [Benares]!

> Hail Lord Krishna! Hail the eternal religion [*dharma*]! Hail the religion
> of the Vedas! Hail Lord Mahavira! Hail Lord Buddha! Hail Banda Bair-
> agi! Hail Guru Gobind Singh! Hail the great sage Dayananda! Hail the
> great sage Valmiki! Hail the martyred *kar-sevaks*! Hail Mother India!

In ringing tones Rithambra invokes the various gods and revered figures
from Indian history, ancient and modern. The gods and heroes are not ran-
domly chosen. In their careful selection, they are markers of the boundary of
the Hindu community she and the *sangh parivar* would wish to constitute today and believe existed in the past. Such a commemoration is necessarily
selective since it must silence contrary interpretations of the past and seek to
conserve only certain of its aspects. The gods and heroes are offered up as
ego ideals, to be shared by members of the community in order to bring
about and maintain group cohesion. Identity implies definition rather than
blurring, solidity rather than flux or fluidity, and therefore the question of
boundaries of a group become paramount. Rithambra begins the construction of Hindu identity by demarcating this boundary.

In the context of the preceding year's agitation around the construction
of the Ram temple, the god Ram occupies the highest watchtower on the
border between Hindu and non-Hindu. Rithambra starts by praising Ram's
wife, the goddess Sita, and his greatest devotee, the monkey god Hanuman,
who are then linked to contemporary concerns as she hails Ram's birthplace
where the *sangh parivar* wishes to construct the controversial temple and
around which issue it has sought a mobilization of the Hindus.

The five-thousand-year-old religion, however, with a traditional lack of
central authority structures such as a church and with a diffused essence, has
over the centuries thrown up a variety of sects with diverse beliefs. It is
Rithambra's purpose to include all the Hinduisms spawned by Hinduism.
The presiding deity of the Shaivite sects, Shiva, is hailed, as is Krishna, the
most popular god of the Vaishnavas.

The overarching Hindu community is then sought to be further en-
larged by including the followers of other religions whose birthplace is India.
These are the Jains, the Buddhists, and the Sikhs, and Rithambra devoutly
hails Mahavira, Buddha, and the militant last guru of the Sikhs, Guru Gobind
Singh who, together with Banda Bairagi, has the added distinction of a lifetime of armed struggle against the Mughals. Nineteenth-century reformist
movements such as the Arya Samaj are welcomed by including its founder
Dayananda Saraswati in the Hindu pantheon. The Harijans or "scheduled"
castes, the former "untouchables" of Hindu society, are expressly acknowledged as a part of the Hindu community by hailing Valmiki, the legendary

author of the Ramayana who has been recently elevated to the position of the patron saint of the Harijans.

From gods and heroes of the past, a link is established to the collective heroism of the *kar-sevaks*, men and women who in their bid to build the temple died in the police firing at Ayodhya. The immortal gods and the mortal heroes from past and present are all the children of Mother India, the subject of the final invocation, making the boundaries of the Hindu community co-terminous with that of Indian nationalism.

I have come to the Hindus of Bhagyanagar [Hyderabad] with a message. The saints who met in Allahabad directed Hindu society to either bend the government to its will or to remove it. The government has been removed. On the fourth of April, more that two and a half million Hindus displayed their power at the lawns of Delhi's Boat Club. We went to the Parliament but it lay empty. The saints said, fill the parliament with the devotees of Ram. This is the next task of Hindu society.

As far as the construction of the Ram temple is concerned, some people say Hindus should not fight over a structure of brick and stone. They should not quarrel over a small piece of land. I want to ask these people, "If someone burns the national flag will you say 'Oh, it doesn't matter. It is only two meters of cloth which is not a great national loss.' "The question is not of two meters of cloth but of an insult to the nation. Ram's birthplace is not a quarrel about a small piece of land. It is a question of national integrity. The Hindu is not fighting for a temple of brick and stone. He is fighting for the preservation of a civilization, for his Indianness, for national consciousness, for the recognition of his true nature. We shall build the temple!

It is not the building of the temple but the building of India's national consciousness. You, the wielders of state power, you do not know that the Ram temple is not a mere building. It is not a construction of brick and stone. It is not only the birthplace of Ram. The Ram temple is our honor. It is our self-esteem. It is the image of Hindu unity. We shall raise its flag. We shall build the temple!

Hindi is a relatively passionate language. Its brilliant, loud colors are impossible to reproduce in the muted palette of English. As the Ram temple takes shape in Rithambra's cascading flow of language, as she builds it, phrase by phrase, in the minds of her listeners, it evokes acute feelings of a shared social loss. The Ram temple, then, is a response to the mourning of Hindu society: a mourning for lost honor, lost self-esteem, lost civilization, lost Hindu-ness. It is the material and social counterpart of the individual experience of mourning. In a more encompassing formulation, the Ram birthplace temple is like other monuments which, as Peter Homans perceptively observes, "engage the immediate conscious experience of an aggregate of egos by re-presenting and mediating to them the lost cultural experiences of the past; the experiences of individuals, groups, their ideas and ideals, which coalesce into what can be called a collective memory. In this the monument is a symbol of union because it brings together the particular psychological circumstances of many individuals' life courses and the universals of their otherwise lost historical past within the context of their current or contemporary social processes and structures."[18] The temple is the body in which Hindu identity is sought to be embodied.

Some people became afraid of Ram's devotees. They brought up Mandal.* They thought the Hindu will get divided. He will be fragmented by the reservations issue. His attention will be diverted from the temple. But your thought was wrong. Your thought was despicable. We shall build the temple!

I have come to tell our Hindu youth, do not take the candy of reservations and divide yourself into castes. If Hindus get divided, the sun of Hindu unity will set. How will the sage Valmiki look after Sita? How will Ram eat Shabri's berries [ber]?** Those who wish that our bonds with the backward castes and the Harijans are cut will bite dust. We shall build the temple!

Listen, Ram is the representation of mass consciousness. He is the god of the poor and the oppressed. He is the life of fisherman, cobblers, and washermen.*** If anyone is not a devotee of such a god, he does not have Hindu blood in his veins. We shall build the temple!

Marking its boundary, making it aware of a collective cultural loss, giving it a body, is not enough to protect and maintain the emerging Hindu identity. For identity is not an achievement but a process constantly threatened with rupture by forces from within and without.

Constant vigil is needed to guard it from that evil inside the group which

*Mandal refers to the reservation policy announced by the government of V. P. Singh at the height of the temple agitation. The policy sought to increase reservations in federal and state employment and admission to educational institutions for the backward castes at the expense of the upper castes.
**The sage Valmiki, reputedly a hunter belonging to a low caste, gave asylum to Sita in his forest abode after she was banished by Rama. Shabri was a poor untouchable who fed berries to Ram during his exile.
***All of them belong to the lowest castes.

seeks to divide what has been recently united, to disrupt and fragment what has been freshly integrated. Rithambra addresses the feeling of threat and singles out the political forces representing this threat which must be defeated at the coming battle of the ballot box.

My Hindu brothers! Stop shouting that slogan, "Give one more push and break the Babri mosque! The mosque is broken, the mosque is broken!" What mosque are you talking about? We are going to build our temple there not break anyone's mosque. Our civilization has never been one of destruction. Intellectuals and scholars of the world, wherever you find ruins, wherever you come upon broken monuments, you will find the signature of Islam. Wherever you find creation, you discover the signature of the Hindu. We have never believed in breaking but in constructing. We have always been ruled by the maxim, "The world is one family" [*vasudhe kuttumbkam*]. We are not pulling down a monument, we are building one.

Scholars, turn the pages of history and tell us whether the Hindu, riding a horse and swinging a bloody sword, has ever trampled on anyone's human dignity? We cannot respect those who have trod upon humanity. Our civilization has given us great insights. We see god in a stone, we see god in trees and plants. We see god in a dog and run behind him with a cup of butter. Hindus have you forgotten that the saint Namdev had only one piece of bread to eat which was snatched by a dog. Namdev ran after the dog with a cup of butter crying, "Lord, don't eat dry bread. Take some butter too!!" Can the Hindu who sees god even in a dog ever harbor resentment towards a Muslim?

Wherever I go, I say, "Muslims, live and prosper among us. Live like milk and sugar. If two kilos of sugar are dissolved in a quintal of milk, the milk becomes sweet!" But what can be done if our Muslim brother is not behaving like sugar in the milk? Is it our fault if he seems bent upon being a lemon in the milk? He wants the milk to curdle. He is behaving like a lemon in the milk by following people like Shahabuddin and Abdullah Bukhari.* I say to him "Come to your senses. The value of the milk increases after it becomes sour. It becomes cheese. But the world knows the fate of the lemon. It is cut, squeezed dry and then thrown on the garbage heap. Now you have to decide whether you will act like sugar or like a lemon in the milk. Live among us like the son of a human being and we will respectfully call you 'uncle.' But if you want to be

*Widely regarded as two of the leaders of Muslim fundamentalism in India.

have like the son of Babar then the Hindu youth will deal with you as Rana Pratap and Chatrapati Shivaji* dealt with your forefathers." Those who say we are against the Muslims, lie. We are talking of the birthplace of Ram, not constructing at Mecca or Medina. It is our birthright to build a temple to our Lord at the spot he was born.

We have religious tolerance in our very bones. Together with our three hundred and thirty million gods, we have worshipped the dead lying in their graves. Along with Ram and Krishna, we have saluted Mohammed and Jesus. With *vasudhe kuttumbkam* as our motto, we pray for the salvation of the world and for increase in fellow feeling in all human beings. We have never said, "O World! Believe in our Upanishads, Believe in our Gita. Otherwise you are an infidel and by cutting off the head of an infidel one gains paradise." Our sentiments are not so low. They are not narrow-minded. They are not dirty. We see the world as our family.

Here, in the construction of the Hindu identity, we see the necessary splitting that enhances group cohesion. The process involves idealizing on the one hand and scapegoating and persecutory processes on the other. What is being idealized is the Hindu tolerance, compassion, depth of insight, and width of social concern. These are the contents of a grandiose Hindu group self which makes the individual member feel righteous and pure. It raises each member's sense of worth for belonging to this group.

The increase in self-esteem can be maintained only by projecting the bad, the dirty, and the impure to another group, the Muslim, with which one's own group is then constantly compared. This process is at the root of scapegoating and, as Rafael Moses reminds us, this indeed is how the original scapegoat was conceived of in religion: the animal was driven away with all the community's badness inside it so that the community of believers could remain pure and clean (like milk, I am tempted to add). [19] Of course, as a good vegetarian Hindu, *sadhavi* Rithambra conceives the Muslim scapegoat not as an animal but as a lemon. As we shall see below, the Muslim is not only the object of scapegoating but also the subject of persecutory fantasies in collective Hindu imagination.

Today, the Hindu is being insulted in his own home. The Hindu is not sectarian. How could he be if he worships trees and plants! Once [the Mughal emperor] Akbar and [his Hindu minister] Birbal were going

---

*Popular embodiments of Hindu resistance to Mughal rule.

somewhere. On the way they saw a plant. Birbal dismounted and prostrated himself before the plant saying, "Hail mother *tulsi!*" Akbar said,
"Birbal, you Hindus are out of your minds, making parents out of trees
and plants. Let's see how strong is your mother!" He got off his horse,
pulled the *tulsi* plant out by its roots and threw it on the road. Birbal
swallowed this humiliation and kept quiet. What could he do? It was
the reign of the Mughals. They rode farther and saw another plant.
Birbal again prostrated himself saying, "Hail, father! Hail, honored father!" Akbar said, "Birbal I have dealt with your mother. Now, let me
deal with your father too." He again pulled out the plant and threw it
away. The plant was a nettle. Akbar's hands started itching and soon
the painful itch spread all over his body. He began rolling on the
ground like a donkey, with tears in his eyes and his nose watering. All
the while he was scratching himself like a dog. When Birbal saw this
condition of his king, he said, "O Protector of the World, pardon my
saying that our Hindu mothers may be innocent but our fathers are
hard-bitten." Akbar asked, "Birbal, how do I get rid of your father?" Birbal said, "Go and ask forgiveness of my mother *tulsi*. Then rub the paste
made out of her leaves on your body and my father will pardon you."

I mean to say that the long-suffering Hindu is being called a religious zealot today only because he wants to build the temple. The
Muslims got their Pakistan. Even in a mutilated India, they have special
rights. They have no use for family planning. They have their own religious schools. What do we have? An India with its arms cut off.* An
India where restrictions are placed on our festivals, where our processions are always in danger of attack, where the expression of our opinion is prohibited, where our religious beliefs are cruelly derided. We
cannot speak of our pain, express our hurt. I say to the politician, "Do
not go on trampling upon our deepest feelings as you have been doing
for so long."

In Kashmir, the Hindu was a minority and was hounded out of the
valley. Slogans of "Long live Pakistan" were carved with red hot iron
rods on the thighs of our Hindu daughters. Try to feel the unhappiness
and the pain of the Hindu who became a refugee in his own country.
The Hindu was dishonored in Kashmir because he was in a minority.
But there is a conspiracy to make him a minority in the whole country.
The state tells us Hindus to have only two or three children. After a

---

*The reference is to a comparison between the maps of India before and after the partition.

while, they will say do not have even one. But what about those who have six wives, have thirty or thirty-five children and breed like mosquitoes and flies?

Why should there be two sets of laws in this country? Why should we be treated like stepchildren? I submit to you that when the Hindu of Kashmir became a minority he came to Jammu. From Jammu he came to Delhi. But if you Hindus are on the run all over India, where will you go? Drown in the Indian Ocean or jump from the peaks of the Himalayas?

What is this impartiality toward all religions where the *mullahs* get the moneybags and Hindus the bullets? We also want religious impartiality but not of the kind where only Hindus are oppressed. People say there should be Hindu-Muslim unity. Leave the structure of the Babri mosque undisturbed. I say, "Then let's have this unity in case of the Jama *masjid** too. Break half of it and construct a temple. Hindus and Muslims will then come together."

You know the doctors who carry out their medical experiments by cutting open frogs, rabbits, cats? All these experiments in Hindu-Muslim unity are being carried out on the Hindu chest as if he is a frog, rabbit or cat. No one has ever heard of a lion's chest being cut open for a medical experiment. They teach the lesson of religious unity and amity only to be Hindus.

In Lucknow there was a Muslim procession which suddenly stopped when passing a temple where a saffron flag was flying. The *mullahs* said, "This is the flag of infidels. We cannot pass even under its shadow. Take down the flag!" Some of your liberal Hindu leaders and followers of Gandhi started persuading the Hindus, "Your ancestors have endured a great deal. You also tolerate a little. You have been born to suffer. Take down the flag." Luckily, I was also there. I said to the leader who was trying to cajole the Hindus into taking down the flag, "If I took off your cap, gave four blows to your head with my shoe and then replaced the cap, will you protest?" This is not just our flag, it is our honor, our pride. Religious impartiality does not mean that to appease one you insult the other. Hindu children were riddled with bullets in the alleys of Ayodhya to please the Muslims. The Saryu river became red with the blood of slaughtered *kar-sevak*s. We shall not forget.

It is true that for the strengthening of cultural identity, belief of the group members in an existing or anticipated oppression is helpful, if not nec-

---

*The best known Indian mosque, located in Delhi.

essary. Yet for the eight hundred million Hindus who are relatively more advanced on almost every economic and social criteria, to feel oppressed by
Muslims who are one-eighth their number demands an explanation other
than one given by the theory of relative deprivation. This theory, as we
know, argues that a group feels oppressed if it perceives inequality in the distribution of resources and believes it is entitled to more than the share it receives. There is a considerable denial of reality involved in maintaining that
the Hindus are relatively deprived or in danger of oppression by the Muslims. Such a denial of reality is only possible through the activation of the
group's persecutory fantasy in which the Muslim changes from a stereotype
to an archetype; he becomes the "arch" tyrant. As in individuals, where persecution anxiety often manifests itself in threats to the integrity of the body,
especially during psychotic episodes, Rithambra's speech becomes rich in
the imagery of a mutilated body. Eloquently, she conjures up an India—the
motherland—with its arms cut off, Hindu chests cut open like those of frogs,
rabbits, and cats, the thighs of young Hindu women burnt with red-hot iron
rods; in short, the body amputated, slashed, raped. It is the use of metaphors
of the body—one's own and of one's mother (India)—under assault that
makes an actual majority feel a besieged minority in imagination, that an-
chors the dubious logos of a particular political argument deeply in fantasy
through the power of mythos.

> They said, "Let's postpone the mid-term elections till the Hindu's anger
> cools down." I say, "Is the Hindu a bottle of mineral water? Keep the
> bottle open for a while and the water will stop bubbling?" It is nine
> hundred thousand years since Ravana kidnapped Sita and challenged
> god Ram. But to this day we have not forgotten. Every year we burn his
> effigy and yet the fire of our revenge burns bright. We will not forget
> *mullah* Mulayam* and his supporter Rajiv Gandhi. I have come to tell
> the young men and mothers of Bhagyanagar, listen to the wailing of
> the Saryu river, listen to the story told by Ayodhya, listen to the sacri-
> fice of the *kar-sevaks*. If you are a Hindu, do not turn your face away
> from the Ram temple, do not spare the traitors to Ram.
>
> After the incident on the ninth of November, many Hindu young
> men came to me. "Sister," they said, "Give us weapons to deal with *mul-
> lah* Mulayam." I said, "Why waste a bullet to deal with an eunuch?" Ram
> had become tired shooting his arrows. Ravana's one head would fall to
> be immediately replaced by another. Vibhishna [Ravana's brother]

---

*The chief minister of Uttar Pradesh.

said, "Lord, you will not kill this sinner by cutting off his heads. His life is in his navel." My brother Hindus, these leaders have their lives in their chairs [of power]. Take away their power and they'll die—by themselves. They are only impotent eunuchs. When Ram was banished from Ayodhya many citizens accompanied him to the forest and stayed there overnight. In the morning, Ram said, "Men and women of Ayodhya, go back to your homes." The men and women went back but a group of hermaphrodites, who are neither men nor women, stayed back and asked, "Lord, you have not given us any instructions." Ram is kind. He said, "In the future Kaliyuga you will rule for a little while." These, neither-men-nor-women, are your rulers today. They will not be able to protect India's unity and integrity.

Make the next government one of Ram's devotees. Hindus, you must unite in the coming elections if you want the temple built. Hindus, if you do not awaken, cows will be slaughtered everywhere. In the retreats of our sages you will hear the chants of "Allah is Great." You will be responsible for the catastrophes for history will say Hindus were cowards. Accept the challenge, change the history of our era.

Many say, Rithambra you are a *sanyasin.* You should meditate in some retreat. I tell them raising Hindu consciousness is my meditation now and it will go on till the saffron flag flies from the ramparts of the Red Fort.*

The feeling of helplessness which persecution anxiety engenders reverses the process of idealization, reveals the fragility of the group's grandiose self. The positive self-image of the Hindu—tolerant, compassionate, with special insight into the relationship between the divine and the natural worlds, between human and divine—exposes another, negative side: the specific Hindu shame and fear of being cowardly and impotent to change the material or social conditions of life. Indeed, we should always look closely at a group's specific form of self-idealization to find clues to its particular moment of self-doubt and self-hatred. What a group most idealizes about itself is intimately related to its greatest fear. For the Hindu, the positive self-image of tolerance has the shadow of weakness cleaving to it. Are we tolerant or are we merely weak? Or tolerant *because* weak?

The crumbling self, with its unbearable state of helplessness, demands restoration through forceful action. Rithambra channels this need for *agens* into a call for collective and united action in the political arena. She holds out

*The symbol of political power in India.

the possibility of some kind of self-assertion through the coming electoral process where all the persecutory anti-Hindu forces, from within and without the Hindu fold, can be engaged and defeated. With this prospect, the negative self-image begins to fade, the group self becomes more cohesive. The Muslim, too, though remaining alien, becomes less demonic and more human, although still a cussed adversary.

> They ask what would happen to the Muslims in a Hindu India? I tell them the Muslims will not be dishonored in a Hindu state nor will they be rewarded to get their votes. No umbrella will open in Indian streets because it is raining in Pakistan. If there is war in the Gulf then slogans of "Long Live Saddam Hussein" won't be shouted on Indian streets. And as for unity with our Muslim brothers, we say, "Brother, we are willing to eat *sevian* [sweet noodles] at your house to celebrate *Id* but you do not want to play with colors with us on Holi. We hear your calls to prayer along with our temple bells, but you object to our bells. How can unity ever come about? The Hindu faces this way, the Muslim the other. The Hindu writes from left to right, the Muslim from right to left. The Hindu prays to the rising sun, the Muslim faces the setting sun when praying. If the Hindu eats with the right hand, the Muslim with the left. If the Hindu calls India "Mother," she becomes a witch for the Muslim. The Hindu worships the cow, the Muslim attains paradise by eating beef. The Hindu keeps a mustache, the Muslim always shaves the upper lip. Whatever the Hindu does, it is the Muslim's religion to do its opposite. I said, "If you want to do everything contrary to the Hindu, then the Hindu eats with his mouth; you should do the opposite in this matter too!"

After the laughter subsides, Rithambra ends by asking the audience to raise their fists and repeat after her. "Say with pride, we are Hindus! Hindustan [India] is ours!"

The conclusion of Rithambra's speech complements its beginning. Both the beginning and the end are concerned with the issue of drawing the boundaries of the group of "us" Hindus. Whereas Rithambra began with a self-definition of the Hindu by including certain kinds of Hinduisms—as personified by heroes, gods, and historical figures—she ends with trying to achieve this self-definition through contrasts with what a Hindu is decidedly not—the Muslim. At the start, the boundary was drawn from inside out; at the end, its contours are being marked off by reference to the "them," the Muslims, who lie outside the psychogeographical space inhabited by "us." It is, of course, understood that "their" space is not only separate and different but also devalued. In her enumeration of differences Rithambra cleverly contrives to end at a note which associates the Muslim with certain denigrated, specifically anal, bodily parts and functions.

I have suggested here that the construction/revival of the new Hindu identity in the text of Rithambra's speech follows certain well-marked turnings of the plot which is motivated, energized, and animated by fantasy. To recapitulate, these are: marking afresh the boundaries of the religious-cultural community, making the community conscious of a collective cultural loss, countering internal forces which seek to disrupt the unity of the freshly demarcated community, idealizing the community, maintaining its sense of grandiosity by comparing it to a bad "other" which, at times, becomes a persecutor and, finally, dealing with the persecutory fantasies, which bring up to the surface the community's particular sense of inferiority, by resort to some kind of forceful action.

In describing these psychological processes, I am aware that my own feelings toward the subject could have colored some of my interpretations. This is unavoidable, especially since I am a Hindu myself, exposed to all the crosscurrents of feelings generated by contemporary events. My own brand of Hinduism, liberal-rationalist (with a streak of agnostic mysticism) can be expected to be critical of the new Hindu identity envisaged by the *sangh parivar.* Thus, to be fair (the liberal failing par excellence), one should add that the Hindu is no different from any other community or even nation which feels special and superior to other collectivities, especially their neighbors and rivals. This sense of superiority, the group's narcissism, its self-aggrandizement, serves the purpose of increasing group cohesion and thus the enhancement of self-esteem of its members. Rafael Moses, reflecting on the group selves of the Israelis and the Arabs, asks: "And is perhaps a little grandiosity the right glue for such a cohesion? Is that perhaps the same measure of grandiosity which is seen in the family and does it serve the same purpose, thereby strengthening the feeling of specialness and of some grandiosity which all of us harbor in ourselves?"[20]

The *sangh parivar* cannot be faulted for fostering a Hindu pride or even for trying to claim a sense of superiority vis-à-vis the Muslim. These are the normal aims of any group's narcissistic economy. Perhaps we recoil from such aims because narcissism, both in individuals and groups, is regarded with much misgiving. A person who is a victim of passions, sexual and aggressive, may be pitied and even seen by some as tragically heroic. An individual propelled by narcissism, on the other hand, is invariably scorned as mean and contemptible. Whereas the perversions of sex may evoke sympathy, the miscarriages of narcissism, such as a smug superiority or an arrogant self-righteousness, provoke distaste among even the most tolerant. The question is not of the *sangh parivar's* fostering of Hindu narcissism (which, we know, serves individual self-possession) but of when this narcissism becomes deviant or abnormal. The answer is not easy for I do not know of any universal, absolute standards which can help us in charting narcissistic deviance or pathology in a group. One would imagine that the promotion of persecutory fantasies in a group to the extent that it resorts to violence against the persecuting Other would be deviant. Yet we all know that a stoking of persecutory fantasies is the stock in trade of all nations on the eve of any war and continues well into the duration of hostilities.

One could say that a group wherein all individual judgment is suspended and reality-testing severely disturbed may legitimately be regarded as pathological. This, however, is an individualistic viewpoint which looks askance at any kind of self-transcendence through immersion in a group. In this view, spiritual uplift in a religious assembly, where the person feels an upsurge of love enveloping the community and the world outside, would be regarded with the same grave suspicion as the murkier purposes of a violent mob. It is certainly true that transcending individuality by merging into a group can generate heroic self-sacrifice, but it can also generate unimaginable brutality. To get out of one's skin in a devotional assembly is also at the same time to have less regard for saving that skin when part of a mob. Yet to equate and thus condemn both is to deny the human aspiration toward self-transcendence, a promise held out by our cultural identity and redeemed, if occasionally, by vital participation in the flow of a community's cultural life.

It is, however, evident that it is this group pride and narcissism which have made it possible for the Hindutva forces to offer another vision of India's future as an alternative to those offered by the modernists and the traditionalists. The modernists are, of course, enthusiastic votaries of the modernization project although the Left and Right may argue over which economic form is the most suitable. Both factions, however, are neither interested in nor consider the question of cultural authenticity as important. The traditionalists, on the other hand, including the neo-Gandhians, totally reject modernity solely on the issue of cultural authenticity. The Hindutva forces have tried to offer yet another alternative by reformulating the project of modernity in a way where its instrumentalities are adopted but its norms and values are contested. The pivotal issue for them is not the acceptance of global technoscience or the economic institutions and forms of modernity but their impact on and a salvaging of Hindu culture and identity—as they define it. Cultural nationalism, though, will always have priority whenever it conflicts with economic globalism. It is apparent that such an approach to modernity will have great appeal to the emerging middle classes and sections of the intelligentsia which are committed neither to what I can only call universal modernism nor to a postmodern traditionalism.

The danger of stoking group narcissism, Hindu *garv* ("pride") in our example, is that when this group grandiosity (expressed in a belief in its unique history and/or destiny, its moral, aesthetic, technological, or any other kind of superiority vis-à-vis other groups) is brought into serious doubt, when the group feels humiliated, when higher forms of grandiosity such as the group's ambitions are blocked, then there is a regression in the group akin to one in the individual. The negative part of the grandiose self which normally remains hidden, the group's specific feelings of worthlessness and its singular sense of inferiority, now come to the fore. If all possibilities of self-assertion are closed, there is a feeling of absolute helplessness, a state which must be changed through assertive action. Such a regression, with its accompanying feelings of vulnerability and helplessness, is most clearly manifested in the sphere of group aggression which takes on, overtly and covertly, the flavor of narcissistic rage. As in the individual who seeks to alter such an unbearable self state through acts as extreme as suicide or homicide, the group's need for undoing the damage to collective identity by whatever means, and a deeply anchored, unrelenting compulsion in the pursuit of this aim give it no rest. Narcissistic rage does not vanish when the offending object disappears. The painful memory can linger on, making of the hot rage a chronic, cold resentment till it explodes in all its violent manifestations whenever historical circumstances sanction such eruptions. I am afraid Ayodhya is not an end but only a beginning since the forces buffeting Hindu (or, for that matter, Muslim) grandiosity do not lie within the country but are global in their scope. They are the forces of modernization itself, of the wonderful attractions and the terrible distortions of the mentality of Enlightenment.

It would also be easy to dismiss Rithambra's—and the *sangh parivar's*— evocation of the Hindu past from a postmodern perspective which considers every past a social construction that is shaped by the concerns of the present. In other words, there is no such thing as *the* past since the past is transformable and manipulable according to the needs of the present. Yet as the French sociologist Emile Durkheim pointed out long ago, every society displays and even requires a minimal sense of continuity with the past.[21] Its memories cannot be relevant to its present unless it secures this continuity. In a society in the throes of modernization, the need for continuity with the past, a sense of heritage, essential for maintaining a sense of individual and cultural identity, becomes even more pressing, sharply reducing the subversive attractions of a viewpoint which emphasizes the plasticity and discontinuities of the past. It is this need for a continuity of cultural memory, of a common representation of the past in times of rapid change, even turbulence, which the *sangh parivar* addresses with considerable social resonance and political success.

SEVEN

The Muslim Fundamentalist Identity

Even though the appellation "fundamentalist" is often used for stigmatiz-
ing particular groups, especially of Muslims, there is no other word
which is a satisfactory substitute. This lies in the nature of the phenomenon
itself which, with its pious passions, strong beliefs, and inflexible values, will
inevitably imbue any neutral and originally descriptive term with negative or
positive connotations. As a phenomenon, many hold the opinion that religious fundamentalism is an attempt by a religious community to preserve its
identity by a selective retrieval of doctrines, beliefs, and practices from a sacred past.[1] Although a nostalgia for the sacred past is a hallmark of fundamentalist rhetoric, the retrieved fundamentals are very often pragmatically
refined and modified. Contemporary fundamentalism is both a revival and a
construction, both derivative and original.

Muslim fundamentalism in India shares some of the abiding concerns of
Islamic fundamentalism elsewhere in the world but also has some distinct
local flavors. As the political scientist M. S. Agwani points out, there is not
one but many fundamentalisms in India of which the major varieties are associated wit the names of Deoband, Nadwah, Tablighi Jamaiat, and Jamaiat-
i-Islami.[2] Muslim fundamentalism is thus not monolithic but divided into
factions which differ not only on the means of bringing about the desired
Islamic revival but sometimes also on the preferred ends. Although they all
agree that the precepts of earliest Islam, valid for all times and climes, must
govern a person's private and collective life, that nationalism, secularism, and
materialism are un-Islamic, and that such popular practices as saint worship
at *dargah*s (shrines) and devotional music in Muslim social and religious life
are undesirable imports from Hinduism, they disagree on the desired relationship between religion and the state, or the extent of totalitarian practice
needed to enforce religious orthodoxy.

For me, fundamentalism is the third Muslim response to the loss of collective self-idealizations and the fracture in self-representation brought on by historical change. If the victim is unable to hate, the fundamentalist cannot stop hating. Whereas in the Andalus syndrome the group cannot stop mourning, one of the components of fundamentalism is the phenomenon of the "inability to mourn,"[3] an emotional state where the natural process of grieving is blocked by undue anger.

Meeting the Mullahs

The men who have traditionally spearheaded the fundamentalist response of Muslim societies and who are widely regarded as representatives of Islamic conservatism are professional men of religion, the *ulema*, with various degrees of religious learning, who are also known as *mullah*s in Persia and India. In some ways, my encounter with the *mullah*s was psychologically the most difficult. The meeting itself was undemanding since besides our animating minds the encounter only involved a disembodied voice on the *mullah*'s part and ears on mine. The *mullah*s—Qari Hanif Mohammad Multanwale, Syed Mohammad Hashmi, Maulana Salimuddin Shamshi, Riyaz Effendi, and others—came to me through their sermons recorded live at different times during the last decade at various mosques and reproduced in hundreds of thousands of inexpensive audiocasettes which are widely available in the Muslim neighborhoods of Indian towns and cities.

The encounter with the *mullah* proved difficult on two counts. First, there was the persistence of my Hindu childhood image of the *mullah* as the wild-eyed man with a flowing beard who spewed fire and brimstone every Friday afternoon in the mosque with an intent to transform his congregation into a raging mob baying for the blood of the Hindu infidel—mine. Second, the *mullah*'s rhetoric, based on older models from the heyday of Islam in the Middle East, was unpleasantly foreign to me. Openly emotional, using the full register of the voice from a whisper to the full-throated shout, screaming and on occasion weeping as he is overtaken by religious enthusiasm, the *mullah*'s style of public speaking (as of the Hindu zealot) was distasteful to me. My adult sensibility, influenced by psychoanalytic rationalism, recoils at the hectoring tone, the imperative voice, and the moral certainty which recognizes only the black of unbelief (*kufar*) and the white of faith and has neither time nor tolerance for the shades of grey.

Influenced emotionally by fantasies from a Hindu past and cognitively by the concepts of a Western-inspired liberalism, my first reaction to the *mul-*

lah was to label him a "fanatic," the word itself an eighteenth-century European coinage meant to denounce rather than describe the religious zealot. The temptation to rip open the *mullah's* facade of a just man gripped by religious passion to reveal the workings of other, baser motives was overwhelming. Indeed, the speeches of most *mullahs*, expressing contempt and indifference for everything other than the object of their passion and an unshakeable certitude in the rightness of their beliefs, seem to be verily designed for a psychoanalytically inspired hatchet job. The temptation to pathologize the *mullah* as an obsessional, if not psychopathic or even paranoid, had to be resisted if I wished to understand Muslim fundamentalism without resort to reductionist psychological clichés.[4] The first step in such an understanding was to listen to the *mullah*.

Sung in many voices and with varying lyrics, the music of the fundamentalist theme song is easily recognizable from one *mullah* to another. After a couple of obligatory *ayats* from the Qur'an in Arabic as a prelude, signifying that both the speaker and the listener are now in the realm of the sacred, the fundamentalist generally begins with a lament for the lost glories of Islam as he compares the sorry plight of Muslims today with their earlier exalted status. There may be a sizable presence of Muslims in all parts of the globe, says one *mullah*, and the mosque and the Qur'an found in every country. Yet nowhere does one hear that Muslims are thriving, successful, or on the ascendant. A hundred and sixty million Muslims are being whipped by two-and-a-half million Jews, says another. Look at the sorry fate of Iraq, a land made sacred by the blood of the Prophet's grandsons. At one time Sultan Salah-al-din Ayubi (Saladin) commanding a force of thirteen thousand in the battle for Jerusalem faced Richard's army of seven hundred thousand and killed three hundred thousand Christians on a single day. Once, in the battle for Mecca—and the first battle of Islamic history is every *mullah's* preferred illustration—the Prophet with a ragtag force of three hundred and thirteen (a number which along with the word "Karbala" has become the most effective symbol of political mobilization), including women, children, and old men, defeated the one thousand armed warriors of Abu Jahl, many of them on horseback at the battle of Badr. Today, with all the oil, dollars, and weapons in the world, Muslims are slaves to the dictates of Western Christian powers even in the thirty-six countries of which they are the putative rulers. Once, when the Muslim saint Khwaja Moinuddin Chisti died in Ajmer, nine million *kafirs* (here, the Hindus) began reading the *kalma*, that is, became Muslims. Once, at the sight of Imam Rahimullah's funeral cortege, twenty thousand Jews converted to Islam. Today, Muslims have trouble keeping their own faith alive.

The choice of historical illustrations from the early history of Islam, including their legendary elaboration, to bring home the fact of Muslim degeneration and distress in the modern world is a pan-Islamic phenomenon. Few if any civilizations have attached as much importance to history as has Islam in its awareness of itself.[5] "Recognize your history (*tarikh*)!" is the common fundamentalist exhortation, in contrast to the Hindu revivalist's implied suggested, "Live your myth!" From the Prophet's time to the present, it has been Islam which has distinguished between self and other, between brother and stranger, between the faithful and the alien *kafir*, the unbeliever. It is therefore not surprising that in fundamentalist discourse it is the wider, Arab-centered history of Islam rather than the history of Indian Muslims through which a collective Muslim identity is sought to be shaped.

After listing the symptoms of Muslim distress, the *mullahs* proceed to diagnose the disease. The bad condition of the Muslims, they aver, is not due to any major changes in the outer circumstances of Muslim lives but because of a glaring internal fault: the weakening or loss of religious faith. Muslims have lost everything—political authority, respect, the wealth of both faith (*din*) and the world (*duniya*)—because they did not keep their pact with Mohammed. At one time Allah gave Muslims the kingdom of the world only in order to test them whether they would continue to remain His slaves. Muslims have failed Allah's test. It was their religious zeal which made a small, unarmed group of Muslims succeed on the battlefield against overwhelming odds. (Now the *mullah* begins to address the listener more directly.) Today, you do not respect the Qur'an. You do not respect the Prophet who is so pure that not a single fly came near him during his lifetime, a man whose sweat smelt more divine than shiploads of perfume. You may think of yourselves as Muslims but look into the mirror of the Qur'an and you will see you are not.

The Arabs lose to the Jews in Palestine because they are fighting for land, even if it is their own land. They are not fighting for Islam, for the Prophet. Sultan Salah-al-din fought for Islam and won Palestine. On eve of the battle against Richard, he said to his soldiers: "Paradise is near, Egypt is far." He did not defend Islam by the sword but by his character as a Muslim. The Christians, as is their wont, used to send beautiful young women to seduce and corrupt Muslim generals, their priests assuring the girls forgiveness for all sins incurred in service of Christianity. Saladin rejected thirteen of the most beautiful Christian girls sent to his palace; in fact, the Christian women, impressed by the Sultan's steadfastness, read the *kalma*. On the other hand the Muslims lost India, not to the British, but because the last Mughal emperors like Mohammed Shah Rangile and Bahadur Shah Zafar were sunk in the quagmire of wine, women, and poetry.

After the diagnosis the physicians proceed to pathogenesis. The disease is caused by the process of modernity which the Muslim body has not resisted. There is no difference today between the home of a Muslim and that of a Hindu, Jew, or Christian. The sickness of television has entered Muslim homes where families fritter away whole evenings in ungodly entertainment rather than in reading from or discussing the Qur'an. Some of them say, "We watch television only for the news." I ask, "What news? Of murders and accidents? Is there any news to gladden the heart of the faithful? Where is the news that a Muslim country has conquered an infidel land?" People walk about the streets singing songs from movies, prostitute's songs, rather than with the *kalma* on their lips. They follow educated people who are the thieves of religion, who teach the separation of religion from life and from politics.

Muslims have now taken to these deeply offensive modern fashions. They no longer give a revered name such as Fatima, that of the Prophet's daughter, to their own daughters but prefer instead to name the little girl after some movie actress, a prostitute. Look at the Western-style trousers that men wear, with pockets in indecent places. You see men bending forward and taking out money from the hip pocket, next to the buttocks. In winter you can see them sliding their hands into the side pockets and taking out peanuts or cashews from the these disgusting places and putting them in the mouth.

In olden days a ruler would never permit the presence of a woman in official rooms or at public functions. A *mullah* would not perform the wedding ceremony where women were present. Now some of the rulers cannot even to go the toilet without a woman. Instead of only bowing before Allah, Muslims now bow before graves of various *pirs* ("holy men") who are three feet underground. No wonder Islam is bending under the assault of Kufar; Arabs are bowing before Jews and Christians, you before the Hindus. What is this preoccupation with worldly wealth and success? Allah says, I did not bring you into the world to make two shops out of one, four out of two, two factories out of one, four out of two. Does the Qur'an want you to do that? Does the Prophet? No! They want you to dedicate yourself to the faith, give your life for the glory of Islam.

The remedy suggested by the *mullahs* is a return to the fundamentals of the faith as contained in the Qur'an. The Qur'an is Allah's book, the light given by God to lift the darkness of mankind. Nothing can be added to or subtracted from the book. No arguments, no discussion, no objections, no asking for proofs. It is eternal and unchanging. It is not like the clothes you wear which are different for summer and winter. Follow every rule of the faith, not just the ones which are convenient. It is not what you want or wish but Allah's wish that has to be complied with. It is not your likes but what is liked by the Prophet that must be done. All that is needed to live your life is contained in the examples from the life of the Prophet. All you need is faith—in Allah, the Prophet, the Book, angels, judgment day, paradise, and hell—and effort. If you cannot get worldly wealth without putting in an effort, how can you obtain paradise without it? Tell your daughters to offer *namaz* daily in the house; you won't be able to tell them once they are burning in hell.

Psychologically, then, fundamentalism is a theory of suffering and cure, just as modern individualism is another theory of suffering and its cure. The core of psychological individuality is internalization rather than externalization. I use "internalization" here as a sensing by the person of a psyche in the Greek sense, an animation from within rather than without. Experientially, this internalization is a recognition that one is possessed of a mind in all its complexity. It is the acknowledgment, however vague, unwilling, or conflicted, of a subjectivity that fates one to episodic suffering through some of its ideas and feelings—in psychoanalysis, murderous rage, envy, and possessive desire seeking to destroy those one loves and would keep alive— simultaneously with the knowledge, at some level of awareness, that the mind can help in containing and processing disturbed thoughts. Fundamentalism, on the other hand, identifies the cause of suffering not in the individual mind but in a historical process which, however, is not fatefully deterministic but amenable to human will and eminently reversible. Individual and collective suffering are due to a lapse from an ideal state of religious faith, and the cure lies in an effort, to restore faith in one's inner life to its original state of pristine purity.

Another striking aspect of fundamentalist religious discourse is not so much its warlike anger against the enemy—the modernization process, the infidels—held responsible for the contemporary sorry state of the Muslims, but the turning of this rage inward in a collective self-recrimination and masochistic self-hate. The loss of Muslim greatness is not grieved for, a process that would pave the way for an eventual acceptance of its loss and thus enable the community to face the future without a debilitating preoccupation with the past. Instead, the loss is experienced as a persisting humiliation, a narcissistic injury to the group self which keeps on generating inchoate anger rather than the sadness of mourning. The instances from history in the *mullahs*' sermons are replete with sadomasochistic imagery, betraying an unconscious rage even as they seem to bemoan the lost glories of Islam. Their talk is liberally spattered with blood. Rivers of blood flow in the massacres of Muslims, fountains of the stuff spurt from the chests of children martyred to the faith. The atrocities borne by Muslims, both in modern and medieval periods, are detailed with much relish. It is not the doctors and the officers—the representatives of the modern world—who have sacrificed for the country's independence, says Qari Mohammad Hanif, but the *mullahs*. Detailing incidents not recorded in history books, three thousand *ulema* were laid on the road to Delhi and the British drove road rollers over their chests. Hundreds were sewn into pigskins and burnt alive. Impaling, burning on stakes, being trampled under elephant feet, and the walling in alive of early martyrs is described with an eye for gory detail. The listeners are asked to visualize the plight of the pious woman who had hundreds of nails driven into her palms and feet saying to her infidel torturer, "You can drive a hundred nails into my tongue too and I will still take Allah's name."

In addition to the sadomasochistic imagery, another theme in fundamentalist discourse is the inculcation of guilt. The speeches conjure up images of the ancestors regarding today's generation of Muslims with eyes full of reproach and with a "Thou hast forsaken us!" refrain on dead lips. Skillfully reactivating the guilt vis-à-vis our parents that is our common human legacy from early childhood, fundamentalism stirs anger and guilt in a potent brew.

To trace psychological themes in Muslim fundamentalist discourse is not to reduce this discourse to psychopathology. Illness to the outsider, fundamentalism is a cure for the insider. For many Muslims with an inchoate sense of oppression and the looming shadow of a menacing future, with fractured self-esteem in the wake of historical change that saw an end to their political role and a virtual disappearance of their language, fundamentalism is an attempt, however flawed, to revive the sacred in social and cultural life, to give politics a spiritual dimension, and to recover in their religious verities a bulwark against collective identity fragmentation.

Religious Politics

To look more closely at the psychological processes involved in the fundamentalist mobilization of Muslims, I have chosen as my exemplary text a speech by Ubedullah Khan Azmi, an influential north Indian Muslim leader. Azmi, who has occupied important positions in Muslim institutions, such as the secretaryship of the Muslim Personal Law Conference, an organization through which the conservative section of the community has zealously sought to guard its autonomy in the making and interpretation of civil laws applicable to Muslims, is what I would call a "moderate fundamentalist." By this I mean that, like all fundamentalists, he subscribes to the founding myth that a truly Islamic society existed only in the period of the Prophet and the first four Caliphs, and one must go back to those origins to restore the initial vitality of the community. As a moderate, however, he does not go so far as some others who advocate an opting out of or a rejection of the modern Indian political system, a *jehad* to recover the spirit of Islam's original enterprise. Informed by fundamentalist beliefs, his politics is yet politics as usual in many ways, requiring a constant adaptation to changing political realities. Like many fundamentalist leaders who must operate within secular democracies, Azmi has negotiated a degree of political influence for himself (he is a member of Parliament) by entering into a mutually beneficial alliance with secular politicians of a mainstream political party, the Janata Dal. In such alliances, we know, fundamentalist leaders are willing to be carried along on a wave of purely socioeconomic or political resentment while they mobilize votes for their political allies by playing on religious passions and fears of their constituency, saying and doing things which the secular politician will studiously avoid.[6]

The rhetoric of fundamentalist politics attempts to seduce its target group with a sense of participation in a collectivity with a transcendent purpose, giving a higher value or meaning to life than could be given by any secular politics. The group addressed by the fundamentalist has the very satisfying feeling of being "chosen," with a sense of mission connected with a sacred purpose, sanctified by God, and superior to the adversary's mission which is not similarly blessed or is blessed by a lesser god.

My selection of this particular speech, delivered in 1985, is not because it is remarkable in any way but precisely because it is not. It is an ordinary speech which takes as its springboard an insignificant event, the filing of a petition by an obscure Hindu lawyer in a district court in Rajasthan seeking a ban on the Qur'an. Unlike Rithambra's speaking style which is modeled after Hindu bardic narration, Azmi's rhetoric is in traditional Muslim style, interspersed with Urdu couplets for an audience which likes poetical flourishes in its orators. The speech as reproduced below is necessarily abridged, though not edited to change its essential content, images, or the sequential flow of thoughts.

"[I wish] I did not have to see this day. These are the offspring of Nathuram Godse [Gandhi's assassin] who are talking of banning the Qur'an. The children of Nathuram Godse dream of occupying the

Babri mosque. Ubedullah Khan Azmi declares openly, Look at the lineage of all traitors from the time of Mahatma Gandhi to that of Indira Gandhi and then look at the lineage of those who have been loyal to India from 1945 to 1985. What is the crime for which we Muslims are being punished? Our book is being banned, our personal law is being proscribed, our community's very way of life is being restricted. Beware, history may repeat itself. Balasaheb Deoras may have to read the *kalma* [i.e., become a Muslim], Atal Bihari Vajpaee may have to read the *kalma*, Mister Rajiv Gandhi may have to read the *kalma*.*

> Stars sometimes appear in the waves
> Khalid sometimes leads armies
> Every ages sees the rise of Yazid
> Every age witnesses the birth of Shabbir.**

How much have we served this country! What have we not done to get freedom for this country! The equal rights given to Muslims under Indian law were not given as charity but because we earned them. And today they want to ban the Qur'an? Who led the country to independence? Everyone calls Mahatma Gandhi the father of the nation. Fine, we'll also call him that. Who killed the "father of the nation"? Nathuram Godse. Who killed Indira Gandhi? Beant Singh and Satwant Singh. Were *they* Muslims? *You* eliminated them both.

> Even then you complain of my faithlessness,
> If I am not faithful, you too have not been a caretaker of my heart.

Who did we eliminate? Let me tell you that since you call us "Pakistanis." When Pakistan's tanks rolled into the country then in the form of Abdul Hamid*** we destroyed eight of those tanks. Whenever the country has asked for sacrifice, Muslims have given their blood. We have protected the country at every juncture and today you are questioning our loyalty? You talk of banning the Qur'an which taught us to die for the country's honor. Qur'an gave discipline to the world.

*Deoras was the chief of the RSS while Vajpaee is a prominent leader of the BJP.
**Khalid was the legendary general of the all-conquering Arab armies in the seventh century. Yazid, the first Muslim king, is the personification of evil in Islamic sacred history while Shabbir is another name for Hussain, the Prophet's grandson and Yazid's antagonist in the battle of Karbala.
***A hero of the India-Pakistan war of 1965.

Qur'an gave even the lowest of the low the right to live in dignity.
Qur'an was the first to raise its voice against caste distinctions. Qur'an
was the first to abolish differences between high and low. Qur'an
taught the world that man does not become great on the basis of birth
but on the basis of religious virtue, abstinence, and truth. To ban the
Qur'an means to ban reality, to ban truth. These bribe-takers want corruption to continue. These libertines want the honor of women to be
violated. These drunkards want the looting of India to continue. But
when people come to know the Qur'an, when they understand Qur'an's
laws, then Qur'an will save both the world and the *millat* [religious
community of the Muslims].

The political culture of fundamentalism, perhaps more than secular political cultures, is fundamentally a politics of imagery. The image Azmi first
conjures up is of a besieged Muslim community, under attack from a vile,
treacherous enemy, the Hindu nationalist. Azmi's specific technique is to
project the image of a relentless attack against the central symbol of Muslim
religious identity, the Qur'an. This citadel of the community's identity, idealized as the all-good, the all-just, the all-pure, and the source of all benefi-
cence, is surrounded by a sea of Hindu corruption and debauchery. In
contrast to a Hindu revivalist like Rithambra, who must first define and then
draw up the boundaries of a Hindu community, Azmi does not need to engage in any such boundary-setting exercise. The religious-cultural identity
of the Muslim *qaum* and its sense of "us" versus "them" has been traditionally
clear-cut and relatively enduring. What Azmi attempts to do is to trigger and
stoke a persecutory anxiety in his audience.

In psychoanalytic thought, persecution is an internal event, a subjective,
irrational experience often equated with the pathology of paranoia. Melanie
Klein has related the anxiety it generates—the feelings of disintegration—
to the earliest stages of life, to the baby's experience of a depriving, frustrating breast-mother. But as Meira Likierman has pointed out, the feeling of
persecution is also a normal part of the response to destructive and obstruc-
tive forces which we encounter in the course of everyday life.[7] Connecting
to the individual's primitive persecution anxiety from infancy, damage, loss,
deprivation, frustration are a range of events which constitute a destructive
attack on our sense of identity and represent partial death. Persecution anxiety signals a situation of great danger and carries with it the fear of the group's
symbolic death, and annihilation of its collective identity. It is only when this
particular anxiety courses through and between members of a group, making

individuals feel helpless, frightened, and paralyzed, that people become loosened from their traditional cognitive moorings and are prepared to give up previously held social, political, or economic explanations for their sense of aggrievement and become receptive to the religious critique Azmi has to offer. Persecutory anxiety is one of those strong emotions which can take people away from "knowing" back to the realm of "unknowing"—from a "knowledge" of the cause of their distress to a state where they do not know what it is that gives them suffering and pain though they *do* know that they are suffering and in pain. One antidote to this paralyzing anxiety is anger, preferably in a violent assertion that is psychically mobilizing, as Azmi continues:

> Even the talk of banning the holy Qur'an shows what dangerous conspiracies are being hatched to damage our faith.

> Awake O Indian Muslims before you disappear completely
> Even your story will not find a mention in other stories.

> What steps should we take under these conditions? The Muslim will not come to the court to prove the truth of the Qur'an. The Muslim will come out with the shroud tied to his head to protect the Qur'an. We will cut off tongues that speak against the Qur'an. We will tear off the skin of those who look askance at the Qur'an.

After having tried to erase previous cognitive structures through a heightening of persecution anxiety and dealt with the paralyzing fear engendered by this anxiety through fantasized violence, what the fundamentalist has before him is a newly born group without memory and with but inchoate desires. Azmi proceeds to shape the identity of this freshly minted group by offering it a series of narcissistically enhancing self-images—"This is who you are!"—particularly in relation to the elder sibling, the Hindu.

> After thirty-five years of oppression the Indian Muslim has remained loyal to the country. If there is anyone loyal from Hindustan to *kabristan* [graveyard], then it is the Muslim. You [the Hindus] die, we die. What happens after death? You are cremated. Next, your ashes are thrown into the Ganges. Where does the river flow to? You flow from here and reach Pakistan. Ashes scattered by the wind can land anywhere. When you die, mother India does not care. When we die, the motherland says, "My dear son, you will not leave me to go any-

where else. If you have lived on top of me, after death you will sleep in my lap."

There are three kinds of sons. One son, who according to the law of the land and in light of his faith fulfills his obligations toward his parents is called *put* [son]. Another is called *suput* (good son) who not only fulfills his obligations but sacrifices his all for the happiness of the parents. The son who shoots his mother, cuts her throat, kills both his father and mother—he is called *kuput* [bad son]. Now look at the sons of this motherland and decide who is the good and who is the bad son. The Muslim who believes in Qur'an and calls India his own country is the *suput*. When after the formation of Pakistan there was trouble in Kashmir then it was Brigadier Usman Ali from my town of Azamgarh who was one of the first to fall to Pakistani bullets. When his twitching corpse fell to earth at the border the motherland said, "This is my son who sacrificed himself to protect my honor."

When Abdul Hamid stopped the Pakistani tanks which would have rolled on to Delhi and had his flesh torn to ribbons then the Indian earth said, "This is my *suput*. And they who killed Mahatma Gandhi, the liberator of the country, killed Indira Gandhi who sacrificed so much for the honor of the nation—what will you call them, *put*, *suput*, or *kuput*? You decide.

While on the surface the whole tenor of the speech is concerned with distancing the Muslim from the Hindu enemy, on the more unconscious level it betrays the existence of an unwanted relationship with the same foe—an intimacy held at bay by disdain, even hate, but an intimacy nonetheless. Viewing oneself as the "good son" of the mother, as opposed to the Hindu "bad son," is an unconscious acknowledgment of their connectedness, even when this connection exists only in an unending and obsessive competition. After exorcising doubt—including self-doubt—about Muslim loyalty to the country (vis-à-vis loyalty to the religious community outside the borders of the nation), the self-images offered to the group in the following passages are of a grandiose variety, of an exhilarating Muslim superiority. The enhancement of collective self-esteem then serves to increase the security of the group self by countering the deathly threat to its survival.

Like spokespersons of all ethnic groups in conflict around the world, Azmi's vision of Muslims and Hindus is of two groups in eternal competition to answer the question of which is more civilized, stronger, and, generally, better.[8] As his evidence for Muslim superiority, he offers Muslim virtues in comparison with Hindu vices. First, this superiority consists of a heightened Muslim apperception of the aesthetics of life, in the Muslim's greater resonance for sensory and sensuous experience and in greater artistic giftedness.

> And you who raise slogans about Muslim loyalty, who talk of a ban on the Qur'an, have you ever looked at your own face in the mirror? It was the believers in the Qur'an who taught you the graces of life, taught you how to eat and drink. All you had before us were tomatoes and potatoes. What did you have? We brought jasmine, we brought frangipani. We gave the Taj Mahal, we gave the Red Fort. India was made India by us. We lived here for eight hundred years and we made India shine. In thirty-five years you have dimmed its light and ruined the country. A beggar will not be grateful if made an emperor. Lay out a feast for him and he will not like it. Throw him a piece of bread in the dust and he will get his appetite back. Do not force us to speak out. Do not force us to come in front of you as an enemy.

> God, look at their ignorance to believe we have no words
> When out of pity we gave them the power of speech.

Azmi's attempt to sharply differentiate the Hindus from the Muslims, suggesting that the Muslims consider themselves as having come to India from outside the country eight hundred years ago (and from a superior racial stock), is partly a consequence of the current antagonism between the two communities. In such a hostile situation, the fundamentalist exhorts the Muslims to shun contamination with any of the Hindu symbols and strive to keep their shared Islamic identity intact and pure. The fundamentalist is loath to acknowledge any Muslim similarity to the Hindu and focuses only on the differences which, he seeks to persuade those yet unconvinced, are of stubborn emotional importance.

From the relative level of sophistication of the two civilizations, the battle for superiority now shifts to the arena of power as Azmi offers up the image of a powerful Muslim nation, much stronger than the Hindu enemy.

> There is a limit to our patience and tolerance. These wicked people should understand that we can sacrifice all we have, including our lives, but not our honor. We cannot compromise the glory of the Qur'an. Today the whole world is in turmoil. Some madmen are disturbing the peace of the world. This is not a challenge to the two hundred twenty million Muslims of India but to the over a billion Muslims of the world. That is why I request you to remain alert. Today's tense atmosphere

should make every Muslim who is still living unawares a true Muslim.
They are banning the Qur'an. Has the time not come that you become
regular in saying your *namaz* as ordained by it? They are thinking of
banning the Qur'an. Has the time not come that you keep your *rozas*
even in the heat of summer? The more they talk of banning the Qur'an,
the more you should live according to it. Give your life a religious cast.

   The secret of Muslim strength does not lie in the sheer number of Muslims all over the world, a *millat* of which the Indian Muslims are also a part, a
notion of a pan-Islamic collectivity which is the stuff of the Hindu nationalist's nightmares. For the Muslims, the offer of such a collective identity helps
to counteract the feeling of being an embattled minority in one particular
country. The real secret of Muslim strength, however, lies in the superiority
of Islam over the religion of the Hindus. Our religion makes us stronger, their
divisive faith makes them weaker. Our religion is of the future, theirs mired in
an outdated past. We are stronger than we think, they weaker than what they
or we might believe.

   Why do they talk of a ban of the Qur'an? Why are they so afraid of the
Qur'an? They are afraid because their religion is one of touchables-
untouchables. Qur'an gives a religion of universal equality. They have
no place in their hearts for their own people. Let them allow a Harijan
to drink water from their wells. These high-caste people who talk of
Rama and Sita, let them first permit Harijans to enter their temples.
In contrast, look at the Qur'an. It gives every human being a right to
equality on basis of his humanity. That is why thirteen thousand Harijans, thirteen thousand tribals, converted to Islam in Meenakshipuram
in Madras. They did not know what is written in the Qur'an. They only
knew that Qur'an gives people of low caste the right to sit together
with people of higher castes on terms of equality. So these Harijans
who have been given so many benefits by the state are ready to throw
them away. We do not want benefits which give us food and clothing
but which leave our hearts enslaved. We want freedom of our minds,
freedom for our souls. We are prepared to tolerate slavery of every kind
but not of the soul. You, enslavers of the soul, Qur'an liberates the soul!
That is why we believe in the Qur'an which gives life to the soul, makes
a black like Billal the chief of a fair-skinned tribe.* Today, when Muslims are being massacred everywhere, when there is talk of doing away

---

*Billal was a black slave and a favorite of the Prophet.

with Muslim personal law, when the honor of our mothers and sisters is
being violated, when our children are being martyred, when our very
existence is unbearable to others, thirteen thousand Harijans chose to
convert to our religion. Because man wants freedom for the soul. A bird
will be unhappy even if confined in a palace of gold. Its soul craves for
the freedom of the garden. Islam gives that freedom. The result is that
not only in Islamic but also in non-Islamic countries, people are flock-
ing to convert to Islam. No one is asking them or telling them to become Muslims. It is because of its teachings that people are taking
refuge in the Qur'an.

Do you think Qur'an can be finished off by merely banning it? We
have lived with the Qur'an for fourteen hundred years. We have passed
under arches of swords. We have come through the battlefield of Karbala. We have passed through the valleys of Spain, through the hills of
Gibraltar, through the plains of India. We can say with pride that in
spite of thousands of ordeals it has undergone, the Muslim nation remains incomparable. The love it has for the Qur'an is unmatched by
that of any other community for its religious books. No one loves his
religion more than the Muslim loves Islam. We need to maintain relationships with Muslims all over the world. We have tried and succeeded in developing these relationships. We can then deal with any
challenge that comes from either inside or outside the country. Our
faith grows stronger with each challenge it faces and makes us more
powerful. The fox which wakes up a sleeping lion should first look after
its own safety. Anyone who dares to challenge the Qur'an should be
aware that either he or his father or his offspring will have to become a
Muslim.

It is the voice of Mohammed, the command of God, which can
never be altered.
The world may change a thousand times, the Qur'an never.

In summary, the psychological process involved in Muslim fundamentalist politics, which has as its goal the replacement of political, economic,
and social bases of politics with a religious critique, consists essentially of
two steps. First, there is an attempt to erase previous cognitive structures, as
they relate to political life and issues, through the generation of a strong persecution anxiety in the group. Second, on the now relatively clean slate of
the group's political psyche, the fundamentalist politician proceeds to draw
a group self-portrait—offers the Muslims a collective identity—which

emphasizes the community's superiority in relation to the enemy group, the nationalist Hindus. Although this superiority may have many other features, such as the strength to be derived from an identification with a larger, powerful pan-Islamic community, its core is a conviction in the inherent superiority of the group's religion, Islam, and of all its symbols. To maintain this feeling of superiority and the strength it gives to the members of the community, it is considered essential for the individual to be zealous in the observance of religious duties, accept the priority of religion in all areas of life, and to acknowledge the demands of religion as having the first call on individual loyalty.

To conclude: The reasons for the attraction of the fundamentalist identity for many Muslims are not difficult to fathom. Apart from providing a forum for resistance to perceived domination and repression, fundamentalism offers a narcissistic enhancement for a sense of self-esteem fractured by the workings of a historical fate. Besides giving a sacred meaning and transcendent purpose to the lives of the hurt, the dislocated, and the shipwrecked, fundamentalism also makes a masochistic reparation for guilt feelings possible. In defining an Other as a competitor with a deadly intent toward one's own group, fundamentalism provides a focus for undue anger and unresolved hate. Little wonder that many are willing to pay the costs of a fundamentalist identity—a considerable denial of reality, the closing of one's eyes and mind to the structures of the contemporary world, and the renunciation of a pleasure-seeking attitude in favor of a religiously disciplined life.

EIGHT

Religious Conflict in the Modern World

Our times are witness to a worldwide wave of religious revival. Islam, Hinduism, Buddhism, the new religions in Japan, born-again Christians in the United States, and the Protestant sects in Latin America are undergoing a resurgence which is regarded with deep distrust by all the modern heirs to the Enlightenment. Although a secular humanist might find most manifestations of the current religious zeal personally distasteful, he or she is nonetheless aware that the revitalization of religion at the end of the twentieth century constitutes a complex attempt at the resacralization of cultures beset with the many ills of modernity. As Andrew Samuels reminds us, this fragmented and fractured attempt at resacralization to combat the sense of oppression and a future utterly bereft of any vision of transcendent purpose is not only a part of the new religious fundamentalisms but also integral to the so-called left-leaning, progressive political movements.[1] One can discern the search for transcendence even in concerns around ecological issues and environmental protection where at least some of the discourse is comprised of elements of nature mysticism.

However, if we look closely at individual cases around the world, we will find that the much-touted revival is less of religiosity than of cultural identities based on religious affiliation. In other words, there may not be any great ferment taking place in the world of religious ideas, beliefs, rituals, or any marked increase in the sum of human spirituality. Where the resurgence is most visible is in the organization of collective identities around religion, in the formation and strengthening of communities of believers. What we are witnessing today is less the resurgence of religion than (in the felicitous Indian usage) of communalism where a community of believers not only has religious affiliation but also social, economic, and political interests in common which may conflict with the corresponding interests of another com-

186

munity of believers sharing the same geographical space. Indeed, most secular analysts and "progressive" commentators have traditionally sought to uncover factors other than religion as the root cause of an ostensibly religious conflict. This has been as true of the anti-Semitic pogroms in Spain in the fourteenth century, of sixteenth-century Catholic-Protestant violence in France, of anti-Catholic riots in eighteenth-century London, as of twentieth-century Hindu-Muslim riots in India.[2] The "real" cause of conflict between groups in all these instances has been generally identified as a clash of economic interests; the explanation embraces some version of a class struggle between the poor and the rich.

The danger to the material existence of an individual can indeed be experienced as an identity-threat which brings a latent group identity to the forefront. This heightened sense of identity with the group provides the basis for a social cohesiveness which is necessary to safeguard the individual's economic interests. But there are other threats besides the economic one which too amplify the group aspect of personal identity. In an earlier chapter, I described the identity-threat which is being posed by the forces of modernization and globalization to peoples in many parts of the world. Feelings of loss and helplessness accompany dislocation and migration from rural areas to the shanty towns of urban megalopolises, the disappearance of craft skills which underlay traditional work identities, and the humiliation caused by the homogenizing and hegemonizing impact of the modern world which pronounces ancestral cultural ideals and values as outmoded and irrelevant. These, too, are conducive to heightening the group aspects of identity as the affected (and the afflicted) look to cultural-religious groups to combat their feelings of helplessness and loss and to serve as vehicles for the redress of injuries to self-esteem.

The identity-threat may also arise due to perceived discrimination by the state, that is, disregard by the political authorities of a group's interests or disrespect for its cultural symbols. It can also arise as a consequence of changing political constellations such as those which accompany the end of empires. If Hindu-Muslim relations were in better shape in the past, with much less overt violence, it was perhaps also because of the kind of polity in which the two peoples lived. This polity was that of empire, the Mughal empire followed by the British one. An empire, the political scientist Michael Walzer observes, is characterized by a mixture of repression for any strivings for independence and tolerance for different cultures, religions, and ways of life.[3] The tolerance is not a consequence of any great premodern wisdom but because of the indifference, sometimes bordering on brutal incomprehen-

Empires

sion, of the imperial bureaucrats to local conflicts of the peoples they rule. Distant from local life, they do not generally interfere with everyday life as long as things remain peaceful, though there may be intermittent cruelty to remind the subject peoples of the basis of the empire—conquest through force of arms. It is only with self-government, when distance disappears, that the political questions—"Who *among us* shall have power here, in these villages, these towns?" "Will the majority group dominate?" "What will be the new ranking order?"—lead to a heightened awareness of religious-cultural differences. In countries with multireligious populations, independence coincides with tension and conflict—such as we observe today in the wake of the unraveling of the Soviet empire.[4]

The identity-threats I have outlined above do not create a group identity but merely bring it to the fore. The group aspect of personal identity is not a late creation in individual development but exists from the beginning of the human life cycle. Although Freud had no hesitation in maintaining that from the very first individual psychology is a social psychology as well, psychoanalysts, with their traditional emphasis on the "body-in-the-mind," have tended to downplay the existence of the "community-in-the-mind."[5] They have continued to regard the social (*polis*) aspect of man's being as an overlay which compromises the wishes and needs of the self or, in case of the crowd, is destructive of individual self and identity. Erikson has been one of the rare psychoanalysts who has called for a revision of this model that differentiates so starkly between an individual-individual and the individual-in-mass who has no individuality at all: "Yet that a man could ever by psychologically alone; that a man 'alone' is essentially different from the same man in a group; that a man in a temporary solitary condition or when closeted with his analyst has ceased to be a 'political' animal and has disengaged himself from social action (or inaction) on whatever class level—these and similar stereotypes demand careful revision."[6]

Such revisions would begin with the idea that the inner space occupied by what is commonly called the "self"—which I have been using synonymously with "identity"—not only contains mental representations of one's bodily life and of primary relationships within the family but also holds mental representations of one's group and its culture, that is, the group's configuration of beliefs about man, nature, and social relations (including the view of the Other). These cultural propositions, transmitted and internalized through symbols, have strong emotional impact on those who grow up as members of a particular cultural group. The self, then, is a system of reverberating representational worlds, each enriching, constraining, and shaping the others, as they jointly evolve through the life cycle. A revision of psycho-

analytic notions of the self, identity, and subjectivity would also acknowledge that none of these constituent inner worlds is "primary" or "deeper," that
is, there is no necessity of assuming some kind of hierarchical ordering of
aspects of identity or an "archaeological" layering of the various inner worlds,
although at different times the self may be predominantly experienced in one
or other representational mode. It is not only the brain that is bicameral.

At some point of time in early life, like the child's "I am!" which heralds
the birth of individuality, there is also a complementary "We are!" which an-
nounces the birth of a sense of community. "I am" differentiates me from
other individuals. "We are" makes me aware of the other dominant group (or
groups) sharing the physical and cognitive space of my community. The self-
assertion of "We are," with its potential for confrontation with the "We are" of
other groups, is *inherently* a carrier of aggression, together with the consequent fears of persecution, and is thus always attended by a sense of risk and
potential for violence. (The psychological processes initiated by an awareness of "We are," I suggest, also provide an explanation for the experimental
findings of cognitive psychologists that the mere perception of two different
groups is sufficient to trigger a positive evaluation of one's own group and a
negative stereotyping of the other.)

The further development of the social-representational world or the
group aspect of identity has some specific characteristics which I have discussed in detail at various places in this book in the context of Hindu-Muslim
relations. To abstract briefly: this aspect of identity is powerfully formed by
the processes of introjection, identification, idealization, and projection during childhood. On the one hand, the growing child assimilates within itself
the images of the family and group members. He or she identifies with their
emotional investment in the group's symbols and traditions and incorporates
their idealizations of the group which have served them so well—as they will
serve the child—in the enhancement of self-esteem for belonging to such an
exalted and blessed entity. On the other hand, because of early difficulties in
integrating contradictory representations of the self and the parents—the
"good" loving child and the "bad" raging one; the good, caretaking parent
and the hateful, frustrating one—the child tries to disown the bad representations through projection. First projected to inanimate objects and animals
and later to people and other groups—the latter often available to the child
as a preselection by the group—the disavowed bad representations *need* such
"reservoirs," as Vamik Volkan calls them. These reservoirs—Muslims for
Hindus, Arabs for Jews, Tibetans for the Chinese, and vice versa—are also
convenient repositories for subsequent rages and hateful feelings for which
no clear-cut addressee is available. Since most of the "bad" representations

[handwritten marginal note:] Is this to argue that it's static?

Where did this "disapproval" originally come from? Why does it seem so natural?

"arise from a social disapproval of the child's "animality," as expressed in its aggressivity, dirtiness, and unruly sexuality, it is preeminently this animality which a civilized, moral self must disavow and place in the reservoir group. We saw this happening in the Hindu image of the dirty, aggressive, and sexually licentious Muslim, and we encounter it again and again in both modern and historical accounts of other group conflicts. Thus in sixteenth-century France, Catholics "knew" that the Protestants were not only dirty and diabolic but that their Holy Supper was disordered and drunken, a bacchanalia, and that they snuffed out the candles and had indiscriminate sexual intercourse after voluptuous psalm singing. Protestants, on their part, "knew" that Catholic clergy had an organization of hundreds of women at the disposal of priests and canons who, for the most part, were sodomites as well.[7]

The psychological processes involved in the development of "We are" not only take recourse to the group's cultural traditions—its myths, history, rituals, and symbols—to make the community a firm part of personal identity but also employ bodily fantasies as well as family metaphors to anchor this aspect of identity in the deepest layers of individual imagination. The "pure" us versus a "dirty" them, the association of a rival group with denigrated, often anal, bodily parts and functions, representations of one's group in metaphors of a body under attack or as a "good" son of the mother(land) while the rival group is a "bad" son, are some of the examples from Hindu and Muslim discourse which I have discussed in earlier chapters.

We must, however, also note that there are always some individuals whose personal identity is not overwhelmed by their religious or cultural group identity even in the worst phases of a violent conflict. These are persons capable of acts of compassion and self-sacrifice, such as saving members of the "enemy" group from the fury of a rampaging mob even at a considerable danger to their own physical safety. There are yet others—the fanatics—whose behavior even in times of peace and in absence of any identity threat seems to be exclusively dictated by the "We are" group aspect of their identity. What the social and psychological conditions are that make one person wear his or her group identity lightly whereas for another it is an armor which is rarely taken off is a question to which the answers are not only of theoretical interest but also of profound practical importance and moral significance.

Religious Identities and Violence

The development of religious identity follows the same lines through which the more global aspects of individual and group identities are also constructed. The individual track, which may be called religious selfhood, is an incommunicable realm of religious feeling which quietly suffuses what D. W. Winnicott termed "the isolated core of the true self" requiring isolation and privacy, a core which "never communicates with the world of perceived objects [and] must never be communicated with."[8] In an integrated state, religious selfhood is a quiet self-experience, marked by a calmness of spirit that comes from being alone in the presence of the numinous. With its access to preverbal experience which can link different sensory modalities of image, sound, rhythm, and so on, religious selfhood deepens religious feeling and consolidates religious identity. In a state of fragmentation or threatened disintegration, religious selfhood is prey to a variety of dysphoric moods. For a few, the saints, whose religious identity constitutes the core of their being, the dysphoria can extend to the state of utter despair, the "dark night of the soul."

Together with religious selfhood, the "I-ness" of religious identity, we have a second track of "We-ness" which is the experience of being part of a community of believers. Religious community is the interactive aspect of religious identity. In contrast to the quietness of religious selfhood, the individual's experience of religious community takes place in an alert state. Optimally, this facet of religious identity expands the self and creates feelings of attunement and resonance with other believers. A threat to the community aspect of religious identity, however, gives birth to communalism, intolerance, and the potential for social violence. In the communal phase, the feelings of intimacy and connectedness characterizing the religious community are polluted by an ambiance of aggression and persecution. Whereas both the selfhood and community facets of religious identity are only partially conscious, the change from community to communalism is accompanied and, indeed, initiated by a heightened awareness of "We-ness," making the community aspect of religious identity hyperconscious. This awareness can be put in the form of declarations similar to the ones Oscar Patterson suggests take place in the inner discourse of an individual who, as a consequence of a shared threat, is in the process of self-consciously identifying with his or her ethnic group.[9] First, I declare to all who share the crisis with me that I am one with them—a Hindu, a Muslim. Second, from my multiple identities I choose the identity of belonging to my religious community though (paradoxically) I have no other choice but to belong. Third, this is my most basic and profound commitment and the one which I am least likely to abandon.

Communalism as a state of mind, then, is the individual's *assertion* of being part of a religious community, preceded by a full *awareness* of belonging to such a community. The "We-ness" of the community is here replaced by the "We *are*" of communalism. This "We are" must inevitably lead to intolerance of all those outside the boundaries of the group. The intolerance, though, is not yet religious conflict since it can remain a province of the mind rather than become manifest in the outer, public realm; its inherent violence can range from a mild contempt to obsessive fantasies around the extermination of the enemy-Other rather than find explosive release in arson, rioting, and murder. The psychological ground for violence, however, has now been prepared. In mapping the sequence of religious violence from the inner to the outer terrain, I do not mean to give group psychology primacy but only precedence. Riots *do* start in the minds of men, minds conditioned by our earliest inner experience of self-affirmation and assertion.

For the outbreak of violence, the communal identity has to swamp personal identity in a large number of people, reviving the feelings of love connected with early identifications with one's own group members and the hate toward the out-group whose members are homogenized, depersonalized, and increasingly dehumanized. For social violence to occur, the threat to communal identity has to cross a certain threshold where the persecutory potential becomes fully activated and persecutory anxiety courses unimpeded through and between members of a religious group. Amplified by rumors, stoked by religious demagogues, the persecutory anxiety signals the annihilation of group identity and must be combated by its forceful assertion. Acting demonstratively in terms of this identity as a Hindu or Muslim, though, threatens members of the rival community who too mobilize their religious identity as a defense. The spiral of threats and reactive counter-threats further fuels persecutory anxiety, and only the slightest of sparks is needed for a violent explosion.

The involvement of religious rather than other social identities does not dampen but, on the contrary, increases the violence of the conflict. Religion brings to conflict between groups a greater emotional intensity and a deeper motivational thrust than language, region, or other markers of ethnic identity. This is at least true of countries where the salience of religion in collective life is very high. Religious identity, for instance, is so crucial in the Islamic world that no Muslim revolutionary has been able or willing to repudiate his religious heritage.[10] To live in India is to become aware that the psychological space occupied by religion, the context and inspiration it provides for individual lives, and its role in fostering the cultural identity and survival of different groups—Hindus, Muslims, Sikhs, Christians, Parsis—is very different from the situation, say, in the United States. An Indian atheist cannot go along with an American counterpart's casual dismissal of religion as "important, if true" but must amend it to "important, even if not true."

With its historical allusions from sacred rather than profane history, its metaphors and analogies having their source in sacred legends, the religious justification of a conflict involves fundamental values and releases some of our most violent passions. Why this is so is not only because religion is central to the vital, "meaning-making" function of human life, causing deep disturbance if the survival of all that has been made meaningful by our religious beliefs is perceived to be under attack. Religion excites strong emotions also because it incorporates some of our noblest sentiments and aspirations—our most wishful thinking, the skeptic would say—and any threat to a belief in our "higher" nature is an unacceptable denuding of self-esteem. Our wishful construction of human nature that "man is naturally good or at least good natured. If he occasionally shows himself brutal, violent or cruel, these are only passing disturbances of his emotional life, for the most part provoked, or perhaps only consequences of the inexpedient social regulations he has hitherto imposed on himself,"[11] is matched by our equally wishful constructions around religion. Religion, we like to believe, is about love—love of God, love of nature, and love of fellow man. Religion, we feel, is essentially about compassion and strives for peace and justice for the oppressed. Indeed, freedom from violence, an enduring wish of mankind, is reflected in various religious visions of heaven.

This construction is confronted with the reality that violence is present in all religions as a positive and even necessary force for the realization of religious goals Religious violence has many forms which have found expression in the practice of animal or human sacrifice, in righteous and often excruciatingly cruel punishment envisaged for sinners, in the exorcism of spirits and demons, killing of witches or apostates, and in ascetic violence against the self.[12] The point is, as John Bowker has vividly demonstrated, that every religion has a vision of divinely legitimized violence—under certain circumstances.[13] In the Semitic religions, we have the Holy War of the Christians, the Just War of the Jews, and the Jehad of the Muslims where the believers are enjoined to battle and destroy evildoers. In other religions such as Hinduism and Buddhism, with their greater reputation for tolerance and nonviolence, violence is elevated to the realm of the sacred as part of the created order. In Hinduism, for instance, there is a cycle of violence and peacefulness as the Kali Age is followed by the Golden Age. Buddhist myths talk of Seven Days of the Sword where men will look on and kill each other as beasts, after which peace returns and no life is taken. Although Islam (es-

pecially in its current phase) and medieval Christianity have had most violent reputations, the question as to which religions have unleashed the greatest amount of violence is ultimately an empirical one.[14] In any event,
fundamentalists can unleash any violence contained in a religion even if the
religion is rarely perceived to have a violent potential, as amply demonstrated by our experience of Buddhist violence in Sri Lanka and Hindu
violence in India. Moreover, as Natalie Davis has observed of Catholic-
Protestant violence in sixteenth-century France and as we saw in case of the
Hyderabad riots, so long as rioters maintain a given religious commitment
they rarely display guilt or shame for their acts of violence.[15]

Rhythms of religious ritual, whether in common prayer, processions, or
other congregational activities, are particularly conducive to breaking down
boundaries between members of a group and thus, in times of tension and
threat, forging violent mobs. I have called these instruments of the community's violence "physical" groups since the individual's experience of group
identity here is through unconscious bodily communication and fantasies
rather than through the more consciously shared cultural traditions. Physical
groups seem to come into existence more effortlessly in religious than in
other kinds of conflict.

Histories and Futures

In this book, I have attempted to contribute a depth-psychological dimension to the understanding of religious conflict, especially the tension between Hindus and Muslims. I am aware that this may be regarded by some as
"psychologizing" an issue which demands social and political activism and
which could well do without the introduction of psychological complexities,
that "pale cast of thought," which can only sow doubt and sap the will for
unself-conscious action. In retrospect, I realize I have gone about this task in
consonance with my professional identity as a clinician, though not as a psychoanalyst with an individual patient but more akin to the psychotherapist
with a family practice who is called upon for assistance in a disintegrating
marriage. I looked at the history of the Hindu-Muslim relationship, made a
diagnostic assessment of what has gone wrong, and considered the positive
forces in the relationship which were still intact. At the end, it is time to
weigh the possible courses of action.

The awareness of belonging to either one community or the other—
being a Hindu or Muslim—has increased manifold in recent years. Every
time religious violence occurs in India or in some other part of the subconti-

nent, the reach and spread of modern communications ensure that a vast
number of people are soon aware of the incident. Each riot and its aftermath
raise afresh the issue of the individual's religious-cultural identity and bring it
up to the surface of consciousness. This awareness may be fleeting for some,
last over a period of time for others, but the process is almost always accompanied by a preconscious self-interrogation on the significance of the
religious-cultural community for the sense of one's identity and the intensity
of emotion with which this community is invested. For varying periods of
time, individuals consciously experience and express their identity through
their religious group rather than through traditional kinship groups such as
those of family and caste. The duration of this period, or even whether there
will be a permanent change in the mode of identity experience for some,
depends on many factors, not the least on the success of revivalist and fundamentalist political and social groupings in encouraging such a switch. They
do this, we saw in our analysis of the speeches by Rithambra and Azmi, by
stoking the already existing persecution anxiety—its combination of aggression and fear weakening the individual sense of identity. The needed support
to a weakened personal identity is then provided by strengthening its social,
group aspect through an invitation to the person to identify with a grandiose
representation of his or her community. The shared "contemplation" and
growing conviction of the great superiority of Hindu or Muslim culture and
ways is then the required tonic for narcissistic enhancement and identity
consolidation around the religious-cultural community as a pivot.

As for the future, there is more than one scenario for the likely evolution
of Hindu-Muslim relations. The Hindu nationalist, who views the conflict as
a product of Hindu and Muslim cultural and institutional traditions, believes
the only way of avoiding future large-scale violence is a change in the
Muslim view of the community's role, traditions, and institutions so that the
Muslim can "adapt"—the word meaning anything from adjustment to
assimilation—to the Hindu majority's "national" culture. To ask the Muslims
to recognize themselves in the Hindu nationalist history of India, to expect
them to feel their culture confirmed in Hindu symbols, rituals, and celebra-
tions is asking them to renounce their cultural identity and to erase their collective memory so that they become indistinguishable from their Hindu
neighbors. To be swamped by the surrounding Hindu culture has been historically the greatest fear of the Indian Muslim, articulated even by some medieval Sufis who are commonly regarded as having been closest to the Hindu
ethos. Such an assimilation is feared precisely because it is so tempting, holding the promise of a freedom from fear of violence and an active and full

participation in the majority culture and life, especially now when the majority is also politically dominant. The Hindu nationalist's dilemma is that the Muslims continue to decline an offer the nationalist believes they cannot refuse. The nationalist finds that the Muslim is too big to be either swallowed or spit out. Even if the Muslim was willing to undertake the exercise in assimilation voluntarily, a highly improbable scenario, the task would involve the immensely difficult understanding of how religious-cultural traditions are transmitted and internalized and how these processes can be effectively interfered with and halted.

The secularist, who views the conflict as rooted in social-structural considerations, especially economic, is more sanguine on the future of Hindu-Muslim relations. In the long run, the secularist believes, the inevitable economic development of the country will alter social-structural conditions and thus assign the conflict, as the cliché would have it, "to the dust heap of history" as religious identities fade and play less and less of a role in private and public life. A skeptical note on the belief in the primacy of political and economic structures in the shaping of consciousness, however, needs to be sounded. Cultural traditions—including the ideology of the Other—transmitted through the family can and do have a line of development separate from the political and economic systems of a society. This is strikingly apparent if one takes the case of Germany where recent studies indicate that, after living for forty years under a radically different political and economic system, the political orientation and values of the young in relation to the family in eastern Germany are no different from those of their counterparts in the western part of the country; cultural socialization patterns within the family have survived the change in political system relatively untouched and are stronger than the logic of the political superstructure.[16]

The optimistic realist, a breed with which I identify, believes that we are moving toward an era of recognition of Hindu-Muslim differences rather than pursuing their chimerical commonalties. We are moving toward a multiculturalism, with majority and minority cultures, rather than the emergence of a "composite culture." Such a multiculturalism is neither harmful nor dangerous but necessary, since it enables different religious groups to deal with the modernizing process in an active way rather than making them withdraw in lamentation at the inequities of modernization or endure it as passive victims. The problem is to ensure that one identity, Hindutva, does not dominate or assimilate other religious-cultural identities which are also embarked on the same quest as the Hindus. I can understand the validity of the nationalist call to the Hindus to find new meaning in customs, practices, and sym-

[margin handwritten note:] Moving towards? Hasn't this been the case always? The difference now being on

bols of Hindu culture. But by the same logic why should this be denied to the Muslims who, too, are engaged in the same struggle to find meaning in the modern world? The realist would say that the solution is to build a state which protects the equal rights of Hindus and Muslims to be different. The realist believes that we must work toward building a polity which respects the beliefs of both Hindus and Muslims, however odd or perverse they may seem to each other and however scornful they may be of the other community in private. Being a skeptic, the realist is also aware that the creation of such a public realm may be a long-drawn-out affair accompanied by much tension and open conflict between the communities which will strain the social and political fabric of the country. *the status quo, + dig in with greater*

This realist agrees with the Hindu nationalist that clouds of violence loom over the immediate future of Hindu-Muslim relations. I am convinced, though, that achieving the desired goal of a truly multicultural polity will ultimately generate much less tension than the permanent discord which is the probable consequence of the nationalist vision. I can only hope that the violence is short-lived and that it will hasten the creation of a common, tolerant public realm. Our experience of needless suffering and cruelty can sometimes have the effect of jolting us out of accustomed ways of interpreting the world and making us more receptive to fresh ideas and new social-political arrangements. When stress and anxiety are at their greatest there is perhaps enough survival need in humans to make them suddenly reasonable. I hope the poet Theodore Roethke is right that "In a dark time, the eye begins to see."[17] Though a realist, I am not a cynic since, unlike a cynic, I still have hope. And even if hope turns out to be illusory, I know that in the words of the Mahabharata, "Hope is the sheet anchor of every man. When hope is destroyed, great grief follows, which is almost equal to death itself." This applies not only to individuals but also to communities and nations.

[handwritten margin notes:]
Hide the problem by a state of adequacy, marked by repressed reservoirs of tension. Push with greater resilience + determination.

Certainly. Everyone hopes for this but doesn't act.

APPENDIX 1
THE GIESSEN TEST STATEMENTS

1. I have the feeling that I am
   relatively impatient   3 2 1 0 1 2 3   relatively patient

2. I think I tend to
   seek the company   3 2 1 0 1 2 3   avoid the company
   of others   of others

3. I believe I tend to
   try to dominate others   3 2 1 0 1 2 3   to be dominated by others

4. I believe that a change in
   my outward circumstances
   would affect my emo-
   tional state
   very greatly   3 2 1 0 1 2 3   very little

5. I have the feeling that I
   worry about my personal
   problems
   very little   3 2 1 0 1 2 3   a great deal

6. I think I tend to
   suppress my anger   3 2 1 0 1 2 3   let my anger out in some
                                                way

7. I have the feeling that I
   care about outdoing
   others
   very much   3 2 1 0 1 2 3   very little

8. I feel that I am
   not at all shy   3 2 1 0 1 2 3   shy

9. I have the impression that
   people are generally
   very satisfied with my   3 2 1 0 1 2 3   very dissatisfied with my
   work   work

10. I think I tend to have
    very great trust in others 3 2 1 0 1 2 3   very little trust in others

11. I have the feeling I show
    my need for love
    very strongly   3 2 1 0 1 2 3   very little

12. I think I tend to
    avoid getting very close   3 2 1 0 1 2 3   want to get very close to
                                                another person

13. I think that compared to others I am
quite good at dealing with money   3 2 1 0 1 2 3   quite bad at dealing with money

14. I believe I am
rarely depressed   3 2 1 0 1 2 3   often depressed

15. I have the feeling that I generally give away
a lot about myself   3 2 1 0 1 2 3   very little about myself

16. I seem to find it
hard to be liked by others   3 2 1 0 1 2 3   easy to be liked by others

17. I think it is relatively
easy for me to feel tied to someone for long   3 2 1 0 1 2 3   hard for me to feel tied to someone for long

18. I believe I tend to be
not too particular about the truth   3 2 1 0 1 2 3   rather particular about the truth

19. I seem to find it
fairly easy to come out of my shell   3 2 1 0 1 2 3   rather hard to come out of my shell

20. I believe I tend to behave
younger than my age   3 2 1 0 1 2 3   older than my age

21. I seem to be
rather disorganised   3 2 1 0 1 2 3   rather too organised

22. I think I get involved in arguments
very often   3 2 1 0 1 2 3   very rarely

23. I think I have a tendency to expect others
to see me as inferior   3 2 1 0 1 2 3   to think highly of me

24. I have the feeling I tend to make life
difficult for myself   3 2 1 0 1 2 3   easy for myself

25. I seem to feel
rather far removed from other people   3 2 1 0 1 2 3   very close to other people

26. I believe that compared with others I have a
very good imagination   3 2 1 0 1 2 3   very poor imagination

27. I think I care
very little about looking nice   3 2 1 0 1 2 3   very much about looking nice

28. I seem to find it
quite hard to work closely with other people   3 2 1 0 1 2 3   quite easy to work closely with other people

29. I think I
rarely blame myself for   3 2 1 0 1 2 3   always blame myself for
things   things

30. I believe I can offer a partner
very much love   3 2 1 0 1 2 3   very little love

31. I think in my behaviour
towards others I am
fairly submissive   3 2 1 0 1 2 3   particularly self-willed

32. I believe I worry myself
about other people
relatively little   3 2 1 0 1 2 3   relatively often

33. I have the feeling that I
am not very successful at   3 2 1 0 1 2 3   am quite successful at
achieving my aims in life   achieving my aims in life

34. Compared with others I
believe that in love I
have very strong feelings   3 2 1 0 1 2 3   experience relatively little

35. I think I am
quite good at acting   3 2 1 0 1 2 3   very bad at acting

36. I believe that others generally see me
as strong   3 2 1 0 1 2 3   as weak

37. I have the feeling that it is
very hard for me to make   3 2 1 0 1 2 3   very easy for me to make
myself attractive to others   myself attractive to others

38. I believe that compared
with others I find it
quite easy to keep my   3 2 1 0 1 2 3   very hard to keep my
mind on one thing   mind on one thing

39. I seem to find it
very hard to get into high 3 2 1 0 1 2 3   very easy to get into high
spirits   spirits

40. I feel
quite relaxed with the op- 3 2 1 0 1 2 3   very awkward with oppo-
posite sex   site sex

APPENDIX 2
THE MORALITY INTERVIEW

Nineteen Cases of Hindu-Muslim Interaction

Normal Time Interactions
1. A Muslim (M) has many Hindu (H) friends.
2. A (M) regularly eats dinner at his (H) friend's house.
3. A (M) rents his house to a (H).
4. A (M) works in a factory where most of the workers are (H).
5. A (M) boy marries a (H) girl.
6. A (M) girl goes to a movie with a (H) boy.
7. A (M) goes to a *pandit* to learn the Gita.
8. A (M) is converted to Hinduism.
9. A (M) girl elopes with a (H) boy.
10. Some (M) boys beat up a (H) boy who was whistling at (M) girls.
11. A (M) throws a dead cow in front of a temple.
12. Some (Ms) attack some (Hs) who were making fun of Allah.

Riot Time Interactions
13. Some (M) beat up a (H) walking through the alley.
14. Some (Ms) rape a (H) girl.
15. Some (Ms) set fire to a (H) house in their area.
16. Some (Ms) loot (H) shops.
17. A (M) man kills a (H) woman.
18. Some (Ms) stab and kill two (H) men.
19. A (M) family gives shelter to some (Hs).

The informant's understanding of each case is sought to be elicited through a standard set of interview questions. The questions are designed to assess different features of the respondent's understanding of the morality of a particular situation.

The Standard Interview

1. Is the behavior wrong?
2. How serious is the violation?
   a. Not a violation.
   b. A minor offense.
   c. A somewhat serious offense.
   d. A very serious offense.
3. Is it a sin?

4. What if no one knew this had been done? It was done in private or secretly. Would it be wrong then?

5. In (another city) people do (the opposite of the practice endorsed by the informant) all the time. Would (name of the city) be a better place, if they stopped doing that?

6. What if (name of informant's society) wanted to change the practice? Would it be okay to change it?

7. Do you think a person who does (the practice) should be stopped from doing that? Should he or she be punished? How?

The first question asks about the existence or nonexistence of a transgression. The second and third questions assess the perceived seriousness of the violation, should one exist. The fourth question, concerning self-regulation in absence of external monitors, tells us whether the violation is regarded as being of a moral order or a matter of convention. Questions five through seven tap the perceived universality (versus relativity) and unalterability (versus alterability) of the moral code being violated. The eighth question concerns sanctions and identifies cases where the informant believes the individual has a right to freedom of choice. In addition, the answers to this question give further clues as to the seriousness of one violation as compared to others.

NOTES

Chapter One

1. In the profession of this belief, physicists did not limit themselves to the field of natural science. In his 1929 lecture on "Light and Life," Niels Bohr made an explicit analogy between quantum mechanics and psychology when he observed that the necessity of considering the interrelationship between the measuring instrument and the object of inquiry in physics paralleled the difficulty in psychology where the content of consciousness changed as soon as attention was directed to it; see Niels Bohr, "Light and Life," *Nature* 131 (1933): 421–33 and 457–59.

Wolfgang Pauli, who is regarded by many as occupying a place next only to Einstein in the hierarchy of the great modern physicists, was categorical in his conclusion that the natural sciences had taken a historically wrong turn by accepting Cartesian ideas and ways of thought engendered by Newtonian physics. The observer in modern physics, he felt, was still too separated from the phenomena observed. In so far as a content of consciousness was itself an observation, the vital question of separation of subject and object was not restricted to the narrow field of physical inquiry but but was relevant for all human sciences; Pauli, "Phänomen und physikalische Realität," *Dialektika* 17 (1957): 36–48.

2. For a history of the city, see S. M. Alam, *The Growth of Hyderabad City—A Historical Perspective* (Hyderabad: Azad Oriental Research Institute, 1986); D. Prasad, *Social and Cultural Geography of Hyderabad City* (New Delhi: Inter-India Publications, 1986).

3. Jean-Baptiste Tavernier, *Travels in India*, trans. V. Ball, ed. W. Crooke (1676, Delhi: Oriental Books, 1977), 122–24.

4. S. C. Dube, *Indian Village* (New York: Harper Colophon Books, 1967), 187.

5. François Martin, *Memoirs of François Martin (1670–1694)*, trans. L. Vardarajan, vol. 1, pt. 2 (Delhi: Manohar, 1983), 761–62.

6. Ibid.

7. Tavernier, 127.

8. Ratna Naidu, *Old Cities, New Predicaments: A Study of Hyderabad* (Delhi: Sage, 1991), 15.

9. Tavernier, 140.

10. Muzaffar Alam, "Competition and Co-existence: Indo-Islamic Interaction in Medieval North India," *Itinerario* 13, no. 1 (1989): 51.

11. Naidu, chap. 5.

12. The secularist view has been articulated in a host of academic and popular publications for over fifty years. Its most sophisticated proponents are a group of historians at the Jawaharlal Nehru University in New Delhi. For an older statement of

the view, Nehru's *The Discovery of India* is still one of the best introductions. For a recent summary, see Amartya Sen, "The Threats to Secular India," *New York Review of Books,* 8 April 1993, 26−32. For the viewpoints of the activists, see Mehdi Arslam and Janaki Rajan, eds., *Communalism in India: Challenge and Response* (Delhi: Manohar, 1994).

13. C. A. Bayly, "The Pre-history of 'Communalism'? Religious Conflict in India 1700−1860," *Asian Studies* 19, no. 2 (1985): 184−85.

14. This view is most forcefully advocated by Marxist and neo-Marxist historians. See, e.g., Gyanendra Pandey, *The Colonial Construction of Communalism in North India* (Delhi: Oxford University Press, 1990).

15. For some of the more recent versions of the Hindu nationalist viewpoint, see Koenraad Elst, *Ayodhya and After: Issues before Hindu Society* (Delhi: Voice of India, 1991); K. D. Prithipaul, "Reason, Law and the Limits of Indian Secularism," *International Journal of Indian Studies,* July−December 1992.

16. Marc Gaborieau, "From Al-Beruni to Jinnah," *Anthropology Today* 1, no. 3 (1985).

17. See, e.g., Tara Chand, *Influence of Islam on Indian Culture* (Allahabad: The Indian Press, 1963). For more recent formulations, see Rasheeduddin Khan, ed., *Composite Culture of India and National Integration* (Simla: IIAS, 1988). See also Gyanendra Pandey, ed., *Hindus and Others* (Delhi: Viking, 1993).

18. Bayley, 184−85.

19. Alam, 46. See also his "Assimilation from a Distance: Confrontation and a Sufi Accommodation in Awadh society," unpublished manuscript, Centre for Historical Studies, Jawaharlal Nehru University, 1992.

20. Ibid., 51.

21. Ibid., 55.

22. Abbé J. Dubois, *Hindu Manners, Customs and Ceremonies,* ed. and trans. H. K. Beauchamp (1906; Calcutta: Rupa, 1992), 48.

23. François Bernier, *Travels in the Mogul Empire (1656−1668)* (New Delhi: S. Chand, 1972), 33.

24. Dubois, 134.

25. Erik Erikson, *Toys and Reasons* (New York: Norton, 1977).

26. Bayly, 192−95.

27. Dubois, 341−42. The Hindus constancy to their faith in the face of Muslim oppression or blandishments is also attested to hold true in the case of north India by Alam, 48−49.

28. Ibid., 343.

29. Raymond Grew, "On the Prospect of Global History," unpublished manuscript for the Conference on Global History at Bellagio, Italy, July 16−21, 1991.

30. Ian Austin, *City of Legends: The Story of Hyderabad* (Delhi: Viking, 1991).

Chapter Two

1. Peter Marsh, "Rhetorics of Violence," in P. Marsh and A. Campbell, eds., *Aggression and Violence* (New York: St. Martin's Press, 1982), 102−17.

2. See Larry Byron et al., "Legitimate Violence, Violence Attitudes, and Rape: A Test of the Cultural Spillover Theory," in R. Prentky and V. L. Quinsey, eds., *Human*

Sexual Aggression: Current Perspectives, Annals of New York Academy of Sciences, vol. 528 (New York: New York Academy of Sciences, 1988), 80–85.

3. Erik Erikson, *Identity: Youth and Crisis* (New York: W. W. Norton, 1968).

4. See Rita R. Rogers, "Intergenerational Exchange: Transference of Attitudes down the Generations," in J. Howells, ed., *Modern Perspectives in the Psychiatry of Infancy* (New York: Brunner/Mazel, 1979), 339–49.

5. Bert N. Adams and M. Bristow, "Ugandan Asian Expulsion Experiences: Rumor and Reality," *Journal of Asian and African Studies* 14 (1979): 191–203.

6. Ralph L. Rosnow, "Rumor as Communication: A Contextualist Approach," *Journal of Communication* 38, no. 1 (1988): 12–28.

7. Krishan Baldev Vaid, *Guzra hua Zamana* (Delhi: Radhakrishna, 1982) 430–36; my translation.

8. Asghar Ali Engineer, ed., *Communal Riots in Post-independence India* (New Delhi: Sangam Books, 1985).

9. Eric Hobsbawm, *Nations and Nationalism since 1870* (Cambridge: Cambridge University Press, 1990).

10. Ashutosh Varshney, "Contested Meanings: India's National Identity, Hindu Nationalism and the Politics of Anxiety," *Daedalus* 122, no. 3 (1993): 227–61. See also Ainslee T. Embree, *Utopias in Conflict: Religion and Nationalism in Modern India* (Berkeley and Los Angeles: University of California Press, 1990).

11. Varshney, 238.

12. Howard Schuman and J. Scott, "Generations and Collective Memories," *American Sociological Review* 54 (1989): 380.

13. Maurice Halbwachs, *On Collective Memory* (Chicago: University of Chicago Press, 1992).

14. See John C. Turner, "Towards a Cognitive Re-definition of the Social Group," in Henri Tajfel, ed., *Social Identity and Intergroup Relations* (Cambridge: Cambridge University Press, 1982); and Tajfel, "Social Psychology of Intergroup Relations," in W. G. Austin and S. Worchel, eds., *Annual Review of Psychology*, vol. 33, 1982.

15. Vamik D. Volkan, "An Overview of Psychological Concepts," in V. Volkan et al., eds., *The Psychodynamics of International Relationships* (Lexington: Lexington Books, 1990), 31–46.

16. Howard Stein, "On Professional Allegiance in the Study of Politics," *Political Psychology* 7 (1986): 248. See also John Mack, "The enemy system" in Volkan, *The Psychodynamics of International Relationships*, 57–89. Wendy Doniger (personal communication) illustrates this dual nature of certain objects, places, people, by citing the Israeli poet Yehuda Amichai who intervened in an argument over whether Jerusalem is a symbol or a real city inhabited by real people, with the remark that Jerusalem is a symbol—but a symbol with a sewage system.

17. Sigmund Freud, "The taboo of virginity" (1918), in *The Standard Edition of the Works of Sigmund Freud* (London: Hogarth Press, 1957), 11: 191–208.

18. See Natalie Z. Davis, *Society and Culture in Early Modern France* (Cambridge: Polity Press, 1987), 152–88.

19. Ikram Ali Malik, *Hindu-Muslim Riots in the British Punjab (1849–1900)* (Lahore: Gosha-i-adab, 1984), 3–5. See also Sandra Freitag, *Collective Action and Community: Public Arenas and the Emergence of Communalism in North India* (Delhi: Oxford University Press,

1990). For an account of the more recent riots, see M. J. Akbar, *Riot after Riot* (New Delhi: Penguin Books, 1988).

20. Sarah J. Moore, *Rioting in Northern India* (Ph.D. diss., University of Pennsylvania, 1976), 53.

21. Phyllis Greenacre, "Crowds and Crisis," *The Psychoanalytical Study of the Child* 27 (1972): 147.

22. See Stephen Reicher, "The Determination of Collective Behavior," in Tajfel, *Social Identity and Intergroup Relations,* 40–82.

23. Moore, 62.

24. "Riots and the Recent Phase of Communal Violence in Hyderabad," *Bulletin of the Henry Martyn Institute of Islamic Studies,* Jan.–March, 1994.

25. Davis shows this to be one of the implicit motivations of a crowd in the case of Catholic-Protestant violence in sixteenth-century France.

26. Romesh C. Majumdar et al., eds., *The History and Culture of the Indian People,* vol. 5 (Bombay: Bharatiya Vidya Bhawan, 1964), 22.

27. Volkan, 44.

28. Cited in Javed Alam, "Traditions in India under Interpreted Stress: Integrating Its Claims," *Theses Eleven* 39 (1994).

Chapter Three

Dieter Beckman, E. Brahler, and H. E. Richter, *Der Giessen Test,* 4th ed. (Bern: Verlag Hans Huber, 1991).

2. Samuel J. Klausner, "Violence," in Mircea Eliade, ed., *The Encyclopedia of Religion,* 15: 268–71.

3. Joseph S. Alter, *The Wrestler's Body: Identity and Ideology in North India* (Berkeley and Los Angeles: University of California Press, 1992). Much of the information on the wrestler's physical regimen and ethical attitudes is derived from this excellent study.

4. J. S. Alter, "The Sanyasi and the Indian Wrestler: The Anatomy of a Relationship," *American Ethnologist* 16, no. 2 (1992): 317–36.

5. Ibid., 326.

6. K. P. Singh, "Swasth Vibhagon par Kharch Bar Raha Hai, aur Nai Nai Bimariyan bhi Bar Rahi hain," *Bhartiya Kushti* 17 (1980): 21, cited in Alter, "The Body of One Colour: Indian Wrestling, the Indian State, and Utopian Somatics," *Cultural Anthropology* 8, no. 1 (1993): 64.

7. For an elaboration of this viewpoint, see R. Gladston, "The Longest Pleasure: A Psychoanalytic Study of Hatred," *International Journal of Psychoanalysis* 68 (1987): 371–78.

Chapter Four

1. M. N. Srinivas, *Social Change in Modern India* (Berkeley and Los Angeles: University of California Press, 1966).

2. Napoleon Chagnon, *Yanomamo: The Fierce People* (Forth Worth: Harcourt Brace, 1983).

3. Sudhir Kakar, *The Inner World: A Psychoanalytic Study of Childhood and Society in India* (Delhi: Oxford University Press, 1978), chap. 3.

4. Christopher Bollas, "Generational Consciousness," in *Being a Character: Psychoanalysis and Self Experience* (New York: Hill and Wang, 1992).

5. For a comprehensive discussion of the theory and its problems, see Thomas F. Pettigrew, "The Intergroup Hypothesis Reconsidered," in M. Hewston and R. Brown, eds., *Contact and Conflict in Intergroup Encounters* (Oxford: Basil Blackwell, 1986): 169–95.

6. David Lowenthal, "The Timeless Past: Some Anglo-American Historical Preconceptions," *Journal of American History* 75 (1989): 1263–80.

7. Dube, 187.

8. Dubois, 218.

9. Owen Berkeley-Hill, "Hindu-Muslim Unity," in *International Journal of Psychoanalysis*, 6 (1925): 287.

10. Ibid., 287.

11. Sudhir Kakar, *Shamans, Mystics and Doctors* (New York: A. Knopf, 1982; repr. Chicago, University of Chicago Press), chap. 3.

12. Robert A. LeVine and Donald T. Campbell, *Ethnocentrism: Theories of Conflict, Ethnic Attitudes and Group Behavior* (New York: John Wiley, 1972).

13. See A. Majeed and E. S. K. Ghosh, "A Study of Social Identity in Three Ethnic Groups in India," *International Journal of Psychology* 17 (1982): 455–63.

14. Erik Erikson, "Womanhood and Inner Space," in *Identity: Youth and Crisis*.

15. The relevant studies are: A. Sharma and S. Anandlakshmy, "Prejudice in the Making: Understanding the role of socialization," in D. Sinha, ed., *Socialization of the Indian Child* (New Delhi: Concept, 1981): 101–16; A. K. Singh, "Development of Religious Identity and Prejudice in Indian Children," in A. deSouza, ed., *Children in India* (New Delhi: Manohar, 1979), 231–44. Other studies have shown a significant correlation between parents' prejudice and that of children, with female children tending to be more influenced by the mother's prejudices, and the fathers of prejudiced boys being significantly more authoritarian: See M. K. Hasan, "Child-rearing Attitudes and Some Personality Traits of the Parents of Prejudiced School Children" *Manas* 24, no. 1 (1977): 1–10, and "Parental Influence on Children's Prejudice," *Social Change* 13, no. 2 (1983): 40–46. For an overview of similar studies from all over the world in the case of ethnic groups, see Nimmi Hutnick, *Ethnic Minority Identity* (Oxford: Clarendon Press, 1991).

16. Luce Irigaray, *Je, tu, nous: Pour une culture de la différence* (Paris: Biblio-Poche, 1994).

Chapter Five

1. Annes Jung, *Night of the New Moon: Encounters with Muslim Women in India* (Delhi: Penguin Books, 1993), 59.

2. Rollo May, *Power and Innocence* (New York: Dell, 1972), 29.

3. Bernard Lewis, *The Political Language of Islam* (Chicago: University of Chicago Press, 1988), 4.

4. R. D. Meade and L. Singh, "Changes in Social Distance during Warfare: A Study of India/Pakistan War of 1971," *Journal of Social Psychology* 90, no. 2 (1973): 325–26.

5. For an interesting description of the behavior of various kinds of victims, see R. A. Ball, "The Victimological Cycle," *Victimology* 1, no. 3 (1976): 379–95.

6. Mushirul Hasan, "Minority Identity and Its Discontents: Responses and Repre-

sentations," paper read at International Congress of Asian Studies, Hong Kong, August 1993.

7. Akbar S. Ahmed, *Discovering Islam* (New Delhi: Vistaar Publications, 1990), 158–60. See also Imtiaz Ahmed, ed. *Modernization and Social Change among Muslims* (Delhi: Manohar, 1983).

8. Gilani Bano, *Aiwan-e-ghazal* (Hyderabad, 1976).

9. See R. A. Shweder, M. Mahapatra and J. G. Miller, "Culture and Moral Development," in J. Kagan and S. Lamb, eds., *The Emergence of Moral Concepts in Early Childhood* (Chicago: University of Chicago Press, 1987); R. A. Shweder, "Beyond Self-constructed Knowledge: The Study of Culture and Morality," in *Merril-Palmer Quarterly* 28 (1982): 41–69; R. A. Shweder and N. C. Much, "Determinants of Meaning: Discourse and moral socialization," in R. A. Shweder, *Thinking through Cultures* (Cambridge, Mass.: Harvard University Press, 1991).

10. R. Dworkin, *Taking Rights Seriously* (Cambridge, Mass.: Harvard University Press, 1977).

11. E. Fromm, *Psychoanalysis and Religion* (New Haven, Conn.: Yale University Press, 1950); G. Obeyesekere, *Medusa's Hair* (Chicago: University of Chicago Press, 1981).

12. Kakar, *The Inner World*, 37.

13. A. K. Ramanujan, "Is There an Indian Way of Thinking?" in M. Marriott, ed., *India through Hindu Categories* (Delhi: Sage Publications, 1990).

14. For an elaboration on the uses of empathy, see Rafael Moses, "Empathy and Disempathy in the Political Process," *Political Psychology* 5 (1985): 135–40.

Chapter Six

1. Kakar, *The Inner World*.

2. Anthony Smith, *The Ethnic Origins of Nations* (Oxford: Basil Blackwell, 1986).

3. For a similarity in the Islamic world, see Bassam Tibi, *The Crisis of Modern Islam* (Salt Lake City: Utah University Press, 1988).

4. For brief biographies of the first and second RSS "supremos," see Walter V. Andersen and S. Damle, *The Brotherhood in Saffron* (Delhi: Vistaar Publications, 1987).

5. The social-psychological effects of modernization have been discussed in E. James Anthony and C. Chiland, eds., *The Child in His Family: Children and Their Parents in a Changing World* (New York: Wiley, 1978).

6. Quoted from a *sangh parivar* journal in an article, "Woman of Saffron," in *The Times of India*, February 1993.

7. See Tu Wei-Ming, "Beyond the Enlightenment Mentality," unpublished paper given at the Second International Conference on Global History at Technical University, Darmstadt, Germany, (July 1992), 4.

8. Erik H. Erikson, *Insight and Responsibility* (New York: W. W. Norton, 1964).

9. Sigmund Freud, "Group psychology and the analysis of the ego" (1921) *Standard Edition*, vol. 18.

10. Ernest Wolf, *Treating the Self* (New York: Guilford Press, 1988), 48.

11. Asghar Ali Engineer, ed., *Communal Riots in Post-independence India* (New Delhi: Sangam Books, 1985), 238–71.

12. Paul Brass, *Ethnicity and Nationalism* (New Delhi: Sage Publications, 1991), 15.

13. See Peter Homans, *The Ability to Mourn* (Chicago: University of Chicago Press, 1991), 309.

14. The clearest description of the concept of complementarity is by Klaus Meyer-Habich; see his "Komplementarität," in J. Ritter and K. Gruender, eds., *Historisches Wörterbuch der Philosophie* (Basel: Schwaber, 1967), 4: 933–34.

15. Don Miller, *The Reason of Metaphor* (Delhi: Sage Publications, 1991), 169.

16. For Rithambra's biographical details, see "Virtuous Virago," *The Times of India*, 19 July 1992, and "Hindutva by the Blood of Her Words," *The Daily*, 9 June 1991.

17. On the poetic function of rhetoric, see John Shotter, "The social construction of remembering and forgetting," in D. Middleton and D. Edwards, eds., *Collective Remembering* (London: Sage, 1990), 124.

18. Homans, 277.

19. Rafael Moses, "The Group Self and the Arab-Israeli conflict," *International Review of Psychoanalysis* 9 (1982): 56.

20. Sudhir Kakar, *Shamans, Mystics and Doctors* (New York: A. Knopf, 1982), Ch. III.

20. Moses, "The Group Self," 63.

21. Emile Durkheim, *The Elementary Forms of Religious Life* (1912; New York: Free Press, 1965).

Chapter Seven

1. See Martin E. Marty and R. Scott Appleby, eds., *Fundamentalisms and the State*, vol. 3 of the Fundamentalism Project (Chicago: University of Chicago Press, 1993), 3. For a review of scholarly discussion of and unhappiness with such terms as "fundamentalism" and "revivalism," see Sadik J. Al-Azm, "Islamic Fundamentalism Reconsidered: A Critical Outline of Problems, Ideas and Approaches, Part 1," *South Asia Bulletin* 13 (1993): 93–121.

2. M. S. Agwani, *Islamic Fundamentalism in India* (Chandigarh: Twenty-first Century India Society, 1986). See also M. Ahmad, "Islamic Fundamentalism in South Asia: The Jamaat-i-Islami and the Tablighi Jamaat," in M. Marty and R. Scott Appleby, eds., *Fundamentalisms Observed* (Chicago: University of Chicago Press, 1991), 457–530.

3. For a discussion of a community or a nation's inability to mourn—in this case Germany after the Second World War—see A. Mitscherlich and M. Mitscherlich, *Die Unfähigkeit zu Trauern* (Munich: Piper Verlag, 1968). See also V. Volkan, *The Need to Have Enemies and Allies: From Clinical Practice to International Relationships* (Northvale, N. J.: Jason Aronson, 1988).

4. For a psychopathological treatment of fanaticism, see A. Haynal, ed., *Fanaticism: A Historical and Psychoanalytical Study* (New York: Schocken Books, 1983).

5. Lewis, *The Political Language of Islam*, 7.

6. Marty and Appleby, *Fundamentalisms and the State*, 631.

7. Meira Likierman, "The function of anger in human conflict," *International Review of Psychoanalysis* 14, no. 2 (1987): 143–62.

8. For a fuller discussion of competition between ethnic groups, see V. D. Volkan, D. A. Julius, and J. V. Montville, *The Psychodynamics of International Relationships* (Lexington, Ky.: Lexington Books, 1990).

Chapter Eight

1. Andrew Samuels, *The Political Psyche* (London: Routledge, 1993), 11–12.

2. See Philippe Wolff, "The 1391 Pogrom in Spain: Social Crisis or Not?" *Past and Present* 50 (1971): 4–18; George Rudé, *The Crowd in History: A Study of Popular Disturbances in France and England, 1730–1848* (New York, 1964); Janine Estèbe, *Tocsin pour un massacre* (Paris, 1968). For the "clash of economic interests" theory of religious-ethnic conflicts in South Asia, see Veena Das, ed., *Mirrors of Violence* (Delhi: Oxford University Press, 1990).

3. Michael Walzer, "Nations and Minorities," in C. Fried, ed., *Minorities: Community and Identity* (Berlin: Springer Verlag, 1982), 219–27.

4. The leading proponent of the theory that the international environment, especially the ending of colonial rule, is responsible for ethnic conflict is D. Horowitz; see his *Ethnic Groups in Conflict* (Berkeley and Los Angeles: University of California Press, 1985).

5. Sigmund Freud, "Group Psychology and the Analysis of the Ego" (1921), *Standard Edition*, vol. 18.

6. Erikson, *Identity: Youth and Crisis*, 46. See also Janine Puget, "The Social Context: Searching for a Hypothesis," *Free Associations* 2, no. 1 (1991).

7. Davis, 156–60.

8. D. W. Winnicott, "Communicating and Not Communicating Leading to a Study of Certain Opposites," in *The Maturational Process and the Facilitating Environment* (New York: International Universities Press, 1963), 187. For a succinct discussion of contemporary psychoanalytic thinking on self and relatedness, see Alice R. Soref, "The Self, in and out of Relatedness," *The Annual of Psychoanalysis*, vol. 20 (1992), 25–48.

9. Oscar Patterson, "The Nature, Causes and Implications of Ethnic Identification," in Fried, 25–50.

10. David Rapoport, "Comparing Militant Fundamentalist Movements," in Marty and Appleby, *Fundamentalisms Observed*, 443.

11. Sigmund Freud, "New Introductory Lectures", (1933), *Standard Edition*, 22: 104.

12. See Heinrich von Stietencorn, "Angst und Gewalt: Ihre Funktionen und ihre Bewältigung in den Religionen," in Stietencorn, (hrsg.) *Angst und Gewalt: Ihre Praesenz und ihre Bewältigung in den Religionen* (Düsseldorf: Patmos Velag, 1979), 311–37.

13. John W. Bowker, "The Burning Fuse: The Unacceptable Face of Religion," *Zygon* 21, no. 4 (1986): 501–18.

14. Rapoport, op. cit.

15. Davis, 165.

16. Hans Bertram, "Germany—One Country with Two Youth Generations?" Paper presented at the Seminar on Childhood and Adolescence, Goethe Institut, Colombo, Sri Lanka, 17–21 February, 1994.

17. Cited in Kanan Makiya, "From Cruelty to Toleration," unpublished paper read at the conference on *Religion and Politics Today*, organized by the Rajiv Gandhi Foundation, New Delhi, January 30–February 2, 1994.

INDEX